The Prison Memoirs
of a Japanese Woman

Autobiographies and Memoirs of Women
from Asia, Africa, the Middle East, and Latin America
Geraldine Forbes, Series Editor

SHUDHA MAZUMDAR
MEMOIRS OF AN INDIAN WOMAN
Edited with an Introduction by Geraldine Forbes

CHEN XUEZHAO
SURVIVING THE STORM
A Memoir
Edited with an Introduction by Jeffrey C. Kinkley
Translated by Ti Hua and Caroline Greene

KANEKO FUMIKO
THE PRISON MEMOIRS OF A JAPANESE WOMAN
Translated by Jean Inglis
Introduction by Mikiso Hane

Kaneko Fumiko
The Prison Memoirs of a Japanese Woman

**Translated by
Jean Inglis**

Introduction by Mikiso Hane

An East Gate Book

M. E. Sharpe, Inc.
Armonk, New York
London, England

Library of Congress Cataloging-in-Publication Data

Kaneko, Fumiko, 1902–1926.
[Nani ga watakushi o kō saseta ka. English]
The prison memoirs of a Japanese woman / author Kaneko Fumiko ;
translator Jean Inglis.
p.   cm.
Translation of: Nani ga watakushi o kō saseta ka.
ISBN 0-87332-801-9
1. Kaneko, Fumiko, 1902–1926.   2. Japan—Biography.   I. Title.
CT1828.K32A3   1991
952.03′2′092—dc20
91-14196
CIP

Printed in the United States of America

MV   10   9   8   7   6   5   4   3   2   1

Contents

Introduction

MIKISO HANE

KANEKO FUMIKO (1903–1926) wrote her memoir, translated here, while she was in prison, having been convicted of a plot, the authorities charged, to assassinate the emperor.

Her life, as her memoir shows, was one of misery, privation, and hardship from early childhood. Her parents were not legally married, and they did not register her birth in their family register. Ever since the Meiji Restoration, the government had required each household to have its family members registered at the local government office. A child born out of wedlock often was registered as the child of the mother's parents. This was not done for Fumiko until 1912, when she was registered in her maternal grandfather's family register as his daughter. A person not recorded in any register was in effect a nonperson. To attend school, gain employment, or have any legal standing, a person had to submit a household registration certificate. Thus, when Fumiko first enrolled in school she did not have any legal status, so she was not allowed to enroll as a bona fide student; she was permitted to attend only as an auditor.

Not only did Fumiko not have any legal status, but she was virtually an orphan. Her father drank heavily and failed to hold a steady job. He gambled, had a violent temper, and beat his wife often. He eventually abandoned his family and went off with his wife's sister. Fumiko's mother in turn drifted from man to man. She and her family were in a continuous state of poverty, and she even considered selling Fumiko to a brothel.

In 1912, when Fumiko was nine, she was sent to Korea to be placed in the care of her paternal grandmother, who was living with her daughter. Fumiko's aunt's husband was a member of the Japanese colonial administration in Korea, which had been annexed by Japan in 1910.

Fumiko's grandmother treated her in a heartless, almost sadistic fashion as an unwanted member of the family. She was punished harshly for the most trivial reasons and was kept in virtual penury. At one point, as her memoir reveals, she even contemplated committing suicide. The only people from whom Fumiko was able to gain some comfort and support were the Koreans in her family circle. This no doubt accounts for her identification with the Korean students and activists she encountered in Tokyo after she returned to Japan.

After annexing Korea, Japan imposed harsh administrative measures against the Korean people. The police and military forces were employed to crush any resistance to the Japanese occupation; large tracts of farmland were confiscated from the Korean farmers, reducing them to tenancy and poverty. Many left their homeland to seek employment in Japan, where they were used as construction workers and miners, often under harsh conditions. In March 1919, just before Fumiko was sent back to Japan, Koreans staged a massive demonstration demanding their nation's independence. At least two thousand Koreans lost their lives, and twenty thousand were arrested.

The heartless treatment she received by her parents and grandmother as well as her observation of the harsh Japanese military administration in Korea undoubtedly conditioned Fumiko to rebel against all authoritarian persons and institutions. Out of the life of hardship, loneliness, and misery emerged a strong personality who eventually turned against all authority and embraced a nihilistic, anarchistic philosophy of life. In response to the officials who interrogated her after her arrest she wrote:

> Having observed the social reality that all living things on earth are incessantly engaged in a struggle for survival, that they kill each other to survive, I concluded that if there is an absolute, universal law on earth, it is the reality that the strong eat the weak. This, I believe, is the law and truth of the universe. Now that I have seen the truth about the struggle for survival and the fact that the strong win and the weak lose, I cannot join the ranks of the idealists who adopt an optimistic mode of thinking which dreams of the construction of a society that is without authority and control. As long as all living things do not disappear from the earth, the power relations based on the principle [of the strong crushing the weak] will persist. . . . So I decided to deny the rights of all authority, rebel against them, and stake not only my own life, but that of all humanity in this endeavor.[1]

Perhaps her life as an underprivileged member of society molded her outlook and personality more than the discrimination that girls and women of Japan had to endure in Meiji and Taisho Japan. But the fact that Fumiko was a female undoubtedly accounted for the way she was treated by her parents and other relatives. Thus, Fumiko suffered not just the economic deprivations and injustices that the underclass members of society endured, but also the restrictions and discrimination that all Japanese women had to put up with. Many strong-willed women like Fumiko struggled desperately to assert their will and fight for their autonomy and personal fulfillment. This is revealed in

---

[1]Mikiso Hane, *Reflections on the Way to the Gallows* (Berkeley: University of California Press, 1988), pp. 121–22.

Fumiko's remarks about why she chose schools attended primarily by men when she went to Tokyo. She was determined not to play second fiddle to men. Women like Fumiko, finding the existing institutions and entrenched interests indifferent if not hostile to their fight for justice and recognition of their right to be treated the same as men, turned to the left-wing reformist or revolutionary movements.

Women under Tokugawa rule were expected to live in accordance with the Confucian ideal of subordinating themselves to men. A Japanese Confucian scholar, Kaibara Ekken (1630–1714), prescribed the ideal behavior for women, especially of the samurai class, in his *Onna daigaku* (Great learning for women). He asserted that from an early age a girl should observe the distinction that divided men and women. As wife, a woman was to serve her husband faithfully as her husband served his feudal lord. "She must look to her husband as lord, and must serve him with all worship and reverence."[2] In all matters she was to obey her husband. A widow was not to remarry, and strict marital fidelity was to be observed. The practice of primogeniture was followed among the samurai class, and women were not accorded any property rights. In the samurai class, the family head had absolute authority over the members of his household, even the power of life and death. A husband could execute an unfaithful wife. The treatment of women was less stringent among townspeople and the peasantry, but rulers encouraged all classes to emulate the samurai class in male-female relations.

When the feudal rule of the Tokugawa shogunate ended with the establishment of the new Meiji government, numerous social, political, economic, and cultural changes

---

[2]Basil Chamberlain, *Things Japanese* (London: Routledge and Kegan Paul, 1939), p. 501.

were instituted, but uplifting the status of women was not on the list of reforms to be implemented. The insurmountable obstacles that prevented women from asserting their individuality remained as the political and legal systems, social mores and customs, and economic imperatives all compelled them to play subordinate roles to men. Fukuzawa Yukichi (1835–1901), an advocate of liberal reforms, remarked concerning the status of women, "At home she has no personal property, outside the house she has no status. The house she lives in belongs to the male members of the household, and the children she rears belong to her husband. She has no property, no rights, and no children. It is as if she is a parasite in a male household."[3]

A number of women participated in the movement to win "freedom and people's rights" in the early Meiji years in the hope that women would benefit if the movement succeeded, but when the Meiji Constitution was adopted in 1889, women were not accorded any political rights. In fact, authorities restricted the rights of women even further. In 1882 the government forbade women from making political speeches; in 1890 it banned them from participating in any political activities, or even listening to political speeches. The civil code of 1898 gave the head of the extended family virtually absolute authority. The head of the household was given the right to control the family property, fix the place of residence of every member of the household, approve or disapprove marriages and divorces, and so on. The wife was treated as a minor under the absolute authority of the household head. One provision stated that "cripples and disabled persons and wives cannot undertake any legal action."[4]

Brothels were sanctioned by the government, and im-

---

[3]Fukuzawa Yukichi Hensenkai, ed., *Fukuzawa Yukichi senshū* (Tokyo, 1951–52), 5:10.

[4]Tanaka Sumiko, *Jyōsei Kaihō no shisō to kōdō, senzen-hen* (Tokyo: Jiji Tsūshinsha, 1975), p. 112.

poverished families sold their daughters to these establishments in most of the towns and cities in Japan. In the realm of education also, girls were discriminated against, although the Education Act of 1872 called for the education of both boys and girls. The reason for educating girls was to prepare them to become "good wives and wise mothers," that is, to perform household duties. Educating girls beyond the elementary school level was not emphasized. Some parents believed that even this level of education was unnecessary or even harmful for girls. A poet, Higuchi Ichiyō (1872–1896), the daughter of a lower-level government official, was not allowed to complete even primary education because her mother believed that "it is harmful for a girl to get too much education."[5] The number of girls attending primary school remained far below that of boys, not reaching the 50 percent level until the end of the nineteenth century. In 1895 there were only thirty-seven schools for girls beyond the primary level, and most of these were operated by missionaries. A college for women was not established until 1911.

One lesson in a morals textbook issued in 1900 read, "Girls must be gentle and graceful in all things. In their conduct and manner of speech, they must not be harsh. . . . Loquacity and jealousy are defects common among women, so care must be taken to guard against these faults. When a girl marries she must serve her husband and his parents faithfully, guide and educate her children." An article in an educational journal published in 1887 asserted, "The male is yang and the female is yin. Consequently, it is only natural that women should remain in the house and be docile."[6] Thus, in the schools for girls, domestic arts such as home economics, sewing, and handicrafts were stressed.

---

[5]Ibid., p. 137.
[6]Ibid., p. 130.

These are not the kind of ideals a person like Fumiko could abide by. She was a woman of strong will and independent mind. This is seen in the life she pursued in Tokyo, as revealed in her memoir. She did not follow the tradition of having her marriage arranged for her as her father attempted. She went to Tokyo to build her own life, continuing her schooling while working as a newsgirl, soap peddler, maid, and waitress. As she indicates, she had been disillusioned with attending a girls' school in central Japan where home economics was stressed. She wanted to study mathematics, English, classical Chinese, and eventually enter medical school, so she chose a school that was attended mainly by men. Her feminism is revealed when she says that she wanted to compete academically with men and win. Even though her formal education was spotty, clearly she was a bright person. She read extensively and was exposed to the ideas of Bergson, Herbert Spencer, and Hegel. She recalls that she was especially impressed by nihilist thinkers such as Max Stirner, Mikhail Artsybashev, Nietzsche, and Kropotokin.

The Tokyo that Fumiko went to in 1920 was an exciting place. It was not only the seat of government, but also the center of the economic, cultural, and intellectual life of Japan. It seethed with liberal and radical ideas. The old-line Meiji autocrats were being replaced by political party leaders and advocates of parliamentary government. The left-wing movement seemingly was on the upswing, stimulated by the victory of the Bolsheviks in Russia in 1917. The first May Day march was staged in the year Fumiko arrived in Tokyo. The radical left had suffered a stinging defeat in 1910–11 with the trial and execution of Kōtoku Shusui, Kanno Sugako, and others who were charged with plotting to assassinate the emperor. But following World War I and the Bolshevik victory, a resurgence of activities by socialists, Communists, and anarchists hit the scene. With the second May Day march in 1921, many women activists joined the group. In 1922 the Communist party was covertly organized, but the government moved swiftly to crush the party and arrest its leaders.

Women who wished to assert their individuality and win equality and justice tended to gravitate to left-wing groups who were challenging established authorities and institutions. Among the most prominent women's organizations was the Sekirankai (Red Wave Society), whose members had close ties to left-wing circles, especially the Communists.

As Fumiko's memoir shows, she encountered a number of Communists and socialists, including Kutsumi Fusako,[7] who appears as Kunō in her memoir. She worked as a waitress at an eatery called Socialist Oden. Fumiko did not join any of the feminist organizations; she stayed outside of the mainstream of organized radical groups. Eventually Fumiko joined with Pak Yeol (1902–1974), a Korean nihilist. Her memoir does not discuss the activities the two engaged in, but the court records of her interrogation reveal her strong political convictions.

Although Fumiko had strong beliefs antagonistic to the established order, she and Pak Yeol did little that was injurious to the authorities or the emperor system, contrary to the charges leveled against them after their arrest. About the only thing they did was organize a two-person nihilist organization which they called Futeisha (Society of Malcontents). And yet they were arrested on September 23, 1923, two days after the Great Earthquake when the entire region centering on Tokyo fell into a complete state of dis-

---

[7]Kutsumi Fusako (1890–1980) joined a Communist labor organizer, Mitamura Shirō, and was active in the movement in the 1920s and 1930s. She later got involved in the spy ring headed by Richard Sorge, a German journalist in Japan who obtained information from a friend in the German embassy and passed it on to the Soviet Union. She was imprisoned in 1941 and remained there until the end of World War II.

order. Taking advantage of the chaos, the government and military authorities set out to crush, and in many instances murder, Communists and labor organizers. Also during the hysteria that resulted from the earthquake, wild rumors spread among the people that disaffected Koreans were taking advantage of the disaster to rob, plunder, and kill people. As a result, vigilante groups were formed, and hundreds of innocent Koreans were murdered. An unofficial estimate held that as many as 2,600 Koreans were killed at this time.[8] Fumiko and Pak Yeol fell victim to this movement directed against leftists and Koreans.

The authorities arrested the two and placed them under "protective custody." They then charged them with high treason. They were accused of plotting to assassinate the emperor, a completely trumped up charge. This was done, some believe, to justify the killing of the Koreans by demonstrating that dangerous Koreans were abroad, posing a threat to society. The two were indicted in July 1925, brought to trial in February the following year, and on March 25, 1926, sentenced to death. But the sentences were commuted to life imprisonment ten days later to show the "merciful benevolence of the emperor." Fumiko refused to accept the commutation, and when the certificate was handed to her she glared at the chief of the prison and tore up the document. Pak Yeol accepted the commutation and remained in prison until the end of World War II.

The two were sent to prison in Utsunomiya in Tochigi Prefecture near Tokyo. Fumiko refused to perform the work she was assigned in prison, but about three months later she asked that she be allowed to work weaving hemp ropes. The next morning, on July 23, 1926, she was found to have hanged herself with the rope that she had woven.

During the course of her interrogation, Fumiko defiantly

---

[8]Imai Seiichi, *Taisho demokurashī* (Tokyo: Chūō kōron sha, 1966), pp. 376–93.

expressed her political beliefs. The authorities no doubt used her rejection of the emperor system to justify her indictment and death sentence. Fumiko audaciously rejected the value system of her society, which oppressed helpless individuals. She expressed the bitterness she felt toward her parents and asserted that she rejected all moral principles, especially filial piety. When questioned about her family she replied, "I have no family in the true sense" and pointed to the fact that she had been abandoned by her parents. "She [Mother] even considered selling me to a whorehouse. . . . My parents bestowed no love on me and yet sought to get whatever benefit they could out of me. . . . [Filial piety] is based on the relationship between the strong and the weak. . . . It is only coated over with the attractive-sounding term 'filial piety.' "

Fumiko asserted that the only path she could pursue was to "deny the rights of all authority, rebel against them, and stake not only my life but that of all humanity in this endeavor." Thus she turned to nihilism and decided to work toward the destruction of all things. Among the institutions that she hoped to destroy was the emperor system. She joined with Pak Yeol, she explained, because they both agreed to work toward the overthrow of the emperor system. "By nature human beings should be equal," but people in Japan are made unequal because of the emperor system. The authorities claim that the emperor is a god, but he is really just like any other human being. "So we thought of throwing a bomb at him to show that he too will die like any other human being," Fumiko told the interrogator.[9]

Such heretical thinking undoubtedly persuaded the judges to condemn Fumiko and Pak Yeol to death despite the fact that they evidently had made no attempt to put their ideas into practice. It appears that all they did was

---

[9]Hane, *Reflections*, pp. 119–24.

talk about overthrowing the existing system.

Fumiko remained defiant to the end. In November 1925 she wrote in her notebook: "The rights of people are being tossed about by the wielders of power as easily as if they are handballs. The government officials have finally thrown me in prison. But let me give them some advice. If you wish to prevent the current incident from bearing fruit, you must kill me. You may keep me in prison for years, but as soon as I am released, I will carry on as before."[10]

The views held by Kaneko Fumiko are remarkable for a young woman of her time. She was hardly twenty, had a limited education, and had grown up in an atmosphere in which patriotism and loyalty to the emperor were viewed as the moral core of Japanese life. Not only is it remarkable that she formulated such a heretical social and political philosophy, but her refusal to grovel before the authorities is even more extraordinary. She refused to cower before the prosecutors and judges, and she expressed her views candidly, courageously, and decisively.

The records of her interrogation were not made public until after the end of World War II. The picture presented to the general public was that of a degenerate, nefarious woman. A photograph of Fumiko sitting on Pak Yeol's lap was passed on to right-wing military officers, who used it to play up the decadent character of the "traitors" and also to criticize the existing party government, to discredit them for pampering the traitors. The public bought the image presented by the authorities. Even the radical and liberal reformers virtually condemned Fumiko to oblivion. Only one women's biographical dictionary listed her. After the war, when some writers sought out her grave, they found it on a Korean hillside in an isolated spot, forgotten even by Pak Yeol, who, after being released from prison, returned to Korea to play an active role in the movement to

---

[10]Ibid., p. 123.

unify North and South Korea. He became a fairly prominent official in North Korea and passed away in 1974.

In prison before her suicide, Fumiko composed some poems. One of them, discovered after her death, reads:

The little weed twisted around my finger.
When I tug at it gently, it cries out faintly,
"I want to live."
Hoping not to be pulled out, it digs its heels in.
I feel mean and sad.
Is this the end of its bitter struggle for life?
I chuckle softly at it.[11]

---

[11]*Nihonjin no jiden* (Tokyo: Heibonsha, 1980), 6:491.

The Prison Memoirs
of a Japanese Woman

Preface

IT BEGAN suddenly at 11:58 A.M. the first of September in the twelfth year of Taisho [1923]. A violent rocking deep in the earth shook the Kanto region on which the capital city of Tokyo rests. Houses creaked and whined, twisted grotesquely, and collapsed. Inhabitants were buried alive, while those lucky enough to flee in time ran about screaming like crazed animals. What had once been a thriving center of the civilized world was in the space of a moment transformed into hell itself.

One aftershock came only to be followed by another violent tremor and yet another aftershock. Fires broke out all over the city, and great columns of smoke billowed up toward the sky as from a giant volcano. Tokyo was soon under a blanket of thick, black vapor.

The terrible tremors left the population in the grip of fear. Then those outrageous rumors started spreading and pandemonium broke out.

It was not long before we were taken in by the police on orders from the capital security officials. I am not free to go into the reasons for my arrest here; suffice it to say that not long after that I was summoned for interrogation to the Preliminary Court of Enquiry of the Tokyo District Court.

I was led by a guard through the door of the court where a judge and stenographer were waiting for me. The court attendant noticed me and began preparing the defendant's seat, during which time I stood silently by the door, the prisoners' thatched head-covering in my hand. The judge stared at me with a cold expression. Even after I was seated he kept on staring at me as if it were imperative for him to see right through to my insides. When he did speak, however, it was in a quiet tone.

"You are Kaneko Fumiko?"

When I answered that this was so, he proceeded to introduce himself in a rather friendly manner.

"I am in charge of your case. My name is Preliminary Court Judge Takematsu."

"I see. I hope you will be lenient," I said with a smile.

The set questioning then began, but the judge seemed to want to make the most of this formal interrogation to find out what he needed for the investigation. I will note down the conversation just as it took place, for it will help in understanding what follows in this account. The judge begins.

"First, where is your original place of abode?"

"The village of Suwa, Higashi-yamanashi County, Yamanashi Prefecture."

"How would you get there by train?"

"Enzan is the nearest station."

"Hmm . . . Enzan," the judge said with a slight tilt of his head. "Then your village is near the village of Ōfuchi. I know Ōfuchi quite well. I know a hunter there. I often go there in the winter."

I didn't know the Ōfuchi he was referring to and said, "I'm afraid you've got me. Actually Suwa Village . . . well, you see, it's my original place of abode, but actually I only spent two years there."

"Hmm. And you weren't born there, were you?" he said.

"No. My parents told me that I was born in Yokohama."

"I see. And what are your parents' names? Where do they live?"

I could not help smiling to myself. The judge was making a point of asking what he must have already known from the police report. Nevertheless, I answered as straightforwardly as I could.

"It's a little complicated, but on the register my father is listed as Kaneko Tomitaro and my mother, Yoshi. But those are really my mother's parents' names, my grandparents."

The judge acted surprised, then asked me about my real parents.

"My father's name is Saeki Fumikazu. I believe he's now in Hamamatsu, Shizuoka Prefecture. My mother's name is Kaneko Kikuno. I'm not absolutely sure, but I think she lives near her parents' home. In the register my mother is listed as my older sister and my father as my brother-in-law."

"Just a minute," the judge interrupted, "that sounds a little strange. I follow the part about your mother being listed as your sister, but if your mother and father have different names and live in different places, it's as if they weren't related at all."

"That's right," I answered despondently. "My mother and father separated a long time ago. Now my father is married to my mother's younger sister, my aunt, and lives with her."

"I see. Well, I suppose there's an explanation. When did your mother and father separate?"

"It must have been thirteen years or so ago. I was around seven at the time."

"And what happened to you then?"

"I went with my mother."

"And your mother brought you up all by herself from then on?"

"No, not really. Not long after my father left, my mother and I were separated too. After that, neither my mother nor my father had much to do with me again."

When I said this I felt my whole history, my entire past,

well up inside. Stupid me, I even had tears in my eyes. The judge may have noticed this, for he said somewhat sympathetically, "You must have had a hard life. We'll get to all that in good time."

He then took up the papers that were on the stenographer's table and began interrogating me about the incident itself. As I said before, however, I cannot write about that here. Indeed, there would not be any point.

But then the judge ordered me to write something about my past life. It seems that there is a provision in the law that says a defendant should be asked not only about what can be used against one, but about things that may stand in one's favor as well. Perhaps by means of this little-used provision the judge hoped to get at something in my background that might account for my having done such an atrocious thing. Of course that may not be the reason at all. He may have simply ordered me to do this out of curiosity. It does not matter. I wrote the record of my upbringing as I was told, and this memoir is that account. I do not know whether it was referred to in the trial or not. But now that the trial is over, it cannot be of any further use to the judge, so I have asked him to return it. I will send it to my comrades in the hope that it will help them to understand me better. Also, if my comrades find it worthwhile, I hope they will publish it.

My greatest wish, though, is that this be read by parents, and not only parents, but by educators, politicians, and socially aware persons as well. I would like all people who wish to better this world to read this.

Father

I CAN REMEMBER back to when I was four years of age. At that time I was living with my natural parents in Kotobuki-chō in Yokohama. Of course at the time I was not aware of what my father did for a living, but from what I heard later I gather that he was a detective at the Kotobuki Police Station. This period looms in my memory as the one all-too-brief period in my life when I knew what true happiness was. For at that time, as I recall, I was the light of my father's life.

Father always took me along with him to the public bath. I would duck under the curtain at the entrance every evening, perched on his shoulders, my arms wrapped around his head. And when he took me to the barbershop, as he always did, he was at my side throughout, pestering the barber with suggestions on how to shave my hairline or eyebrows. If he was not satisfied he would take the razor in hand and shave me himself. Father was the one who chose the material for my clothes, and if something of mine needed taking in at the shoulders or waist, he would point it out to my mother and have her get out her needle and thread to fix it. It was Father, too, who stayed at my bedside when I was sick and nursed me. He was forever putting his hand on my forehead and taking my pulse. I never had to say a word at times like that; my father knew what I wanted just from my look and got it for me.

Father always took great pains when he fed me. He would cut the meat in little pieces so that I could eat it easily and would remove even the tiniest bones from fish. He always tasted the rice or any hot liquid before giving it to me, and if it was too hot he would patiently cool it. My father, in other words, did everything that the mother would normally do in most households.

I realize now that we were not well off, but my first impressions of life were by no means unhappy. Even then our home was rather shabby and we never seemed to have enough, but my father prided himself on being the eldest son in a good family that, he believed, traced its ancestry to some aristocrat or other. He had in fact lived a relatively affluent life and had been indulged by his grandparents when he was young. So although we were actually poor, he acted as if nothing were any different from the old days.

Here, however, my pleasant memories end. I realized at some point that my father had brought a young woman into the house. Now there was constant quarreling and name-calling between my mother and the other woman. My father always took the other woman's side, and I had to look on as he hit and kicked my mother around. A few times my mother left him, sometimes for two or three days at a time. When that happened I was left at my father's friend's house.

I was still little, and this was a very sad time for me, particularly when my mother would go away. But then the woman just disappeared, at least that is how it seemed to me. But we saw less and less of Father after that.

I can recall being taken by my mother to bring Father home from what I now realize was a brothel. I remember Father getting up in his bedclothes and shoving Mother out of the room. But occasionally Father would come home late at night singing at the top of his voice, and my mother would docilely wait on him and hang his clothes up for him on the nail in the wall. But if she came across a candy wrapper or orange peels in the sleeve of his kimono she would glare reproachfully at him and say, "Just look at this. Couldn't you have brought some little thing home for your own child?"

Of course, Father had left the police by this time, but what he did for a living I never knew. I do know that there were always a lot of rowdy men around the house drinking and playing cards, and that Mother was constantly quarreling with Father and grumbling that this was no way to live. This life must have gotten to be too much for Father, for he finally got sick. My mother's family helped out and he was hospitalized. Mother stayed with him, and I was taken to her parents' home where my grandmother and young aunts looked after me for more than six months. Though I was separated from my parents, the time I spent there was quite pleasant.

When Father recovered I was sent home. Now we lived by the sea, which was considered to be more conducive to my father's health as well as my own; for I was a sickly child. The house was located on the coast at Isogo in Yokohama, and we were drenched with salt water and blown by sea breezes from morning to night. This period did in fact transform me into a healthy person, but whether this was a blessing, or nature's cruel scheme to bind me to the life of suffering fate had in store, I cannot say.

When Father and I had recovered, the family moved again. The place was a little way from Yokohama and was one of fourteen or fifteen houses in a village surrounded by rice fields. One morning of the winter that we moved—I remember that it was snowing—my little brother was born.

It was fall and I was six years old when my aunt, Mother's younger sister, came. (Of the intervening period I can only remember that we were constantly moving.) My aunt had some female disease, and because she could not get proper treatment out in the country, she was to stay with us and go to a nearby hospital. She was twenty-two or twenty-three at the time, a trim, pretty woman, lively, friendly, and meticulous in whatever she did. She got along well with people and was dearly loved by her parents. But before long, a strange relationship had developed between this aunt and my father.

Father had a job as a clerk at a warehouse on the waterfront not far from our house. But on this job, as on others he had had, he often stayed home on some flimsy pretext. Consequently we were not very well off, which is why, I gather, my mother and aunt spun hemp thread on a piecework basis at home. Every morning my mother would wrap in a scarf the three or four balls of hemp that they had spun and go off with my little brother on her back to collect their pittance of a wage.

Then a strange thing would happen: no sooner was my mother out of the house than my father would call my aunt into the three-mat room near the entrance where he was sprawled out. My aunt would stay in there a long time, although they could not have had all that much to talk about. My lively curiosity was aroused, and one day I tiptoed up and peeped in through a tear in the paper of the sliding door. What I saw did not particularly shock me, for this was not the first time that I had witnessed a scene like this. From a much younger age I had often seen my parents in loose moments, something that never bothered them in the least. I was thus quite precocious, my interest in sex having been aroused by the time I was four.

The spark of passion seemed to have gone out in Mother. She never got really angry at me, nor did she ever express any strong affection. My father, on the other hand, got extremely angry when he scolded me, while in his tender moments he displayed an affection that was overdone. Which of these two personalities was I drawn to? As a small child I was closer to my father, and if I had not come to realize that he was the cause of my mother's problems I would probably always have been close to him. But at some point I became more attached to my mother and would follow her everywhere, clinging to her sleeve. When my aunt came, however, my father would not let me go out with Mother. He had all sorts of tricks to cajole me into staying home. I realize now that he was trying to cover up what he and my aunt were doing and to allay my mother's suspicions. As soon as Mother left the house, Father would hand me a few sen and send me out to play, to get rid of me. I did not ask for money, but he would give me some, more than usual, and tell me to go out and play and not to come back for a while. But when my mother got home, he would complain about me to her. "This kid is really brash," he would say. "She knows what a softy I am, and as soon as you're gone she pesters me for change and then runs off."

It was the end of the year, New Year's Eve, as I recall. My mother had gone out to buy some things with my little brother on her back. Father, Aunt, and I were sitting around the kotatsu in the living room. It was a wet, damp night, and both my father and aunt were looking depressed, which was unusual for them. At length my father raised his head from the kotatsu and said very solemnly, "Why is my home so unlucky? Isn't this bad luck ever going to change? If only something would turn up in the new year."

People are the pawns of fate, and until one's luck changes there is nothing that can be done to better one's lot. This is what my superstitious father believed and what I had heard him repeat countless times from as far back as I can remember.

The two of them carried on about something for a while, and then my aunt got up and went to get her box of combs from the closet. "I guess this one will do," Aunt said as she took out a comb. "It's a little too good, though," she said, examining it. "It seems a shame."

"You're going to throw the thing out," Father replied, "and there's no rule that says it has to be a certain kind, just as long as it's a comb."

My aunt then put a comb with several broken teeth into her hair and went through the motions of shaking it out.

"You don't have to put it in so tightly. Just slip it in above your bangs," Father said. "If you run around in the vacant lot in front of the house, it will fall out."

Aunt did as she was told and went out. A few minutes later she was back, and the comb had fallen out.

"That ought to do it," Father said. "Bad luck has fled, and my luck will take a turn for the good in the new year." Just then Mother came home.

While Mother took the crying baby from her back and nursed him, my aunt undid the bundle with the shopping. Twenty or thirty pieces of mochi, seven or eight slices of fish, a few small paper bags, a cheap battledore with red decorative paper pasted on . . . that was the entire contents. This was the extent of our preparations for the festive new year.

During the New Year holidays my uncle on Mother's side came to visit. No sooner had he gone home, however, than my grandmother came to take Aunt home with her. But Aunt did not leave and Grandmother had to return home alone. From what I heard later, it seems that Uncle realized when he visited at New Year how things stood between my father and aunt. When he told the family about it, Grandmother was so worried that she came herself to get Aunt and take her home on the pretext that she was arranging a marriage for her. My father, of course, would not hear of this. He even intimated that to marry her off before she had fully recovered would be to endanger her life.

"No," Grandmother had argued, "it will be good for her. The man is rich and has promised that as soon as she becomes his wife she will be put under a doctor's care."

But Father dragged out his old line about fate and said that because of his run of bad luck he had had to pawn all of my aunt's kimonos. Of course he couldn't send her home, he said, with only what she had now. Another excuse was that my aunt's constitution was too weak for farm work. He would not always be so badly off, and in time he would surely be able to make a good match for her in the city. He would marry her off and would himself stand in as the parent. He gave all kinds of excuses like this and in the end managed to prevent my aunt from going home.

Poor Grandmother. Of course she did not believe Father, but she was just a simple country woman and no match for the wily city man and his barrage of lies. She returned home having failed in her mission.

With the God of Misfortune driven off, Father must have heaved a deep sigh of relief. But Mother was more miserable than ever, and there was incessant bickering at home after that. And what of my aunt?

My aunt was not exactly radiating happiness. She would be away for two or three months at a time, and I heard later that she had run away from Father and gone to work as a maid. But Father went around doggedly making enquiries until he tracked her down. The second time Aunt was brought back, we moved again. The place was in Kuboyama in Yokohama on the side of a hill. If you went five or six blocks further you came to a temple and crematorium.

Father, of course, was not working, but we somehow managed to get money with which to rent a house that was fitted out as a shop right at the bottom of the hill in Sumiyoshi-chō. Here Father opened an ice shop. The actual running of the shop fell to my aunt. Father went there during the day "to do the bookkeeping and look after things," as he put it, and Mother and we children stayed at home on the hill. This was only in the beginning, however; it wasn't long before he hardly ever bothered to come home.

My mother, little brother, and myself had been deftly eased out of Father and Aunt's life altogether.

I was seven years old at the time [six in the present age-reckoning system]. I had had my birthday in January, so I was the right age to start school that year. But I could not go to school because I had never been entered in the family register. I have not touched on this matter of not being registered, but I had better go into it here.

My birth had never been registered for the obvious reason that my mother had never been entered in Father's register. Much later I learned from my aunt what I believe is the most probable explanation. According to Aunt, Father never intended to stay with my mother. He deliberately never entered her in his family register because he meant to ditch her as soon as he found a better woman. Of course, he may have just told Aunt this to win her over. Or he may have simply considered it out of the question to register as his wife in the supposedly illustrious Saeki family the daughter of a peasant from Kōshū. Whatever the reason, however, this is how it came about that I had still not been registered at the age of seven.

My mother had lived with Father for more than eight years without saying a word about not being entered in his family register. I could not keep quiet about it, however, because it was preventing me from going to school. I had always enjoyed learning, and now I pestered constantly to be allowed to go to school. Mother finally said that she would register me for the time being as her illegitimate child. But Father, always concerned about appearances, would not hear of this. "What!" he railed. "You mean you'd put her down as an illegitimate child? She'd be ashamed of it for the rest of her life."

Not that Father made the least effort to enter me in his own register and send me to school. And for all his professed concern, he never bothered to teach me so much as a single letter of the kana syllabary. He was too busy drinking, playing cards, and loafing all day. I had reached the age for school, I wanted to go, but I could not. Later in life I came across a passage to the following effect. Perhaps the reader can imagine how I felt when I read it.

> With the glorious Meiji Era, intercourse with the West commenced. Japan awoke like a giant roused from a long sleep and began to walk, leaping over half a century in a single stride. The Rescript on Education was promulgated in the beginning of the Meiji Era, and primary schools were built even in the remotest country districts. The children of every human being, regardless of sex, not physically or mentally unable to attend, received a compulsory education from the state from April of the year in which he or she attained the age of seven. An entire nation was thus showered with the benefits of civilization.

But for unregistered me, these were only empty words. I was not from a remote village: I lived in Yokohama, right next to the nation's capital. I was certainly the offspring of human beings, and there was nothing physically or mentally wrong with me. But I could not go to school. There were schools aplenty: primary schools, middle schools, girls' high schools, colleges, universities, even Gakushūin [school for children of aristocrats]. The sons and daughters of the bourgeoisie in their Western-style clothes, their fancy shoes, some even riding in automobiles, were entering their gates. But me—what good did all this do me?

I had two playmates who lived just a little way up the hill from us. They were both my age and both went to school. Every morning the two of them would go down the hill hand in hand past our house, swinging their arms and singing as they went in their maroon hakama and with big red ribbons perched jauntily at the side of the head. I was miserable with envy as I leaned against the cherry tree in front of the house and watched them go by.

If there had been no such thing as school in this world, I would have gotten through life with a lot fewer tears. But then I would never have seen the joy that I saw on the faces of those children. Of course, at that time I did not yet know that every joy that some experience is paid for by the sorrow of others.

I wanted to go to school with my two friends, but I could not. I wanted to read, to write, but neither of my parents taught me so much as a single letter. Father could not be bothered, and Mother did not know how to read herself. I used to spread out the pieces of newspaper that Mother's shopping was wrapped in and pretend I was reading.

It must have been around summer of that year when, one day, Father chanced to come across a private school not far from my aunt's shop right in Sumiyoshi-chō where we were living. There would be no fuss about my not being registered, so it was decided that I would go here to school.

"School" is too fancy a word to describe this place, which was actually nothing but a six-mat room in a dilapidated row house. The tatami were dirty and ripped, the straw stuffing coming out in places, and a half-dozen or so Sapporo Beer boxes lined up on their sides served as the children's desks. This is where my writing career began. The teacher, "Ossho-san" as the children called her, must have been around forty-five. She did her hair up in a tiny chignon toward the front of her head and wore a striped apron over her soiled yukata.

Every day I walked down the road from the house on the hill past my aunt's shop to this splendid school, my things bundled up in a cloth that was tied across my back. The ten or so other children who treaded the boards covering the sewer in the little alleyway where the school was located probably came from circumstances similar to my own. After Father put me in that private school, the back-alley row house, he took me aside. "Now look, be a good kid," he said, choosing his words. "I don't want you telling any of the men that come over that you go to Ossho-san's school. It wouldn't be good for me if other people found out, see?"

My aunt's shop was doing a good business, but she was not making money. It was impossible to save anything because Father drank and played cards every day. Also, at that time she and Father were so engrossed in each other that people were even talking about it.

Even so, things were not all that bad at my aunt's. It was Mother, my little brother, and I who had a hard time. One day we did not have a single thing to eat. It was supper time and there was not even a grain of rice in the house. My mother took my little brother and me to see Father, who was at a friend's house. But although Mother implored him, Father would not come out of the house to talk to her. I suppose Mother had reached her limit, for she suddenly opened, from the porch, the sliding door into the room and went in. Four or five men were sitting under a bright lamp playing cards. Mother exploded: "I thought so! There isn't a grain of rice in the house, the children and I haven't a thing to eat for supper, and you sit here drinking and playing cards!"

Father stood up, livid with rage. He pushed Mother off the porch, jumped down after her in his bare feet, and started hitting her. If the men had not grabbed him and held him back, calmed my mother, and taken Father back into the room, who knows what he would have done to her. She was saved from a beating, but we had to leave without so much as a grain of rice or a cent to buy any with. We trudged up the hill in silence.

"Hey, wait up!" came a voice from behind. It was Father. He's come with some money for rice, we thought, but that was not it at all. What a cruel, devilish man he was. We were standing there expectantly, waiting for help, and he yelled, "Kikuno, I hope you're satisfied. You did a great job of humiliating me in front of those people. Goddamit, you made me lose everything, and I'm not gonnna let you forget it!"

Father now had one of his wooden clogs in his hand and began hitting Mother with it. Then he grabbed the front of her kimono and threatened to throw her over the ridge. It was dark then, but in the daytime you could see that it was a steep decline with a tangle of bushes and briars at the bottom. My little brother was bawling on Mother's back, and I was circling them helplessly and pulling at Father's sleeve to try to stop him. Then I remembered that a friend of Father's, a man named Koyama, lived just a little way down the hill from there in a wooden row house. I raced to the man's house, screaming at the top of my voice.

"I thought that's who it was," the man said. He had just sat down to supper, but he threw down his chopsticks and flew out of the house to help.

I had barely started in at the private school when it was Bon festival time. Ossho-san told all of the children to bring two *kin* of sugar as a mid-year gift. This was probably the only remuneration she got, but in my case, there was no way that I could comply. Not only were we having a hard enough time just trying to make ends meet, but the house was in such a state of confusion that no one could be bothered about me and my problems at school. Thus I had to leave school before I had even learned all of my katakana.

My aunt's shop had not survived the summer, and the two of them had moved back into our house on the hill. The ruckus at home started up again worse than before, and there was a fight between my parents at least once every three days. I always sided with my mother when my parents fought. I talked back to Father too, and this made him hit me just as he hit Mother. Once when it was pouring rain he shut the two of us out of the house in the middle of the night.

The relationship between Father and Aunt was as cozy as ever. But Aunt's family kept after her to come home, and finally, with Father's agreement, she said she would. Needless to say, this cheered Mother and I no end.

But Father said that he could not let Aunt go without any decent clothes, so he used the money he had gotten when he disposed of the shop to buy her long crepe undergarments, a sash, and a parasol, worth at the time about seventeen or eighteen yen. And just as he had himself overseen my care when I was little, he now insisted on himself purchasing these things for Aunt. But this time it was a woman, not a child, on whom he lavished his care and attention.

It was autumn. Father packed all my aunt's belongings for her and put in the best bedding we had in the house. Mother, my little brother on her back, and I went along to see my aunt off. As we walked along, Mother kept apologizing, tears in her eyes. "I'm so sorry to have to send you home with hardly a stitch on your back, your wedding ahead of you and all. But with our luck down like this, what could I do?"

We went only halfway, then returned home. Father, who saw Aunt all the way to the station, got back in the evening.

What a perfectly wonderful night we had! Even I, young as I was, sensed tremendous relief. How quiet, how peaceful it was! But little did Mother and I guess the all too peaceful time that lay in store. Four or five days later, Father disappeared once again.

"Oh this is too much! The two of them have just run off and left us," Mother uttered through clenched teeth.

Seething with rage, and aware that we were looking for a needle in a haystack, we set out to track them down. And one day we did find them; we spotted the bedding they had taken from home out sunning. A lot of good it did us, though; we only ended up with another clouting from that wooden clog!

Mother

ABANDONED by Father, we were at a complete loss. In the beginning we still had a few things that could be sold to buy food, but these were soon all gone. Father, of course, sent us nothing. We had to live somehow, so I cannot blame Mother for what she did, taking up with an iron-smith by the name of Nakamura. Although I was too young to understand why, I remember that Mother's tone was distinctly apologetic when she told me about the arrangement. "This man brings home a good daily wage of one yen, fifty sen. Things will be much easier for us than before, and you'll be able to go to school and all, see?"

Nakamura came one day with a small bundle of his belongings and that was it: he was living with us. He went off every morning in his overalls and carrying his lunch to a nearby foundry. He was about forty-eight or forty-nine, had graying hair and deep-set, mean eyes. Short and stooped, he cut a very poor figure. My father had been raised like a young lord and looked down on working people. I suppose this attitude had rubbed off on me, for I could hardly stand to speak to this nobody Nakamura, much less become close to him. Even though he was, for the time being at least, my foster-father, I called him "Mister" as I would a stranger. Mother did not bother to correct me; in fact, she herself referred to him derisively as "Whiskers" behind his back.

I used to pick up on his words and talk back to him, and he in turn would use any excuse to harass me. When Mother was out of the house he would sneak some rice for himself and then put the rice tub high up out of my reach. Or he would roll me up in the quilt and throw it in the closet. One night he tied me up with fine rope like a ball and suspended me from the bough of a tree at the edge of a nearby river. Mother must have known that this sort of thing was going on, but there was nothing she could do about it, except, of course, curse my father and aunt for putting us in this situation in the first place. "They'll get what's coming to them one day," she would say, "and end up dead in the gutter."

But the saddest thing that happened to me while we were living with Nakamura had nothing to do with his harassment: my little brother was taken away. One day I overheard Nakamura and Mother talking. "The sooner you take him, the better. As long as he's going to be theirs, he should go before he gets too big," Nakamura said.

"Giving him to a man like that, I can't help but worry. But what else can I do?"

I knew what they were talking about and was so upset that I finally came out and asked, "Mama, are you gonna give Ken to somebody?"

Mother explained that when she and Father separated they had agreed that she would raise me and that my father would take my brother. I was miserable all the same. My brother was the only real friend that I had. But more than that, I wanted someone I could love. I begged: "Mama, please! Starting tomorrow I won't go out and play at all. I'll take care of Ken all the time, from morning 'til night. I'll take such good care of him he'll never even cry. Don't take him to Father's. Please, Mama, please! I'll be so lonesome all by myself."

But Mother would not listen. "It won't work, Fumi. If that child stays it'll be all that much harder for you and me.

And besides, your father has been here asking for him."

No matter how I pleaded, Mother would not budge. The next day when Nakamura was out I brought up the subject again. "Mama, if Ken has to go to Father's, let me go with him. I'm scared to be here with that man all by myself."

But grownups have their own reasoning. Mother turned a deaf ear to my pleas; she seemed incapable of understanding how I felt. This was to be my fate, and in the end there was nothing I could do but submit to this power greater than myself.

Shortly after that Mother put my brother on her back and took him to Father's. They lived in Shizuoka then, and you had to take the train to get there.

Not long after my brother left, we moved again, or rather, we rented a room in someone else's house. The house, which was up against a fence made of charred railroad ties beside the tracks, had just one six-mat room and one four-and-a-half-mat room. There were five in the family, and the man was a longshoreman or something. They lived in the six-mat room and we occupied the smaller room. The place was incredibly dirty. Sooty, yellowed newspaper was pasted on the sliding door, and the straw was coming out of the ripped tatami. The biggest hole was in the tatami beneath the window, and Mother put the long hibachi there to cover it. She put pieces of cardboard over the other holes and sewed them down as best she could with white thread. That kept the dust from rising up into the room.

Nakamura continued to work at the foundry, while Mother had found a job sorting beans at a warehouse by a nearby river. I did not stay home all by myself, however. A primary school in the neighborhood had given in to Mother's earnest entreaties and allowed me to attend school even though I was not registered.

Naturally, I was delighted; I even forgot my loneliness at

losing my little brother. For this was not a fly-by-night school like the one I had gone to before; it was everything I had ever dreamed a school should be. Most of the children seemed to come from good families. The girls had beautiful clothes and wore a different ribbon in their hair every day. Some were even brought to school by maids or houseboys. But once again I had to suffer for this. I hadn't been going there long when we were told not to use slates, which were supposed to be bad for the lungs, but to bring a pencil and notebook to use. For me, however, this would not be easy. Nakamura would never have bought them for me, and Mother was unable to come up with the money right away. I had to miss several days of school until I was able to buy them. Mother wanted to transfer me to a less expensive school but couldn't because of residency regulations.

Then one day Father turned up out of the blue. He must have been selling something at the time for he was carrying a large cloth bundle on his back. His face was haggard; even I was shocked when I saw him. But I was glad to see him, this father of mine whom I had so much cause to resent. He put the bundle down in a corner, and as he sat talking with Nakamura by the hibachi I felt how far above the other man he was. I even wanted to be fussed over by him again, and when Nakamura stepped away for a moment I put my mouth up to Father's ear and whispered, "Buy me a rubber ball." How I longed for a ball like all my playmates at school had!

That night Father took me to the fair. When we had left the path in front of the house he said, "How about a piggy-back ride" and stooped down to put me on his back just as he had put me on his shoulders when I was a little child. At the fair I found some rubber balls at one of the stands, and Father said I could have whichever one I liked. I took two, one large and one small, both with red flower designs. There were many other things hung on the stand, and I gazed at them completely absorbed.

"Anything else you want?" Father asked. I shook my head. "Poor thing . . . ," Father said in a voice that choked as we hurriedly left. "Sure, there are lots of things you still want. And I want to get them for you. But your Father is so poor. Be patient with me, eh, Fumiko."

I felt I was going to cry, but I managed to control myself. Although only a child, I would have been ashamed to cry in front of all those people. We walked around the night fair for a while and then went home. When we had turned off the brightly lit street onto the dark, deserted alley Father spoke again. "Fumiko, your father was bad. Please forgive me. Everything I did was wrong, and it was innocent you that had to suffer. But you know, Fumiko, I'm not always going to be poor like this. And then the first thing I'm going to do is to make you happy. Will you wait until then?"

Father was actually crying now, and he choked when he tried to hold back the sobs. I was crying by this time, too, but not like a child. And when I spoke it was as an adult. "I don't care. I don't care how poor you are. Only take me with you. Please take me to Ken's."

"I know how you feel, I know," Father replied, sobbing now without restraint. "I'd take you if I could. No matter how poor, I wouldn't let you starve. But if I took you with me now your mother would have no one. You're the only one your mother has. So be patient for a while. Listen to what your mother and this father tell you, and wait. Father's going to come for you, he really is."

Father stopped walking and just stood there by the side of the road crying. I clung to his back and cried too. But he did not go on like that for long, and when at length he spoke, his voice was quite controlled. "Well, let's go home now. Your mother will be waiting." He then set off with a firm step. When we entered the alley beside the house he put me down and wiped my tears with a white handkerchief.

Late that night Father hoisted the bundle onto his back again and trudged off for home. After that visit, I would run out to the road in front of the house every evening and scrutinize the people passing by, for I really believed that Father would come for me. But he never did.

We moved again, and the first thing that Mother did was to go to the principal of the primary school in the neighborhood and beg him, tears in her eyes, to admit me. Her request was finally granted.

Compared to the one I had just attended, this school was downright shabby. Most of the pupils were the children of poor people, so I should have been right at home there, yet it was always made perfectly clear to me that I was not wanted.

At the start of class in the morning, the teacher called the attendance. Though I was present as surely as anyone, my name was never called. The names would be called right up to the child next to me, and I would be skipped over. Now, of course, I realize that this was not important, but it is hard when you are a child to be belittled like that. The times that I did not deliberately come late, I would open the desk top and stick my head inside while the teacher took attendance. Or I would open a book and read. When the teacher scolded me for this I merely fidgeted with my hands in my apron.

One morning about a month after I started school there I handed in the envelope with my school fee to the teacher. Presently I was called into the teachers' room. I did not know what I was being summoned for, but I was not worried. My teacher showed me the envelope I had given him and said, "I've got your envelope here, but there's nothing in it. What happened?"

Of course I had not the faintest idea. Mother had put the fee in the envelope, and this I had brought to school. I replied the only way I could: "Nothing happened."

"If nothing happened, why is there no money in this envelope? You bought something on the way to school, didn't you?"

"No."

"Then I suppose you lost the money on the way?"

"No. I had it in my bag. . . ."

The principal, a menacing look on his face, joined the attack. He accused me of spending the money on sweets. Finally they searched my bag, but they found nothing, neither the money nor anything I could have bought with it. They were angrier than ever, convinced that I had spent the money. But no matter how they upbraided me, the fact remained that I simply did not know what had happened to the money; and I stuck to my guns.

The office boy was sent running off to get my mother. Summoned before the principal, Mother was at a loss at first. But it was not long before she realized what must have happened.

"This girl would never do anything like that. Oh no, she would never do that. I put the money in the envelope last night and she put the envelope in her bag so as not to lose it. My husband saw that. She hung the bag up on the wall, and I think my husband may have taken the money out when he went to work. It wouldn't be the first time this has happened."

Mother even went on to give examples. I knew that this had been going on. I had gone home in tears one day because a pencil I had put in my notebook was not there when I got to school. And it was not just once or twice that this kind of thing had happened.

The principal must have been moved by what Mother told him. I was right there, and I can still remember what he said to her. "It's too bad a good girl like this has to be left in that kind of environment. I wonder if you would consider giving her up to me for adoption. I would do everything in my power to take good care of her."

Whether he said this out of genuine sympathy for me, or because it occurred to him that it might solve his own problem of being childless, I do not know. I was delighted, however, because not only were those awful doubts about me gone, but the principal had thought kindly enough about me to make this offer.

Mother thanked him, but of course she could not have parted with me. "This is the only child I have. She is the only joy I have. No matter how hard it is, I want to raise her myself." The principal did not pursue the issue further. Mother took me by the hand and we went home.

Mother and Nakamura must have quarreled after this. He had often gone out drinking before this incident; in fact, it was probably for that that he had needed my school money. But now it got worse. Mother would sometimes find receipts or bills from eating places in the pockets of his work clothes, yet he would get after her to scrimp more on food or complain that she was wasting charcoal.

When we left Nakamura we took our belongings and went to a friend's. Mother left me there during the day while she went out to look for work, and she would issue a warning before leaving in the morning. "You mustn't play out in the street in front; Nakamura might find you." I gather that mother had left Nakamura against his wishes.

Mother traipsed around every day looking for work, but she found nothing in the city to her liking. But a lady friend of hers had an older brother who was supposedly a foreman at a silk mill in the country, and Mother evidently decided to go there. She sounded quite pleased when she told me about it. "This man is apparently a foreman, so he must have a lot of pull. If we entrust ourselves to him, I'm sure he'll be sympathetic and things will work out."

Mother's dependency was so bad it bothered even me, young as I was. She was incapable of taking a step on her own without someone there to support her. But I was only a child; I had to do what Mother said.

We went to the mill, but nothing came of it. There was no one there, foreman or otherwise, for us to depend on. The man in question turned out to be a menial who worked in the kitchen. We spent three months there, however, although the only thing that I can remember about this time is that Father showed up one day with some Korean candy for me.

I was delighted to see him. He had kept his promise and come for me, I thought, so things must be looking up for him. This was not so, however. Father looked awful, even worse than when he had bought me that rubber ball at the night fair.

Mother stopped working at the mill when Father came and we lived with him. The two of them were just like they had been before. Then Father disappeared again. I cannot remember how long he was with us or when he left, so little did we mean to each other by that time.

Back to town we went, Mother having evidently found a job there in a spinning mill. We rented a flat in a row house, and I started back at the school with the sympathetic principal. We had nothing, so of course life was not easy, but with just the two of us and no encumbrances, things went fairly well. Though lonely, our life had a deep intimacy, and I thought that, barring some calamity, the two of us could have gone on like that quite happily. I wanted to pray with all my young, childish heart that we could remain like that forever, but of course this was impossible. There was Mother's ingrained dependency for one thing, and for another, she was the sort of woman, I realize now, who cannot live without a man. This time she took up with a young man. He was twenty-six or twenty-seven, seven or eight years younger than Mother. I knew him because he rented a room at the home of a widow friend of Mother. He wore a blue silk neckerchief and had long, neatly parted hair which he kept plastered down with pomade. He was always lolling around smoking cigars. I think Mother had already decided to live with him when she said to me, "They say he's hard working. And being so young, if he does work hard, you and I will have things easy."

I did not like it at all. I was a little cheeky anyway and tried in a roundabout way to object. "I don't think he's so hard working, Mama. I saw him myself yesterday, and the day before, and the day before that, just hanging around."

But Mother paid no heed. A cold, she insisted, had kept him from going to work the past few days. And anyway, hadn't the widow said that he was unusually industrious?

It could not have been more than three days after this conversation that he came to our house . . . and just never left.

Kobayashi was the man's name. He was a dock worker and about as lazy a man as you could hope to meet. He had been more or less forced on my mother by the middle-aged widow at whose place he was boarding; they had in fact been living as man and wife. Even this woman, who had a record of several convictions, found him too much, so she neatly disposed of him by inveigling Mother into taking him on.

Once Kobayashi got into the house he never left. On the few occasions when he did set off for work, he soon came strolling back, saying that he had been too late and missed out on the work, or some such excuse. Before long Mother quit her job at the factory and the two of them just lay around all day. They tried to get rid of me whenever they could.

One night, past nine o'clock, I was doing homework or something in the corner of our one and only six-mat room. Mother, who was cavorting with Kobayashi in the bedding right beside me, suddenly told me to go buy them some roasted sweet potatoes. She reached under the quilt by her head, pulled out her coin purse, and casually flung it at me. Three or four copper and nickel coins fell out and rolled over the tatami.

"Mama, sweet potatoes at this hour?" I protested. "That sweet potato man closes early; he'll be in bed by now."

Mother was peeved and yelled, "That's not the only sweet potato man. Go to the one next to the bathhouse on the street in back; they'll be open. Now get going!" I shuddered at the mention of this place, for to get there I would have to pass under the big trees in the woods around Hachiman Shrine.

"Mama, can't I get cakes instead? The cake shop is right over there where it's light."

"No! I said sweet potatoes," she yelled. "Do as you're told. Get going, you spineless girl. What's there to be afraid of?"

Mother's menacing look convinced me. "Well, how many should I get?"

"There's five sen by the foot of the table," Mother said from under the covers, motioning with her chin. "Get whatever you can for that." I reluctantly picked up the money, rose, and, grabbing the cloth for shopping, stepped down into the kitchen stoop.

When I opened the door and peered out I flinched; the wind was so strong and the night so dark! The sharp staccato of the fire lookout's wooden clappers could be heard in the distance. Off to the left loomed Hachiman Shrine, pitch black. A deathly stillness hung over the woods that seemed ever so much more impending now than in the daytime. And I would have to go through it all by myself! There was no getting out of it; I would have to go.

I was standing before the door petrified, when Mother suddenly got up and came over. "Will you get going!" She pushed me out and slammed the door behind me. I would just have to resign myself to my fate. Screwing up every ounce of courage, I started running for all I was worth, dreading the worst. I cannot even recall now how I got through those woods. At the shop I had the man wrap the hot sweet potatoes in the cloth and then made another non-stop dash home through the woods, racing as if I were being pursued. I flew into the house.

But the sight that greeted me was such that I had to turn away my gaze and flee once again into the darkness without. My mother had not wanted sweet potatoes at all; she had only meant to get rid of me.

Spring came, and with it the end-of-the-school-year ceremony. Although the school authorities in their benevolence had allowed me to attend classes, I was not to be given a certificate and hence could not pass on to the next class. Mother once again went to the principal to plead on my behalf, and he finally agreed to give me a letter stating that I had completed the first grade. I went to the ceremony in a kasuri cloth kimono that belonged to the son of one of my mother's acquaintances and a saffron crepe obi.

The table at the front of the hall was covered with a white cloth and piled high with certificates and prizes. The teachers and the mothers, dressed in kimonos embroidered with their respective family crests, sat stiffly in rows on either side. The children, who were also decked out in their best, were seated behind the table.

The program began, and after a short speech the principal called the children one by one up to the table and handed each of them a certificate and a prize. The children took them, beaming with pride, and returned to their seats.

I was the last to be called. When I heard my name, I slipped through the rows of children and stood in front of the table, beaming too, of course. I bowed deeply and raised my hands high to receive the certificate. The principal handed me a piece of paper. That is all it was: just a plain piece of paper! The other children had received a proper square certificate with real printing, but for me there was only a piece of folded rice paper on which a few tiny characters had been scrawled in brush and ink. The thing drooped limply in my hands.

How mortified I felt. It was as if this whole ceremony, my classmates with their certificates and prizes, their families and the teachers lined up on either side, the whole thing had been held for the sole purpose of humiliating me. I should never have come in the first place. And to think that I had even had to borrow a boy's kimono to wear!

That was not so bad. But at home things had gone from bad to worse, and we were able to eat only by selling our belongings. Even the food container went, as did the hibachi. One after another, everything that could be turned into cash was disposed of. Finally it was my turn: I was to be sold as a maid in a brothel.

Young though I was, I realized what a hard time we were having just getting food to eat. Yet one day Mother brought home a hair ornament with red plum blossom trim that she had bought for me. This was something that I had always wanted, and I was beside myself with joy. Mother combed out my hair and arranged the ornament in it. As I had only one kimono to my name, I of course had nothing fresh to change into, but Mother smoothed the kimono I was wearing so that it would show to best advantage. She was talking all the while about how badly off we were and what a shame it was to leave me like this until before I knew it I was on the point of tears.

Then, however, Mother suddenly switched to a cheerful tone. "But you know, Fumi, you're lucky that there is someone who is willing to take you. They're not poor like us. You could even end up riding in a fine carriage."

I was forlorn at the thought of leaving Mother and being

given to strangers. But realizing what a hard time Mother was having caring for me, I felt that if there were a place like that that wanted me, I was prepared to go. Naturally, I had no idea what the "carriage" referred to [marriage to a rich man], but the thought of riding in such a vehicle was quite pleasant. Thus it was with mixed emotions that I set out from home with Mother.

The house Mother took me to looked quite nice. The two of us sat on the stoop inside the door and waited a while until a middle-aged woman with a black satin obi appeared and exchanged greetings with Mother in a patronizing tone.

In retrospect, it is clear that the woman handled geishas and prostitutes—was a trafficker in human flesh, in other words. She stared long and hard at me. Then, the merchandise between them, my mother and this middle-aged woman began their bargaining.

"Say what you like, the girl is too young. It's going to be five or six years at the very least before she's good for anything, and in the meantime she'll just be one big expense. We can't just let her play all day, you know; she's got to be sent to school, and she's got to graduate, even if it's only primary school. And then she's going to have to be trained before we can have her waiting on customers. You can see that it's going to mean sinking a lot into her before there is anything to show for it." This was the other side's line of approach. .

And Mother? I think Mother was genuinely distressed. She choked back the tears when she spoke. "I—I'd never see this child become a prostitute for the money. I don't care about the money. It's just that I'm so poor; I thought it might be better for her this way."

"And you're right. If she makes something of herself, a prostitute can end up quite well off." The buyer was hitting Mother in her weak spot, but her opponent too was determined to take advantage of this turn in the conversation.

Mother now took out the copy of Father's family register that she had brought with her for the purpose of impressing the woman with the supposedly high social standing of my family, the so-and-so's on Father's side. "With a family background like this she can be proud of herself; and I'm sure she'll get ahead," Mother concluded.

The woman probably felt that she already had her prey in the trap. Mother was not dissatisfied with the amount offered, and the matter seemed to be just about settled. Although I realized that this arrangement was not what Mother had told me when we set out for this place, I had no idea what either a geisha or a prostitute was. And considering that I was to be sent to school and to be taught good manners, the prospect of coming here did not appear altogether bad.

But when the discussion got around to where I was to be sent, Mother began to have second thoughts. The woman said that I was to go to Mishima, which is on the Tokaido Line. Mother's expression clouded over when she heard that the place was Mishima. "I wonder if it couldn't be someplace closer," Mother all but begged. "Mishima is so far; I'd hardly ever be able to see her."

"No, I suppose not," the other said, somewhat disconcerted. "Unfortunately there's no opening close by. Mishima is the only place that has a position to offer."

Mother asked repeatedly for someplace closer, but the woman refused. Mother finally gave up. "I guess we'll just have to ask your help some other time." Mother reluctantly turned down the offer and we went back to the dark and dreary house. I can just imagine how happy I would have been at that place! I do not think Mother herself believed what she said about it being for my happiness. If she had truly thought so, she would not have turned down the offer just because she could not see me as often as she wished.

Unable to dispose of its last "possession," the household was in desperate straits. The landlord was around practically every day clamoring for the rent, and the neighborhood stores would no longer give us anything on credit. Mother and Kobayashi evidently had a quiet talk at this point, for one night we loaded ourselves down with the remaining items in the house and slipped away in the darkness. We landed at a flophouse on the edge of town; we had finally reached rock bottom. We rented a three-mat room. The occupants who lived on top of one another in the rest of the house included a dockworker, umbrella mender, fortune teller, sleight-of-hand artist, and a carpenter of sorts. Most of the boarders hung around the house day in and day out, and only when they became absolutely desperate did they reluctantly don their happi, smooth the wrinkles in their torn hakama, and set out for work. On the way home they would drink themselves into a stupor on cheap saké, and then a ruckus would start up. They would gamble, try to outdo each other's outlandish boasting, and end up in a big fight.

Kobayashi, lazy enough to begin with, was not about to go after work in an atmosphere like this. I was thoroughly disgusted, though only a child. It finally got to the point where he achieved the feat of spending entire days fast asleep in the corner of the room.

We hardly ever had three meals a day, and not even one, as often as not. My stomach was always empty. To this day whenever I am hungry I recall the time I roamed the streets famished and found some scorched rice thrown out on a garbage heap. I stuffed it into my mouth, praying that no one would discover me. Oh how good it was!

Mother was constantly apologizing to me. "I'm so sorry for all that you've had to go through."

"It's all since that man came to live with us," I would say, making her all the more depressed.

"I thought he was a good worker, that guy. But I've had it; I've learned my lesson. We were better off on our own, no matter what anybody said. If only we had stayed the way we were, just the two of us, we would never have had to stoop this low." Mother hung her head and her speech broke off in places. When she raised her head again, she seemed resigned and her voice was clear. "But I couldn't leave now even if I wanted to. If only I had gone ahead and just left that time I was planning to."

I did not know what she was referring to, but it upset me to see her so bereft of self-respect.

Mother was forever getting after Kobayashi, but to move him would have been like moving a mill stone. She evidently gave up, for she started doing piece work spinning hemp thread. But Mother too quit after a while and lay around listlessly as if there were something wrong with her.

As bad as things were, however, I was a child and, like all children, wanted to go outside and play. One day I was playing by the riverbank with some neighborhood children when Mother came over with heavy steps and called to me.

"What is it, Mama?" I answered.

She asked in a spiritless voice if there were any ground cherry bushes around. Children are kind, and these children all helped in the search. We soon found one at the foot of a nearby bridge. Actually one of the children had known where to look because she had been keeping an eye on it herself, waiting for it to get big. But she pulled it up by the root and gave it to Mother.

"Thank you," said Mother, and then snapped off the root, put it in the sleeve of her kimono and went home.

That night I saw the yellow ground cherry root wrapped in an old newspaper beside the oil lamp on the shelf in our room. I now realize that Mother was pregnant at the time, and I believe that she wanted the ground cherry root to abort herself with.

Kobayashi's Village

FALL came at last. I don't know how they did it, but Mother and Kobayashi managed to get some money and took me with them to Kobayashi's native village. I cannot remember the name of the village, but it was located in Kitatsuru County, deep in the mountains of Yamanashi Prefecture. Kobayashi's family were farmers and at least were able to get by. There were three brothers, not one of them very bright; but of the three, Kobayashi, who was the second brother, was by far the sharpest. When their father died he, rather than the eldest, had taken over management of the finances and after a while had run away with some of the family's money. The family had worried about him but had had no word for a long time. When now he suddenly turned up with an older woman, everyone was pleasantly surprised, and they all went out of their way to do what they could for him.

As I said, I cannot remember the name of the village, but the hamlet was called Kosode. It was a quiet place with fourteen or fifteen families, all of whom were related much as in a clan society. When we arrived, there was no place for us to live, but everyone put their heads together and it was decided that a woodshed located to the west of Kobayashi's sister-in-law's parental home would be cleaned up for us to live in.

The place had been used for storing logs and straw and was now in a state almost beyond repair: the floor was rotten, the walls were crumbling, and the roof leaked when it rained. But after some old planks had been nailed on, a mud mixture plastered on the walls, and the cracks stuffed with straw, it was rendered inhabitable. The shack was a square space the size of a ten-mat room and had a wooden floor. Two old tatami were laid down in the back, and this area served as our living room, dining room, and bedroom. We cut out part of the floor near the entrance for a hearth, but since the place was originally a woodshed, there was neither a door nor doorsill. On summer nights we made do with a straw mat hung over the entrance, but for the cold winter we got a couple of old doors from someone and tied them to the entrance with a rope. On nights when there was a snowstorm, however, this did not keep out the freezing wind and snow, and we often awoke in the morning to find a pile of snow beside the hearth. As if the place were not bad enough, on the other side of our flimsy wall on the left was a stable, while on our right was the outhouse which we shared with the main house, making this about as foul a place as you could hope to find.

But wonder of wonders, once Kobayashi settled down here he actually began to work. For the time being he was to receive a wage for making charcoal for his family. Mother did sewing for the homes in the neighborhood, and in return she brought home daikon, potatoes, and other vegetables, so we were at least assured of something to eat. As for me, for the first time since that humiliating experience at the end-of-school-year ceremony I was going to school. I will have more to say about this land of learning that so enthralled me, but first I had better give an overview of what life was like in the hamlet of Kosode.

To a person from the city accustomed to seven- and eight-story buildings and the brightly lit show windows of Ginza, to someone who rides to assignations or cafés in a private car, to someone who can at will turn on a fan in summer or a heater in winter, what I am about to relate will doubtless seem incredible. Nevertheless, be assured that I am not lying or even exaggerating. As I see it, the prosperity of the city is based on an exchange between country and city, an exchange in which the country is hoodwinked.

Kosode, as I said, was a kind of primitive society consisting of fourteen or fifteen interrelated families. It was located at the base of a fairly steep mountain, but because it faced south it got quite a lot of sunlight. There was not even one rice field in this village, however; there was only the mountain and the gardens that had been carved out on its slopes. From spring to summer the main industry in the village was silk worm cultivation. The fields were planted with a little barley and mulberry as well as vegetables for the villagers' own consumption; sandy soil was planted in wasabi. In winter the men went into the mountains to make charcoal while the women stayed at home and wove straw bags. I would guess that a good 70 or 80 percent of the income of the villagers in this mountain hamlet came from charcoal.

The villagers' diet was of course very plain. Their rice was mixed with barley as is ours, but theirs was inferior to our prison rice. Although ours is only four parts rice to six parts barley, the rice is polished rice. The villagers, however, never saw so much as a grain of polished rice. On the other hand, their rice did not have the insects, tiny stones, and pieces of straw in it that ours does. And there, as here, vegetables were cooked without sugar. The only fish that was available in the village was salmon, and that was so highly salted that you practically jumped out of your skin when you took a bite of it. You were lucky, though, if you got even that once a month.

But please do not suppose that the people were not healthy on this simple diet—they were. And you need only go into the mountains to learn why. The akebi, pears, and chestnuts that are so abundant in the mountains are rich in the "vitamins" that everyone talks so much about these days as well as the sugar and calories so lacking in our diet. The adults picked these things just as the children did. What was left was food for the crows and mice, and what escaped their notice weighed down the branches, was eventually covered with earth, and rotted right on the branch. Should anyone have wanted to hunt them, rabbits and other small animals hopped about on the mountain behind the village or in the woods on the road to school. No one did; however, the children merely chased them for the fun of it.

I was truly close to nature at this time. This period enabled me to appreciate how ideal, how healthy, and how one with nature village life is. Why, then, has the life of the villagers become so wretched? I do not know what it was like in ancient times, but in the Tokugawa Era [1600–1867] and in this present civilized age of ours the villages have been bled for all they are worth for the benefit of the cities.

In my view, if a village can cultivate silk worms, the peasants should spin silk thread and wear silk clothing, even for work. There is no need for them to buy striped cotton "country clothes" and obi from traders from the city. But, of course, the villagers cannot do this. The villagers sell their cocoons and charcoal to the city and then must turn around and buy inferior cotton and hair ornaments, losing the money they earned to the city in exchange.

The temptation, money, is there, and they sell their cocoons and charcoal in order to get it. Merchants from the cities come into the villages to take advantage of them. A peddler bundles up boxes of goods which he carries on his back into a village. There may be ten kimono collars in one box, seaweed and dried goods in another, fancy goods in another, and assorted sweets in another; a few pair of wooden clogs, more seaweed, and groceries are added onto the stack for good measure. He need not bother to peddle from house to house in the village; he simply picks out a relatively prosperous-looking house and temporarily sets up shop there. "The trader is here," someone announces, and in no time word has gotten round the whole village. Then the women flock around to pick up and gaze longingly at everything and ask prices.

"My, that's expensive," someone remarks. "Why, not ten days ago Mrs. Omasa bought this for twenty sen in town." The peddler has an explanation, on which he has all the time in the world to elaborate, as to why the item is really not all that expensive, and how it is different from the other. It is not only a case of deceiving, but of making the customer believe she has to have a particular item, no matter what. The bargaining drags on and on. And why not? Even if the peddler has to spend the night in the village, he still only pays a fourth or a fifth of what he would have to pay for a room in town. It might even work out that he will be welcomed as a guest in someone's house and will not have to pay a thing. It matters little how long it takes; even if he only sells a few things, he still comes out ahead.

Girls buy collars and hair ornaments without telling their fathers. Mothers come with cocoons or hand-spun raw silk or dried persimmons, or wasabi still covered with earth and wrapped in straw, and exchange these things for something worth only a third as much. Year in and year out, villagers have the fruit of their hard labor stolen by such people.

Mail was delivered only once every week or so. In winter when the postman came, he would kick off his shoes, install himself at the kotatsu, and kill time over cups of tea and small talk with the family, or in reading and discussing postcards and showing around photographs that he took out of mail to be delivered to other families. At mealtime he would leisurely get up and make his way home.

When there was mail for the temple, he would ensconce himself in the priest's quarters and keep the priest company over one artless game of go after another, oblivious of the day slipping by.

But let me get back to the subject of school. The village school was located at the edge of a town called Kamozawa and consisted of only a primary school section with perhaps sixty or seventy pupils. This was the most poorly equipped school I had seen since "Ossho-san's" place, and the teacher, if he could be called that, was a heavy drinker who could become quite violent. The school was located about one *ri* from Kosode down a lonely mountain road. The snow was very deep in winter, and the girls and boys wrapped towels around their cheeks and wore boots made from bamboo bark.

Though not many, there were a few items such as pens, paper, and ink that we needed for school. But cash did not exist in this village. A child who needed something would set out for school with one or two bags of home-produced charcoal on his or her back to take to the store beside the school. Children could get the supplies they required from that store until the exchange value of the charcoal was used up. Here was another case of barter. But there is one thing about this that I must not omit. How old do you suppose the children were who toted a whole bag of charcoal on their back over one *ri* up and down the mountain path? Nine-year-old girls did this. I wanted to try too, but for a city girl like me it was out of the question. For one thing, my family had never had that much charcoal for me to have carried around.

While I am at it, let me mention something that, although trivial, someone raised in the city might find hard to imagine. In the village, people never use paper when they go to the toilet. To do so would be the height of extravagance. Even for letter writing, the only paper the villagers had was what was too sooty and ripped to serve anymore for covering on the sliding doors. What did they use instead of paper? They would put branches and chop-stick-length pieces of bamboo in the boxes in their toilets; after use these would be placed in another box. When a lot of dirty sticks had accumulated, they would take them to the stream at the foot of the mountain and wash them to use over again. This is a fact; I am not making it up.

One day in early spring a child was born in our house. The grandmother at Kobayashi's was delighted. The baby was called Haruko, after the season, and her birth celebrated as that of a first-born. The mare was loaded with five or six bags of charcoal and led off, her foal trotting behind, to the town five or six *ri* distant. She returned with a meager bundle on her back of things purchased in exchange for the charcoal: a little rice, some dried sardines, and some cloth-ing. These were in celebration of the first-born. Haruko turned out to be a healthy child.

It was the end of March, and once again I was going to attend a ceremony commemorating the conclusion of the school year. How many times had I been humiliated on this occasion! But this time I would be spared. The teacher had said that this was the country, and that I would be given a certificate just like the other children even though I was not registered. As strapped as we were, Mother man-aged to make me a kimono of striped cotton cloth with a matching jacket for the occasion. I set out for school in my new outfit with all the other children, dancing for joy.

The ceremony, a stark affair, began, and everyone beamed as they received their certificates. In spite of what the teacher had told me, however, I, and only I, did not get one. Up to the very last moment I kept thinking that this time it would be me, this time for sure. . . . Finally I knew there was no point in waiting any more.

The ceremony was over and everyone prepared to go home. I merely stood there in a daze, however. Then the teacher came up to me and waved the certificate and an honor award in front of my nose. "I've got your certificates, two of them, right here. Now if you want them, tell your mother to come and get them, see?"

Around the time of the ceremony the children's families always sent something, usually saké, to the teacher. He was saying in so many words that I could have the certificates in exchange for saké. My family had not sent the teacher anything. We had nothing to send in the first place, and I do not believe that Mother even realized that it was expected.

Oh, how mortified I was! I walked home all alone by a back road to avoid the other children, and when I reached home I cried my eyes out by the hearth. Mother said, to comfort me, not to worry, that she would take the saké and get the certificates for me. But the hurt would not go away. "No, Mama, I don't want them." Nothing she said could dissuade me, and I finally just dropped out of school.

I was desolate. It is impossible adequately to express how I felt at the time, but oh how I cried! I cried until the tears would not come any more. This went on for several days. Then one day, quite out of the blue, my uncle, Mother's younger brother, turned up.

The first New Year's after we arrived in this place I had written a card for Mother to her family; this is how Uncle had known where we were. Mother had told me at the time why she was sending the card. "After all that's happened, I couldn't ask them straight out to come for us, but I think that if they see this card they might come on their own to take us home." She talked about going home frequently after that. "We'll have to put up with a lot of talk if we go home, but it would be so nice not to have to live poor like this. And think how pleased your grandmother and grandfather would be." Mother was convinced that, if only she sent that card, her family, who had worried about us ever since Father had left, would immediately come for us.

"Well, if it isn't Sister!" Uncle said as he stepped in.

"You came! You came!" Mother greeted him, tears rolling down her face.

The two of them just stood there, talking away happy as could be. What I could make of the conversation was that Uncle had wanted to come as soon as they had received our New Year's card. (Even a woman could have made the trip in two days, it seems.) But the snow was so deep that he had had to turn back three times to wait for it to melt. I also understood that, just as Mother had hoped, Uncle had come for the purpose of bringing her home.

As soon as Kobayashi got home, a conference began on the spot. Kobayashi's mother and father and close relations came over to take part. The discussion went on for some time, but the upshot of it was that Mother could go home if that was what she wanted. The problem was what to do with the baby, who was still nursing. Kobayashi's elderly mother scolded Mother. "Couldn't you have given us a little warning? If only you had told us sooner, I'm sure we could have worked something out."

Although I did not grasp at first what "work something out" referred to, I gradually began to understand. Mother's reply provided a clue. "I thought of that, but ... the poor thing."

This reminded me of something I had heard before, a piece of information gleaned from a conversation between Mother and the girl from the house west of ours who had married into a family in a nearby village. "This isn't the sort of thing you talk about, but—well, it really wasn't so hard," she said softly to Mother as the two of them sat beside the hearth. "It was like this ... and she kept staring at the baby and thinking, 'Not yet? Not yet?' ... The woman next door gave birth to a child when she was still unmarried and she got rid of it like that on the quiet to spare the families."

Mother listened in silence, ashen-faced, as if she had sustained a terrible shock. "Poor thing . . . ," she sighed at last.

I was afraid that "something would be done" about Haruko, but after discussing the matter for several days it was decided that we would leave Haruko with Kobayashi's family. The day after the decision was made, Mother and I left with Uncle. Yuki, the youngest daughter at the main house, bundled Haruko in a carrying jacket on her back and went as far as the edge of the village to see us off. The emotional girl was crying so that her eyes were red, but Haruko, the picture of peace and contentment, remained fast asleep in the warm jacket, oblivious of what was happening.

Although we had already gone well beyond the village, we found it impossible to leave them. It was only when we reached the point at the foot of the hill where the road turns that we bade them farewell. But even then Mother's legs would not carry her on. We had only gone four or five steps when she turned and walked unsteadily back again. She took the baby from Yuki's back, sat down on the grassy bank by the side of the road, and, shaking the still sleeping baby awake, forced a nipple into her mouth. Mother was sobbing convulsively, and as she stroked the nursing baby's face and rubbed her cheeks, she repeated the same thing over and over again to Yuki, who was standing beside her, also crying. "Take care of her, Yuki. Please, take care of her. . . ."

It seemed as if Mother would never leave the child, but Uncle, who was about one *chō* ahead, yelled to her, and she finally got up and put Haruko on Yuki's back again. She did not let up her sobbing, though. Every two or three steps Mother and I stopped and looked back, always to find Yuki standing there in the same spot by the turn in the road. At another bend in the road a few *chō* further, Mother and I once again turned to look back, but by this time we could only make out Yuki dimly, wrapped in the morning mist. Haruko's shrill crying, however, cut through the stillness of the mountain morning, hurling accusations, as it were, at the mother and sister who had roused her from her dreams only to go off and leave her.

That was the last time that I was to see my only sister. And that was more than ten years ago. I wonder if Haruko is still alive, or has she already gone to her death?

Mother's Family

THE AFTERNOON of the second day after leaving Kosode we reached a small town called Kubotaira. Only one *ri* now from Mother's family home, we had only to push on a little further, but Mother held back. She would be embarrassed, she said, to return to the village in broad daylight. Uncle went on ahead, while we went to the barber's and then bought a gift for Grandmother. It was dark by the time we reached Mother's home.

Grandmother and Grandfather were of course happy to see us, but their joy was no doubt tinged with sadness. Mother and I felt the same way.

The family consisted of Grandmother and Grandfather, who had partitioned the house and were living in retirement in the back portion; my second aunt, who had married into a shopkeeper's family in a village two *ri* from there; my younger uncle, who no longer lived at home; and the older uncle who had come for us, who was now the head of the family. He had a two-year-old child. I lived with my uncle's family, while Mother got a job at a silk-reeling factory where she had worked when she was young. The idea was that she would work and save money until I got older.

I was lonesome but at least felt secure, and the days went by peacefully enough. But a great misfortune lay in store.

One night that summer I was awakened from a sound sleep by my aunt. Rubbing my sleepy eyes, I followed her into the living room next to the kitchen where, much to my surprise, I found Mother. She was sitting there, her obi undone, eating. She had bought me a muslin summer kimono and a long kimono. I was of course pleased, but I was also worried that she might have quit work again. Nothing had happened here that would have necessitated her coming home, and by all rights she should have been far away in town at her job. Not understanding what it was all about, and not caring to ask, I went back to bed.

It was not long, however, before I found out. Mother had rushed home in response to a telegram: "Father critically ill; come immediately." Grandfather, of course, was fit as could be, and the next day a family council was held in which Mother, "critically ill" Grandfather, Grandmother, Uncle, and Aunt all took part. I was told to go out and play, but I refused to leave.

"He says that there are three children; but that they're all big, so they shouldn't be any care," said Grandfather.

Grandmother picked up the ball. "The family is fairly well off. And best of all is that they're town people; you wouldn't be in the country like here. It would be the best match you've had."

I finally understood that they were talking about a marriage proposal from a well-off man named Furuta who had been married before and who ran a general store near the station in Enzan. What would happen to me, I wondered, if Mother went there. I stared at her nervously, looking for a clue, but this problem seemed not to have even occurred to her. "I suppose you're right," she said, as if she were thinking of something else. The family urged her to accept the offer, and at length she replied, almost nonchalantly, "Oh, I guess I'll give it a try. I wouldn't have to force myself to stay if I didn't like it; I've always got this child to fall back on."

I leaped to my feet, panic-stricken. "Mama, for God's sake, don't go! I beg you, please don't go!" I threw my arms around her neck and cried.

"Forgive me, child."

Everyone tried to console me with a string of arguments about how I would be able to see Mother often since she would be living nearby, and how this marriage would actually be for my good too because it would get me into town, etc., etc. It was finally decided that Mother would go.

So that was how it was to be! She was leaving me, abandoning me to pursue her own happiness, just as Father had once done to the two of us. I have already written of the time that Father appeared and bought me a rubber ball after having gone off and left us. I was so happy to see him then. But he never fulfilled his promise to come back for me, "no matter what." Having long since given up on Father and his love, I had only Mother to depend on, and now she too had deserted me. I cannot help but recall the time she was going to sell me to a brothel. It was supposed to be for my own good, but that was not the real reason. She only wanted to make her own life a little bit easier.

If only I could scream to the world at the top of my voice, I would hurl curses at all the mothers and fathers in the world! "Do you really love your children? Or, once the stage of instinctual mother-love is over, do you not merely pretend to love them while in fact you think only of yourself?" I'd say, "Are you sure your love is not a false love, like my Mother's? She did not really love her child. She calculated, even as she abandoned her, that if her plans did not work out, she would come back one day to live off her child."

I have gotten carried away. But these words come out of the despair that I felt at the time, and that I feel to this very day, and I must be allowed to speak them.

Mother left, and I stayed on at my uncle's and went to

primary school. By this time I had no more illusions about school. And in fact here too they treated me like a piece of unwanted baggage. In gym class, for instance, they always told me that I was "one too many" and made me go to the end of the line, although I was by no means the smallest. It was not so bad if there was an even number of children; but if not, I was always the one left over and stuck at the end. In classroom subjects, with the exception of penmanship and drawing, I was better than anyone else; but I never got a report card like the others did.

The weather was just starting to get chilly when, one day, Mother came over with her youngest stepchild. Though I had cursed when she left, I was glad to see her. When she said she wanted to take me to her new home for a visit, however, I did not want to go. She pressed me, though, and I finally gave in.

Mother's new family sold groceries, kitchen utensils, stationery supplies, and the like. I made friends right away with the children there, but for some reason I did not take to Mother's husband. I had only spent two nights there when I was asking to go home.

"Don't tell me you want to go home already," Mother said sadly. She tried to persuade me to stay, but I insisted that I wanted to leave. Finally she gave up. She took her dressing table out on the veranda where she did up my hair and then gave me a purse of red Chinese brocade and a cord that she took from the top drawer of her dresser. "I thought of you when I came across this material at the bottom of the dresser and made these things up without telling anyone."

Mother then went into the shop and hurriedly wrapped in a cloth three tins of food, a bag of white sugar, and a pair of straw sandals with red leather thongs. Concealing the bundle under her sleeve, she took me by the hand and slipped out of the house. When we reached the mill beside the bamboo thicket outside of town, she tied the bundle securely on my back and then bought me some cheap candy at a nearby shop.

"Eat this on the way, and mind you don't get lost. It's quite a way, you know. Tell them at home that I'll look for a chance and come over and see them again one of these days."

Mother was on the verge of tears. I felt like crying too, but I merely nodded. Yes, I wanted to cry, but something held me back. Oh, how lonely and withdrawn I was becoming.

When I got home, I started in at school again. I did not dislike school even though I was made to feel unwanted. In fact, going to school was the one and only pleasure I had. Then, when winter was almost upon us, my grandmother on Father's side, who lived in Korea, arrived.

My two grandmothers were almost the same age, fifty-five or fifty-six, but the grandmother from Korea had a nice complexion and was in better health. It was her clothes, though, that really made the difference. The Ōshima tsumugi jacket and other finery that she wore as much as proclaimed that here was the matron of a fine family; they certainly made her look younger than Grandmother and the other country women here.

She had come for me: she wanted to take me back to Korea to raise in her home. Why? In Korea she lived with my father's next youngest sister who, it seemed, was not able to have children of her own. When I was three or four years old, it had been decided that, if indeed this aunt did not have children, she would take me to raise as her own. Nothing came of the plan because after Mother and Father separated the family did not know where Mother was. But with Mother's return home, this old plan was revived.

Grandmother also said that she felt some responsibility for my father having left Mother and run off with my aunt. Mainly, however, there was no longer hope for my aunt in Korea to have a child of her own, and the perfect solution seemed to be to take me to raise. The family here believed too that I would be better off in my other, well-off grandmother's home, especially now that it seemed Mother had settled into her new marriage. Thus the matter was quickly settled.

Grandmother from Korea had brought beautiful clothes for me. There was a red satin obi that must have cost thirty-five yen, and things I had never seen the likes of before: a long-sleeved kimono, coat, hakama, and a formal-wear kimono with the family crest, as well as a shawl, wooden clogs, and ribbons. Grandmother said that there were lots more at home.

My not being registered presented a problem for Grandmother from Korea, who had the family's social position to think of. They decided, therefore, to register me as the fifth daughter of my grandmother on Mother's side.

The clothes that she had brought were magnificent beyond my wildest dreams, and I was being told to put them on. Again and again I would lift the sleeves of the kimono and gaze at the gorgeous obi with an exquisite mixture of timidity and joy. "You'll be on your way to Korea soon," everyone said, "so go around in your pretty things to say your good-byes."

I wore the silk crepe outfit, the satin obi, and a red ribbon and made the rounds with my aunt to the school and the homes in the neighborhood. The clothes were so stunning that the neighborhood women slipped over later to the back door, asking if they could have another look. "How wonderful for Fumi," they all said, as if all that I had been through never happened.

Of course, Mother came over too. She was no less delighted than the others. "Wouldn't it be nice, Kikuno," my aunt said, "if we had a photograph?"

"Oh, it would. If only there were a photographer nearby," Mother answered.

"A photo? Oh, we'll have one taken and sent to you as soon as we get home," Grandmother from Korea said, basking in the awe that this remark produced. "A photographer comes to our house once or twice a month; we'll send a photo right away."

"Oh please do!" everyone said.

What Grandmother said next built my hopes up even higher. "But you know, it will only be for a little while that you won't be able to see each other. If she graduates as she should, we'll be sending her to a girls' high school. And if she gets good grades there, we'll send her on to women's college, which means that she'll have to go to Tokyo and so will be able to see her family all the time."

Oh yes, she promised something else as well. If I went with her, she said, I would never be forced to do anything I did not want to do. And the family could rest assured that I would be given not only every necessity, but playthings as well, and anything else that my heart desired. Needless to say, everyone was weeping with joy. I too was of course very happy.

It was a brilliant, cloudless day with a bit of chill in the air when, inundated with the blessings of all, I set out with Grandmother for Korea.

My New Home

I WAS in Korea at last, Korea, bright with the promise of happiness! But did Korea bestow on me what had been promised? The reader will learn the answer in the course of what follows, but I would like to note what I sensed at this point, lest the reader be jarred by the abrupt change. I felt, in a word, slightly disappointed. I sensed that I was to receive only an infinitesimal bit of what I desired from Grandmother: to be loved by her as a grandchild. I was also uneasy, knowing that I possessed very few of the qualities that she expected to find in me. But I had by no means lost hope. I would yet grab hold of the God of Happiness that was waiting for me

I had finally reached Korea and my home there. It was in the town of Bugang in Chung Cheon Bug Do. The family's name was Iwashita. The reader will no doubt wonder at this name, Iwashita, so I had better explain why, if I were a Saeki, the family of my father's mother was named Iwashita, not Saeki.

Grandmother married at the age of fifteen or sixteen in Hiroshima, but her husband died when she was twenty-seven, leaving her with four children, the eldest of whom was only nine years old. Not long after that she lost the two youngest. My father, the eldest, eventually ran away from home, and only a daughter, my aunt, was left. Shortly after this aunt graduated from girls' high school in Hiroshima, she had a proposal of marriage from a naval officer, but Grandmother turned it down. The next proposal was from a government official. Although she had never met him before, Grandmother took one look at the man and knew that this was the one. They practically concluded the marriage on the spot. Although the eldest son, my father, was missing, and it would thus have been only natural to have adopted the man into Grandmother's family, they did not do this; my aunt went into the man's family. But even though my aunt was legally a member of his family, since Grandmother was all alone and happened to like her son-in-law, she went to live with the young couple. The family went by the name of its legal head, Iwashita, not by Grandmother and Father's name, Saeki. Thus my new home was that of the Iwashitas.

Bugang

WHAT was this place where the Iwashitas lived, Bugang, like? It was a small village situated along the Seoul-Pusan railroad. Both Japanese and Koreans lived there, but the majority were Koreans, there being only about forty Japanese families. The two nationalities were not integrated, however, but formed separate, autonomous groups. The Koreans had a ward office and a ward chief who handled all the affairs of the Korean community, while the Japanese had an office that functioned much as a village office in Japan and a person with the rank of village head who handled the affairs of the Japanese population.

The Japanese community consisted of the inn, general store, stationery store, doctor's office, post office, barbershop, nursery, sweet shop, clog shop, a carpenter, and the teachers at the primary school. There were also five households of Japanese military police, three farm families, two brothels, the station chief, four railroad personnel, three or four homes of railroad construction workers, six or seven people who lent money to Koreans at high interest, two dealers in marine products, and two or three families who had small cigarette and penny candy stores.

To understand what this small Japanese community was like, it must be remembered that these people had originally come here to make money. There was no community

spirit as such binding them together. Money was everything. People with money had power; and this lot in effect
ran the village. These people with money and leisure, who
dressed in styles that had been the fashion a few seasons
back in Japan, were the class that threw their weight
around.

The most powerful members of this class had, in addi-
tion to money, fields and paddy land that constituted the
main source of their income. Next in importance were the
military police, station master, doctor, and school teachers.
Their womenfolk were respectfully called *okusan*, while the
wives of those below them, the traders, farmers, laborers,
and carpenter, were all called *okamisan*.

The village could thus be viewed as consisting of two
classes, and these were as distinct from each other as oil
and water. There was rarely interchange between the two.
The circle of people whom one invited to one's home,
whether it be for a service for a dead ancestor or a celebration, was rigidly circumscribed. Within one's class one exchanged not only the sweets eaten at seasonal festivals and
the Star Festival, but even the New Year's rice cakes. This
was not the friendly exchange among villagers related by
ties of blood; it was strictly a matter of obligation. One
gave in return the exact number of items, or something of
equal value, as what one had been given. It was not unusual for families to pinch and save to engage in a showy
exchange of gifts. People were generally vain and ostenta-
tious in public, and the women always wore their most
expensive clothes to festivals, funerals, and the like.

Although Bugang was only a small village, since it was a
stop on the trunk line, groups of dignitaries or government
officials often passed through. On such occasions it was
practically mandatory for school children, the military police, public-spirited citizens, and even women to hurry
down to the end of the station and stand in neat rows to
welcome or see off these VIPs. The men usually turned out

in suits sporting "Red Cross Member" badges, and the women wore kimonos of patterned silk crepe with "Women's Patriotic Society" badges on their breasts. Some people even wore medals that looked just like two-sen coins, commemorating the opening of the Chungju-Bugang highway. By the time they found out which car the VIPs were in, however, the train had usually already passed. Maybe one time in ten the train would stop in the station for a whole minute, and then an official in haori and hakama would present a tray decorated with red crepe paper through the train window with the calling cards of the people who had turned out.

If any big event occurred, the people held a torchlight or masquerade procession. Occasionally they would set up a hut in a vacant lot on elevated land where they would dance, play instruments, sing, and do renditions of plays and kyōgen passages. Customs like these are just what you would expect to find in a new colony. They provided a means for the men and women to have a little fun and broke the monotony. This entertainment, however, was only for those who belonged to the first class; the people of the second class were mere passive onlookers.

The Iwashitas

MY AUNT'S family, the Iwashitas, were thoroughly immersed in this world and were, indeed, one of the most influential families in the village. Although not extensive, their property included five or six pieces of wooded land as well as paddy and dry field land that they rented to Koreans. The income that this land brought in was lent at high interest, once again to Koreans. The Iwashita home was located on high land on the north side of the railroad.

The townspeople's way of referring to their respective neighborhoods was an exercise in mutual self-conceit. The people who lived on the south side of the village referred to their area as the "town" and the north as the "country," while those who lived on the north side called the south side the "working class district" and their own area "uptown."

My aunt's house was in the highest section of "uptown." It was key-shaped, had a low, thatched roof, and was equipped with Korean-style floor heating. There were only four rooms, all four-and-a-half-mat size, two on either side of the house. Although it looked run-down, the house was fairly roomy inside. There were two outbuildings in the back of the house and a storehouse for rice on the other side of a garden planted in vegetables and fruit trees.

My uncle was a quiet, affable man from Nagano Prefecture. He had been in charge of track maintenance on the railroad but had resigned to take responsibility for an accident in which a train derailed and overturned, killing and seriously injuring a number of people. He had been living a quiet life here in the country ever since. My aunt, ten years his junior, was tall, slim, refined, and very shrewd, a no-nonsense, masculine type, so to speak. She loved cards and often invited women of her class over to play. She could also perform on the koto and dance. In the spring she gathered warabi in the mountains and in the fall, mushrooms. In short, she indulged liberally in all the pastimes of the typical bourgeois wife.

The people in the neighborhood referred to my grandmother as the "retired" mistress of the house. She was anything but retired though; she ran the place.

My Life in Korea

I

MOTHER, Grandmother, Aunt, and all the villagers had sent me off with congratulations for the good fortune that awaited me. I too entertained pleasant visions of the future when I went to Korea. But no sooner had I arrived than I realized that the life I was entering upon was not going to be such a happy one after all.

I did not expect anything as fine as a crepe, long-sleeved kimono and obi, but I believed Grandmother would give me the kind of kimono I had often seen middle-class girls wearing. I did not particularly care about the promised toys, but I did suppose I would have the books that I wanted. And I thought, too, that there would be people here who would love me in place of the mother and father I did not have. But none of these things were to be mine.

Naturally I was let down, but I was accustomed to disappointment, so it was not that hard to bear. But shortly after I arrived something happened that made me feel truly desolate. One day a woman whom I had not met came to visit. Noticing me, she said to Grandmother, to flatter her no doubt, what a "nice girl" I was.

Grandmother did not seem pleased at all and responded in the most offhand manner she could affect. "Oh her? She's from a family I know only slightly, very poor people.

She doesn't know how to behave and can't speak but in the most atrocious language. It's enough to make one blush. But I felt sorry for her and ended up taking her in."

I did not object to her referring to the poverty of my family; I knew only too well how desperately poor I was. But why, oh why, did Grandmother not tell the woman that I was her granddaughter, the daughter of her eldest son? My feelings were not as articulate as they are now, but I knew that something was very wrong. And that was not the only occasion; Grandmother explained my presence to everyone that way. I was told to make the same reply if I were asked about myself. Grandmother even added a threat to drive her point home. "You don't know this yet, but as far as the register goes, you're absolutely unrelated to us. So if the truth comes out, you and your family will all have to dress in red." I did not fully comprehend, but I realized that wearing red indicated humiliation and was sufficiently intimidated so that I never told anyone the true situation in all the seven years that I lived there.

They must have felt that my crude way of speaking and uncouth manners would never do for a daughter in their refined home, that I would only sully the family name. But how could I have understood that then? After all, I had gone there fully convinced that I was to be their child.

II

I had been in Korea less than ten days when I started in at the village primary school. It was a one-story, thatched-roof building in the middle of the village. When you opened the waist-high sliding window in the classroom you could see across the fields to the marketplace and the crowds of people, donkeys, cattle, and pigs.

It was a village-run school and there were less than thirty pupils in all. The teacher was a good-hearted old man in his sixties whose only qualification to teach was that he was related to the village doctor. Unfortunately, there was no third grade when I entered the school, so I was put in with the fourth graders. My first-grade schooling, two weeks of which were at that place with the beer cartons for desks, had been all of six months, during which time I had moved no less than four times. Second grade had amounted to five months, and third grade, not even four months. And now here I was in the fourth grade at only nine years of age. I suppose it was expecting a lot to put me in fourth grade, but I was quite pleased about it. Then I was told something that pleased me even more. "Now look, Fumi, for a child of poor people like the Kanekos, it wouldn't matter how you behaved; but from now on, even if only temporarily, you're going to be going to school as the child of the Iwashita family. You've got to keep that in mind and study hard. If you fall behind the peasant children or do anything to make us ashamed of you, you'll be deprived of the family name."

I was delighted, for this meant that I really *was* the Iwashitas' child after all. And sure enough, the other children all called me "Iwashita." Also, thanks to my aunt's family, I received an award for excellence on the yearly exam and had the name "Iwashita Fumiko" inscribed in beautiful writing on my certificate.

When I got to fifth grade, however, lo and behold, the name on my report card and certificate was "Kaneko Fumiko." Had I been stripped of the right to bear the Iwashita name in the space of barely half a year? I had not fallen behind the peasant children in my studies, nor do I recall doing anything that would have cast shame on the Iwashita name. Why, then, was I no longer Iwashita Fumiko? I think I can surmise what happened.

When I started school I was given a room in the vacant house in the garden to use as a study. I was told to close myself in this room as soon as I got home from school and review my lessons there, one hour for each subject. Perhaps it is out of place for me to say this about myself, but I did not need to study. I do not remember where I learned, but I could read sixth-grade readers by the time I was in second grade, and in the third grade I could read the high school morals textbook without difficulty. I was good enough at math that I do not recall ever running up against a single problem in the whole primary school curriculum that gave me trouble. By the time I was eleven or twelve, I could multiply two four-digit figures in my head. And in singing, if the teacher went through a song four or five times, I could remember it perfectly. The only things I was not good at were technical subjects like calligraphy and drawing. There was thus absolutely no reason for me to do review or lesson preparation.

When I got in my room and unburdened myself of my school bag, there was nothing to do except munch on the crackers my aunt had given me and wonder if the time would ever be up. Once I was so bored that I burst out of the room before it was time, hoping to get them to let me off. "I don't have to review, Grandmother. I'll do all right."

My grandmother glared at me and said, "You're not with poor folks like the Kanekos now, and you're not going to get away with lazy ways like one of them."

Although hurt that they had misunderstood my intentions, I screwed up my courage to try again. "But I can read fine without doing any review. I want to read harder, more interesting books." My request was of course turned down.

"I don't want any of your lip. You've got all you can manage with your school books."

This was an order and I had to obey. I did try in the beginning to review my lessons, but it got to be ridiculous and I finally took to amusing myself making dolls or playing with a ball. I would have asked to be allowed to play outside, since I was only playing anyway, but I knew they would scold me, so I contented myself with playing on the sly, my text and notebook open in front of me. Grandmother must have caught on, though, for every once in a while she would creep up on my room and suddenly slide open the door, usually to find me playing. She would give me a terrific scolding. After this had happened five or six times she took away my study time. Needless to say, this was about the biggest blunder I could have made. With this I doubtless gave them their first good reason for judging me unfit to be the Iwashita family successor.

III

The subjects that I was poor in were technical ones like calligraphy, drawing, and, later, sewing. I do not dislike these subjects, and I do not believe I am innately bad at them. But from the start of my school career in Yokohama I was never given the paper, brushes, and pencils for me to become proficient in these subjects, nor was I able to attend school regularly enough. I realized how bad my writing was when I got to Korea, and I determined to work at improving it. But the family would not give me sufficient paper to do this.

I would ask for paper on the day we had calligraphy, but Aunt gave me only two pieces, and these were full of creases. They were actually paper the little gifts she brought home from her social visits had been wrapped in. I am not fastidious, but I could hardly get enthusiastic about writing with paper like that. If I made a mistake, however, there was nothing else to use. For this reason I probably handed in no more than one calligraphy assignment in three from the time I was in fourth grade until I graduated from upper primary school. This is perhaps why my writing is so poor and why, to this day, I cannot even hold a brush properly.

I will never forget an incident in connection with drawing class. In fifth grade we started using paints, so I had to get the family to buy some for me. But knowing how hard it was to get even necessities out of them, I hesitated to ask, and when I did, it was with great trepidation.

"Show me your art book," Uncle said.

I brought my book, and he gave it a cursory inspection. "Well, if this is all you need them for, the paints I've got will do you fine." Uncle gave me three old jars of the basic colors, red, blue, and yellow, and two worn brushes from his paint box.

The paints were used up in no time. Just then the school supply store in the village was selling a new kind of paint that came in sticks that you rubbed down like you would an ink stick. The colors came out nicely, but more important was the fact that it was new and everyone was using it. I wanted this kind of paint too. This was, after all, something that I had to have for school, so after much deliberation I got up the courage one morning to ask for it—a set of paints that cost all of twelve sen.

"If it's something you really need, I'll buy it for you," Uncle said. Aunt also gave her consent, but Grandmother would not allow it.

"Now look here, you," she said, putting down her chopsticks and fixing a menacing scowl on me. "Don't tell me you've forgotten already? You weren't registered. And you know what that means, don't you? If a person isn't registered, it's as good as not being born. People like that can't even go to school. And if they do go, they're only made fun of, aren't they? Well, I felt sorry for you and entered you in our register. If I hadn't helped you, you'd still be unregistered today and wouldn't be able to go to school with everyone else the way you do now. So you just keep in mind the fact that it's only because of our goodness that you're going to school. But you can never seem to remember your place. It's always 'I've gotta have this, I've gotta have that.' Well, you keep that up and you'll be taken right out of school. Just remember that when you open that mouth of yours. It's up to me whether you go to school or not."

I never got the paints, not that it mattered. But how it wounded my pride to hear that word again, "unregistered," which was always being thrown up at me. I write this now as an adult, but the truth is that when I was young I did not know that the reason I could not go to school or, if I did go, was treated differently, was that I was not registered. And not knowing the reason, my humiliation and shame were that much worse. It was only when I went to Korea that I learned I was not registered.

But was it my fault? I did not even know that I was not registered. My parents knew, and they should have been made to suffer the consequences. But I was the one the schools closed their doors to; I was the one people looked down on. Even my own Grandmother, my own flesh and blood, held it over me.

But I had been born. I was alive, all right! Let Grandmother say what she would about "not being born," I was alive, and I knew it.

IV

In the summer of the year that I was in fifth grade, the school was made a public school and an upper primary section was added. The elderly teacher was replaced by a young man who had been to teacher's college. At about this time a large-scale project to move the railroad tracks was undertaken; also, tungsten was discovered in the mountains nearby. This brought an influx of Japanese to the village, and the school enrollment leaped to over one hundred practically overnight. A new school was built on some property owned by my aunt's family at the foot of a hill in the middle of the village. But this new school had only one classroom more than the former one-room schoolhouse had and, like the former, had only one teacher. The education that took place there thus left something to be desired. Because my family would not give me the supplies I needed, I always borrowed paints and pencils from the new teacher, whose name was Hattori. I know he felt sorry for me, but he had to curry the favor of the big wheels in the village; so although he often came to call at my aunt's home, he never took the opportunity to offer his opinion or put in a word on my behalf. I suppose he is to be pitied.

V

When I was twelve or thirteen, I was put to work in the kitchen under Grandmother's command. From the Iwashita family heiress, I had descended to the position of maid. In fact, all of the housework fell to me, from washing the rice out in the winter cold, to getting the fire started under the floor heater, from cleaning the chimney of the oil stove, to scrubbing up in the privy. Not that I am complaining, far from it. I am grateful for the training that I gained. But I am a person too, and a woman at that. One thing happened that was hard to bear.

I do not remember if it was the spring or fall, but the day was cold and wet. Uncle had gone to a gathering of his poetry group, and the male servant, Kō, was pounding rice out by the granary at the end of the yard. Inside, Grandmother was playing the shamisen behind the closed sliding doors, and Aunt was going through her dances. It was a quiet day, and I was alone in the kitchen, squatting in front of the stove. Lulled by the lethargic pounding of the pestle, the drizzle of the rain, and the soulful tones of the shamisen, I was lost in my own melancholy thoughts and savored the quiet that my loneliness afforded.

When the greens I was boiling on the stove were ready, I removed them from the pot and plunged them in cold water. Then I carried the pan out to the drain by the well and was about to pour out the boiling water when suddenly the hot steam hit my bare arms. I sensed that I was not going to manage and, sure enough, the handle came loose and the pan fell and shattered.

Now you've done it! I thought—too late of course. Not that I felt I had done anything bad; in fact, when Grandmother came back in the kitchen I told her straightforwardly about breaking the pot. She started screaming. "What! You broke the pot? You careless lout!"

I cowered and just stood there staring at Grandmother. She lit into me, and when she was done, said that I would have to pay for a new pot. I meekly consented. About two weeks later Grandmother went to town to buy the pot.

The old pot could not have cost more than seventy sen when it was purchased four or five years previous, but prices had skyrocketed in the meantime and now the pot supposedly cost one yen, twenty-five sen. "The lid wasn't broken, so I didn't have to buy that. And since I did some other shopping while I was out, I'll pay for the train fare myself," Grandmother said.

In all the time I was at my grandmother's house, I was only given spending money once, all of ten sen. How then did I pay for this one yen, twenty-five sen pot—out of my maid's salary? As I said, I never received so much as a single sen for my work. The pot was paid for out of the twelve or thirteen yen that my family had scraped together to give me as a farewell gift when I left for Korea.

VI

But there was at least some consolation in the fact that I could buy off a measure of my grandmother's wrath with money when I broke something. It was when I could not pay with money that I had it hard. For sometimes I had it taken out of me in corporal punishment.

I remember the time I was thirteen and it was the second day of the New Year's holiday. The Iwashita family were all gathered around the breakfast table eating the New

Year's soup when, for some reason, one of Grandmother's chopsticks snapped in two. I was the one who had put the chopsticks into each person's paper holder before the holidays, so the blame naturally fell on me.

Grandmother, pale with rage, flung the chopstick at me and launched into a tongue-lashing. "What's all this about? It's a bad omen, I tell you, right at the beginning of the New Year. Fumi, you're trying to wish me dead, aren't you? I'll just have to remember that."

I picked up the chopstick she had thrown at me, and, sure enough, worms had eaten two holes right in the center. I had not noticed, and for that I should indeed have been blamed. But why would I have wanted to wish my grandmother dead? I did not even know that one could wish a person dead by doing something like this.

"I'm sorry. I'm afraid I didn't notice," I said to apologize. But Grandmother would not forgive me.

What should I have done? Based on past experience, I knew that I had two options. I could either keep insisting that it had been an accident, or admit to the charge and promise to be more careful in the future. But I could not very well have said that, yes, I had wished my grandmother dead; I might as well have told them to go ahead and kill me! And besides, it was not true. But Grandmother would not accept my denial. She gave me my usual punishment.

Just the thought of "my usual punishment" is enough to make me shudder. I was immediately sent outside without being allowed to have any New Year's breakfast. It was one of those subfreezing Korean mornings. I was cold and hungry, but not wanting to be seen standing there like a fool, I hid behind the privy. There was a wall on one side, and on the other side the hill had been cut away where a house was to be built. Never once did the rays of the sun reach this spot. The snow that was packed there had turned to ice, and it was impossible to keep from slipping.

The Manchurian winds that blew up from time to time pelted my face with sand and snow.

I tried standing. I tried stooping. I broke down and cried. I tried fantasizing about what a happy life would be like in order to forget how miserable I was. Nothing helped, of course. After a while Grandmother came out to feed the chickens. "Well, how do you like it? Nice to be able to play like this?" Grandmother's face was twisted in an ugly grimace. She made no gesture of reconciliation and walked briskly on by. I ran after her and tugged at her sleeve, asking forgiveness; but she only brushed my hand away. How forlorn I was! It was only at the end of the day, after the family had finished supper, that I was at last pardoned.

In Korea when the temperature plunges in the evening, the cold is something fierce. The skin of my face was hard as a board from cold and exhaustion, and my legs, stiff as poles, were so numb that I felt no pain when I pinched them. I was so hungry that I was dizzy.

I was at last permitted back into the house, but my teeth were chattering so, and I was so completely drained of strength, that I could not even hold a pair of chopsticks.

This sort of thing happened more times than I care to count. But what was particularly bad was when Grandmother deliberately set me up to do something wrong, or when she blamed me for something that she herself had done. But I have said enough about this.

There is one thing that I must add, though. At the end of this punishment, whether deserved or not, I was always made to apologize and to swear that I would never do the misdeed again. Perhaps they thought that this was necessary for them to maintain their dignity. Or maybe they believed it was for my own good.

From my own bitter experience, there is one thing that I would like to say: Make children take responsibility only for what they have actually done! Otherwise you rob them of a true sense of responsibility, you make them servile, and you teach them to be two-faced, in both thought and deed. No one should have to make promises about their actions to another. Responsibility for what one does cannot be entrusted to a custodian. Each person, and that person alone, is the subject of his or her actions. Only when one realizes this will one be capable of acting responsibly, autonomously, and with true conviction, deceiving no one and in fear of no one.

The disciplinary methods my grandmother and the others used turned me into a devious liar. If I broke even a dish, I worried myself sick over it. What with my copious head of hair, I was often breaking combs, for instance; and each time I would worry so much over that one comb that I was unable to eat. Although I did not want to hide what I had done, I was terrified of telling the family. In dread of the abuse, verbal and corporal, that would be heaped on me, I invariably lost the initial chance to make my confession. I would agonize over whether to tell them that day or put it off until the next, until whole days had slipped away, by which time I really was trying to conceal whatever it was that I had done. I would wrap a broken bowl in paper and stuff it down into the bottom of its box, or try to stick a broken comb back together with rice grains and stealthily put it back among the other articles in its case. I was gloomy and depressed. Because of the anxiety and fear in which I lived, I could never be at peace.

VII

In writing of this period in my life, I must say something about the male servant, Kō. Although not a very bright man, Kō was honest, straightforward, and an unusually hard worker. He never tried to get out of work, nor was he the kind of man who could have pocketed, even inadvertently, anything that belonged to his master.

Kō had a wife and three children. His eldest daughter was pretty, and a man had offered to buy her for three *to* of unpolished rice. My grandmother, however, told Kō not to sell her. If he waited until the girl was twelve or thirteen, she said, he could get one hundred yen for her. Although Kō was desperate, he deferred to my grandmother and went on feeding the girl.

Kō was paid around nine yen a month, which was two or three yen lower than the going wage. This arrangement did not last long, however. My grandmother figured that she could make out even better if she paid him partly in rice instead of cash. She gave him some excuse and started paying him two yen of his salary in rice, and very poor quality rice at that, which she estimated at a rate two sen cheaper per five *shō* than usual.

Kō was thus extremely poor. No one in his house had enough to eat, and in the cold of winter his children shivered in hemp rice bags. Even Kō himself, the mainstay of the family, literally owned only the clothes on his back. My grandmother was always getting after him, in fact, about how dirty they were, and how she could not have him disgracing the family. One bitterly cold winter evening Kō, standing outside, had the following conversation through the closed sliding doors with my grandmother inside.

"Ma'am, I apologize for asking, but I wonder if I could have the day off tomorrow. There is something that I really have to do."

Grandmother, who was ensconced in the warm kotatsu, lit into him. "What! Just like that: 'Gimme the day off.' You too, eh? Want to see how much you can get away with. Well, you just keep it up and see what happens."

"Oh, no. It's not that at all. I really can't come tomorrow."

"Is that so? Well, why not? Expecting your rich relatives from Seoul?" Grandmother and Aunt looked at each other and had a good snigger over this little joke.

"No, it's not that. You see," Kō answered, acutely embarrassed, "it's the washing. . . ."

"Washing? Well, if it's only washing, there's no reason you have to do it. That's what your wife is for, isn't it? Talk about spoiling a woman!"

What a contrast: the maliciousness of the two inside and the misery of the poor soul outside! Though I was only a child—no, precisely because I was a child—I hated my grandmother and aunt out of a sense of pure justice more at that moment than I ever have in my whole life.

"It's not that I'm easy on my wife, Ma'am. You see, I only have this one set of clothes; so while my wife is washing them and drying them over the fire, and putting the padding back in and sewing them up again, the only way I can keep warm is to stay under the quilt."

The two of them guffawed. Then—perish the thought that they should give the man something else to put on—they simply granted his request.

Kō was a hard worker, but he was doomed to poverty. He had once been about to quit, figuring that if he went back to the railroad construction job that he had before, he could make seventeen or eighteen yen; but Grandmother would not let him go. She persuaded him that even if he did make seventeen yen, or even eighteen yen, the work was not as good as what he was doing for her. And besides, she said, he should take into account all the largess that fell his way in her employ.

"You've got to remember that you're getting your lodging free; and when you're really pressed, we give you an advance on your wages. Even when you borrow money, you only have to pay the usual market interest of 70 percent. And though it may be small, we're renting you a garden patch, and your pots and pans and things. . . ."

The weak Kō, though knowing full well that he would actually be better off working on the railroad, could not bring himself to quit and was thus stuck with his suffering.

VIII

She came into my life when I was just starting fifth grade. She was one of the twenty or thirty new students who entered the school at that time. Pretty, quiet, mature, and intelligent, I liked her from the start. She must have felt the same way about me, because we quickly became friends and were soon confiding completely in one another. The more I was with her, the more I liked her, and our relationship at school glowed with the warmth of a sisterly intimacy.

Our friendship was my one and only happiness. I was not loved at home, but this child adored me. And in her I found someone I could love. If it had not been for her, I doubt that I would have had the will to go on living. Her name was Tami, and her family had a shop that sold stationery and wooden clogs twelve chō from the school. Her father had died when she was young, after which her mother had been sent back to her own family, leaving Tami and her younger sister to be raised by the grandparents. The grandparents were not unkind, in fact they loved the two girls. Yet I could not help feeling sorry for Tami, having to be raised by her grandparents like that, and wondered if that was why she always looked so withdrawn.

Tami followed me everywhere. If there was a word she did not understand or an arithmetic problem she could not do, she brought it to me. But Tami had a weak constitution and was often absent from school with a cold or fever. In winter she came to school with white cotton wrapped around her neck. When she was sick, I sometimes stopped by to visit her on my way to or from school. Her grandmother liked me for this and often gave me candy or school supplies. Our love deepened as time went by, and I grew fond of her younger sister too.

Tami and I were only able to enjoy one another's company at school, however, for I was not allowed to go over

to friends' homes or to play in the fields in the neighborhood the way the other children did. The other children
would fling down their school bags as soon as they got
home from school and run off to play in a grassy field
barely a block from my aunt's house. If I happened to be
sweeping or doing some other work in the yard, I could
hear them calling out to each other. Their voices raised in
laughter and tears, pouting and anger, and the chanting of
the rock-scissors-paper rhyme were so clear that I could
almost have reached out and touched them. By peeking
through a crack in the fence I could see the boys and girls
chasing about, their obi trailing behind them. What fun
they were having! How free they were! And how sad I was
as I watched them that I too was not a "poor nobody."
Grandmother was always drumming it into me that we
were not "poor nobodies" like them and that we mustn't
take after them. "We're not in the habit," she said, "of letting our children run around wild like that." I had to be
miserable, shut up in the house, thanks to this "refined"
upbringing. And the knowledge that this was just a pretext
to treat me like a slave in my own house made it all the
harder to bear.

The neighbors knew how strict the family was with me
and how hard they made me work, and the neighborhood
children normally did not come by to ask me out to play.
Occasionally, however, when there were not enough to
make up a game, or when for some reason they particularly wanted to include me, I would hear a voice outside
the gate calling to me to come out and play.

And how I wanted to join them! But knowing that this
was out of the question, I kept still and made no reply. If I
were outside when they came, I would dash around the
back and hide, holding my breath. Grandmother, angered
by the children's cries, would go out and tell them she was
not in the habit of letting Fumiko out and not to come over
any more. From the speed with which they ran away, you

would think the children had seen a ghost. Afterward I would be scolded and accused of having put the children up to it, or of trying to get out of work, or told that I had a mean nature. . . .

IX

Not being allowed to play after I got home was one thing, but the day came when I was told that I must come straight home after school let out, which meant losing my five or ten minutes of play on the way home. When school got out early I had five or ten minutes to fool around on the way home, but woe be tied if I ever got caught! Needless to say, I was never allowed to leave for school even as much as five minutes early.

Then something happened that caused me no end of trouble. We, the "uptown" folks, had always cut across the nearby railroad tracks when we went to town or to school. But when the old station master was replaced, this road was blocked off so that we could no longer reach the so-called working class district without making a long detour. People for whom this was too great an inconvenience moved to the south side of the tracks, with the result that there were no Japanese left on the north side except for two or three families of my aunt's standing and a poor barber's family. This would not have mattered except that it meant that the only one I had to walk to school with was the barber's daughter, a girl named Omaki.

This barbershop was a run-down place just half a block down the road from my aunt's house. It consisted of only a small, damp room with a dirt floor at the front of the house and contained only one wooden chair that had a broken leg tied with a rope and a mirror, the surface of which was half cracked off.

Omaki and I walked to and from school together until Grandmother found out, when she put a stop to it. "Fumi, you are not to go to school with the child of people who make their living off the filth of other people's heads."

I had no choice but to obey. In the morning I would take my time over washing and drying the dishes so that I would leave the house late, or sneak out the back way and go to school all alone. That worked on the way to school, but there was no way I could avoid Omaki on the way home; and she invariably wanted to walk home with me. I could not very well have said to her, "I can't walk home with a poor person like you," so I kept to myself and tried to walk a little ahead of or behind her, in dread all the while of what my grandmother would say if she saw me.

One summer day Omaki and I left school a little after noon. We had only gone about half a block when she stopped and said to me, "I'm going to stop in at my uncle's; there's something I want to pick up. Would you wait for me, Fumi? I'll only be a minute." Her uncle had a hardware store right in front of where we were standing. He made a fairly good living and evidently contributed something toward the expenses of Omaki's family.

Here was the perfect chance to make my escape! I mustered my courage and said, "Oh, well in that case, excuse me if I go on home ahead of you; we're pretty busy at my place."

But Omaki loved company. "Oh please," she practically begged, "I won't be a minute. Wait for me, will you?"

What could I say? Reluctantly agreeing to wait, I leaned up against the fence in front of the house. Omaki happily hurried inside. But three, five, seven minutes passed with no sign of her. I was getting worried and beginning to regret that I had agreed to wait. Anxious, and peeved at Omaki, I decided to tell her that I could wait no longer. "I'm going home," I yelled into the house.

"I'm sorry to be so long," she answered apologetically, and then, to hasten her aunt, "Please hurry; I'm keeping Iwashita-san waiting."

Omaki's aunt appeared and said to me, "Oh, did Omaki make you wait for her? I didn't realize. It's so hot out there, please come in. The heat these days is really something, isn't it?"

It was so rare to hear a kind word that when someone did speak to me in a sympathetic tone of voice it was enough to make me break into tears. I forgot my fear and my irritation and went in. I sat in a corner of the shop where I hoped no one could see me from outside; but no sooner was I seated than I started to worry again. I kept looking outside nervously.

And sure enough, luck was against me again. Who should I see bicycling past in front of the house but my uncle. He saw me as well, and he threw me a stony glare as he rode past. I was terrified and felt more dead than alive. I thought for a minute my heart had stop beating, only to find the next minute that it was pounding away. When my wits returned, I jumped to my feet, excused myself, and flew out of the shop.

I ran the seven or eight *chō* to my house in a daze, my school bag bouncing on my shoulder. When I reached the gate, however, I was too petrified to go in. My legs felt like lead. At last I mustered all my courage and entered. My aunt was sewing in Grandmother's room, as she often did. I squatted respectfully in the hall outside and announced politely, shaking all the while with fright, that I was back from school. Aunt flew at me. She pushed me, or rather kicked me, down on the earthen floor of the kitchen. Still not appeased, she jumped down after me in her bare feet and hit me all over the body with her measuring stick. Grandmother joined the attack. "All right. I'll teach you so you'll learn real good," she said as she kicked me with her clogs.

When the beating was over I was too limp to get up; I just lay there where I had fallen and cried, tears my only solace. This corporal punishment over, Grandmother dragged me out to the grain house in the yard, shoved me inside, and padlocked the door from the outside, just as they do in this prison. Sacks of unhusked rice that had been steaming all day under the hot summer sun made it stifling inside. But what confronted me first, when I began to recover from the shock of what had happened, was the pain in the places where I had been hit and kicked. I noticed that my comb had been broken and that my head was cut. And besides this, I had not had any lunch and was ravenously hungry. There was nothing here to eat however. I leaned feebly against the sacks of rice and, picking up a few grains that were spilled out at my feet, peeled the husks off one by one with my fingernails and chewed the grains. But then I remembered what had just happened and began crying all over again. I must have been exhausted, however, for before I knew it I had fallen asleep.

They let me out of the grain bin the evening of the next day. Though her anger had by no means subsided, Grandmother handed me, without a word, some pumpkin. I wolfed it down. When I had finished, my uncle came over and gave me a letter. "Go and take this to school," he said.

I could see that it was addressed to my teacher. "Now, sir?"

"Yes, this minute."

I washed my face, changed, and left the house. Although I did not know its contents, I could imagine well enough that it contained a request to my teacher to admonish me for what I had done. But what *had* I done that was so bad? Our morals textbook enjoined us to be good friends to one another and not to look down on people who came from homes poorer than our own. Why, only two or three days before, our teacher himself had spoken to us on the topic of "friendship." I could remember exactly what he had said. I was sure the teacher would not scold me; in fact, the thought that I was on my way to the only ally I had lifted my spirits.

The teacher had evidently just finished supper. He was strolling in the garden, dressed in a yukata, his child in his arms.

"Good day, Sir."

"Oh, Fumiko," the teacher greeted me with a smile. "You weren't at school today. What happened—get scolded again?"

The teacher knew that I was always being punished for something or other and probably did not think it was all that serious. Or perhaps he said this to show his sympathy. I had thought on the way that if only I could see him and tell him what had really happened, he would be able to tell me what to do. But as soon as he said this to me, I broke down in tears and could not get a word out. Still crying, I took the letter out of my pocket and handed it to him. He took it without a word, broke the seal, and, after giving it a quick glance, rolled it up again and stuffed it back in the envelope.

"I don't know what you've done, but it says that due to some misconduct you're to be taken out of school."

His words struck me like a heavy blow on the chest. My head spun, and I felt as if I were going to fall. The teacher continued.

"But there's nothing to worry about. Of course they won't really keep you out of school, only make you stay home for a while. I'll have a talk with them. But you see, it's hard to get your people to relent once they've said they're going to do something. All you can do is to be patient for a while and do what they tell you."

What could I say to make him understand? And I had no one else to turn to. I felt betrayed and left without saying a word. I cried my eyes out in an empty classroom, but the only response was the sound of my own sobs echoing in the room. I had never felt so acutely how utterly alone I was in the world.

From what the teacher had said, I gather that he and my

uncle had talked about me earlier in the day. At this moment when I had been kicked down to the depths of isolation, I perceived all too clearly the cowardliness and insincerity contained in that word, "teacher," and I realized only too painfully how hollow and deceitful their fine-sounding lectures really are.

X

This was in early June. At the beginning of the new term in September, just as the teacher had predicted, I was allowed to return to school. But on my report card for the first term, the grade for deportment had dropped to "B," the only time this happened in all my years at school. To be going to school again revived my spirits, though, for now I would be able to see my beloved Tami.

Tami was in third grade and her sister, Ai, had just started school. I was in my first year of upper primary school. Seeing the two of them and doing little things for them was my one consolation in life, and how I had missed them! But I only had Tami's company for a brief time after that. The second term had barely begun when she had to stay home for a cold, which often afflicted her. After two or three days I used my lunch hour to run over and enquire how she was. Tami was delighted to see me, but I learned that she was not getting any better; in fact, the doctor said that she had pneumonia. But my visit cheered her and she began talking animatedly. I was afraid that might not have been good for her and decided not to visit for a while. Later I heard from Ai that her condition had worsened and that she now had meningitis. Once again I went to see her during my lunch break.

She was no longer the Tami I knew. There was no hint even of the wan smile with which she had greeted me the last time. She simply lay there, her eyes opened wide in an unseeing stare. When the doctor directed the light of his reflector onto her pupils she did not even blink. It was hopeless. Her grandparents sat there in silent grief. I cried. Tami was dying, and I would never see her again.

Two days later all the children at school accompanied Tami's remains on the long trip to the crematorium in the mountains. I was chosen to go the next day with two or three others to bring back the ashes.

Chance had brought us together in a friendship that lasted only three years, but we seemed to have been meant to share a special intimacy. My own background being what it was, I may have been particularly sympathetic to her having lost her father by death and then later being left by her mother. But whatever the reason, I had come to think of Tami as a younger sister. It was not just that I felt lonely after her death; it was as if something very important had been wrenched away from me. Every time something at home or school reminded me of her, I broke down and cried. A month went by like this.

One day I was leaning against a poplar tree at school while the other children were playing in the yard, when Ai ran up. "Iwashita-san, so this is where you've been," she said, pulling me by the hand. "Everybody's been looking for you; let's go. Hey, what's the matter with you?"

Unable to control myself, I threw my arms around her. "Ai, I've been thinking of your sister."

Her innocent expression was now gone, and she too looked sad. Then she remembered something. "Hey, Iwashita-san, did you see what I brought you the other day?"

"What you brought . . . ? Where?"

"What! You don't know?" she said in an endearing tone. "The sewing box that Sister got. Grandmother said that you were to have it as a memento, and to take it to you."

Tami's sewing box! Of course I knew it. It was a gorgeous black lacquer box with a gold scroll design on it, and it was still brand new. And to think that they had given it to me! How wonderful! I would never let anything happen to it. But Ai would have been disappointed if I had told her that the family had not given it to me yet, so I merely answered, "Oh, that? Yes, I saw it. Thank you."

If I had actually received that box I would have been far too jubilant to have responded so coolly, but under the circumstances, this was the best that I could do. I did not want Ai to know how badly I felt, so I suggested we play with the others. I took her by the hand and we ran off to join in the game.

XI

How I wanted that box! If only I could see it, I thought, it would be like meeting Tami again. As soon as I got home from school that day I found a pretext to search through all the closets and drawers, but the sewing box was nowhere to be found. It had to be there somewhere, I thought, and every day I made up excuses to tidy up closets and clean out rooms. Finally I had to conclude that my mean grandmother had put it someplace where I would never find it, and I gave up searching.

Several months later when I was cleaning in my grandmother's room I discovered a piece of paper that had fallen behind the dresser. My curiosity aroused, I stretched my hand between the dresser and the wall and slowly edged it out. It was a dusty old letter written in a child's hand by a "Sadako."

Sadako was the daughter of my grandmother's older brother and had once been adopted into this family. After a falling out between Grandmother and her brother, however, the daughter had returned to her own home. That was when they decided to take me.

I slipped the letter into my pocket and went to my room to read it. I have forgotten the wording, but not the import. The Iwashitas, it seems, had sent all kinds of gifts to

Sadako, including the clothes I had been dressed up in at my mother's village. I learned, too, from the letter that Tami's sewing box, which I had searched all over for, and which was to be a memento of her, had been sent to Sadako. I also learned that they were paying for Sadako's dancing, sewing, and flower-arranging lessons, while here I was being treated worse than a servant. The salutation at the end of the letter was quite explicit: "My dear Mother."

I will not blubber on like a baby about all the other things that were meant for me but were sent to Sadako. But when I learned that they had sent her Tami's sewing box, how angry, and sad, I was.

XII

It was three years now since the teacher, Mr. Hattori, had come to our school. Young, full of energy, and fond of sports, he had lost no time in installing a swinging log, rotary pole, and other gymnastic equipment in the school yard, all to the great delight of the children. And now he said that we were going to start farming.

He rented a large plot of land behind the school for our garden. We children formed teams of four or five, and each team was allotted a piece of land. Potatoes were chosen to start with because they did not require a lot of care. Excitedly we began digging our plots and making furrows as our teacher showed us on the little plot that he made. We imitated what he did and, after spreading fertilizer on our field, at last were ready to plant. Again, our teacher showed us how on his plot.

"Now listen, all of you," he called out heartily, "in ten days these seed potatoes will be sprouting. Just think of it—sprouts coming from these lumps of mud! And after that, little potatoes. And when we eat the potatoes, they turn into nutrition for our bodies. And, you know, for farmers potatoes are the easiest plant there is to raise. But even so, you can't just leave the seed potatoes to grow up by themselves and expect to get a good crop. You have to give the plants lots of care. And not only with potatoes: farmers have to work hard over all their crops. So you must never make fun of farmers. Without farmers, the Japanese people wouldn't be able to live. And that's true everywhere, not only in Japan."

We hung on his every word, for we were ten times more interested in this than in our classroom subjects.

The seed potatoes soaked up the heat of the sun and started to put forth little sprouts. We children danced for joy at this miracle of creation. The sprouts grew higher and higher. We went out to the fields every chance we got, compared the progress of our own potato sprouts with those of our neighbors, and bragged about who had the tallest. We measured our sprouts with rulers, scraping away the earth to make them look taller. Our schedule stipulated only one period a week for gardening, but this was not enough, so we took time from our other subjects as well. There we would be, fertilizing and weeding away out in the garden, the teacher in his undershirt, the girls barefoot and kimonos tucked up, the boys in nothing but their drawers. Everyone was drenched in sweat and covered with dirt from head to foot, but there was not a one of us who did not love it. Every once in a while the teacher's "Now everyone listen" would ring out, and we would know that he had something to say to us.

"We have to love one another. And not only people; we have to love things too, everything. But real love doesn't come easily; you have to work hard at it. Well, how about it—are you starting to love these plants?"

Another time he said, "Look how much work it takes just to grow one potato. We're spoiled from buying potatoes at the grocer's. We take them home and cook them, we eat them and enjoy them. But we have no idea of the backbreaking work the farmer has to put in to make them." He always wound up his little talk by saying, "So you must never look down on farmers. Farmers have our lives in their hands."

There was no rain. The earth dried up and the sprouts started to wither. All of us got up early and carried water out to our plants. Some even went out in the evening to water them again, that's how caught up we were in the fate of those potatoes. And of course I was right in there with the rest of them.

One day when I got home from school, however, I was called straight into the room where my grandmother and aunt were. My aunt began questioning me. "Fumi, is it true what we've heard: that you've all been playing at being farmers at school?"

"Yes," I answered, trembling, sure that I was going to be scolded for something. My aunt did not seem particularly angry, however. She merely said, as if to herself, "Imagine sending them out, even the girls, in this heat to make like farmers. Why, they're going to rip their clothes for one thing. . . ." Then she said to me, "I guess you'll have to carry through with what you've started. But after this, no more."

Although I was sorry I would not be able to garden in the future, I was relieved at least not to have to quit immediately. Grandmother, however, was of a different opinion.

"No. Not 'after this.' You've got to stop now. We're not paying tuition to have you taught how to farm. It's too bad that you've started, but I think we can manage to live somehow without you having to go out and work as a farmer." I merely listened as she went on. "From tomorrow you're not to have a thing to do with that farming, Fumi. And don't try to tell me that it's one of your school subjects. You can just stay home from school on the day that you have that subject, hear?"

I must have had a spiteful look on my face, for my grandmother got more and more worked up and started bringing up other things to scold me about.

"And another thing. You're always coming home with the thongs on your clogs broken. Well, I know very well what that's from: you hang and swing on that thingamajig and run around with the boys. Always taking after those vulgar poor kids. You're a girl, and you should behave like a girl that has at least a little bit of breeding. So starting tomorrow all that running around is forbidden. That goes for the swing and playing tag, too. And don't think I don't know what you're doing while you're at school. I keep an eye on you from the hill in back of the house. . . ."

Ah! My last bit of freedom was finally to be taken from me. Here I was at twelve, thirteen years of age, the most active period of my childhood, and I was to be forbidden every form of play other than the prescribed exercise period at school, and all because my clothes might fade in the sun, or the thongs of my clogs might break! What a trial it was for a rambunctious tomboy like me to be bound hand and foot like this. Now as an adult, when I hear a mother yell at her child for dirtying her clothes playing in the mud, I want to scream: "Which do you value more, your children or their clothes? It is not the children that exist for the clothes, but the clothes for the children. If soiling clothes is so awful, let the children go around in old clothes."

Adults make their children suffer for the sake of appearances, or to save themselves a little trouble. But it is the job of an adult, especially a mother, to help her child develop its natural abilities. It is a terrible wrong to deprive children of their freedom and rob them of their personalities. Let your children play as they please! To play freely on this earth is the one privilege nature has given to children. If they are allowed to play, they will grow up to be healthy human beings. Of this, at least, I am absolutely certain.

XIII

It was at the end of one of our lessons four or five days after Grandmother had handed down this sentence. Looking down at us from his platform, Mr. Hattori said in a disarmingly casual tone, "Well now, what are they saying at home about our taking up gardening? I'll bet some thought it was a good idea, but others might have said, 'Oh, we don't want our children doing anything like that.' "

Nobody spoke up. The teacher called on a boy named Hosoda. "How about at your place, Hosoda? Didn't your brother say anything?"

This boy, who lived with an elder brother suffering from consumption, said, "My brother's glad. He says it'll make me strong."

"My father, too . . ."

The children were murmuring among themselves, but no one ventured to speak out. The teacher looked as if he were going to call on someone, and I had an awful feeling that it would be me. I stared down at my desk, trying to be as inconspicuous as possible. And sure enough . . .

"What about your family, Iwashita-san? I'll bet your grandmother said something."

Perhaps, I thought, he had heard something. But even if not, he knew my family well enough that I could not have lied. Yet if I told the truth . . .

"Yes. Well, umm . . . Grandmother said that I'd get my clothes faded doing farming."

A sarcastic smile spread over his face. "Hmm, I see. Well, I guess for somebody who dresses in clothes fit for a queen . . . ," he said peevishly. Then, textbook under his arm, he rattled open the classroom door and stalked out in a huff.

Everyone's eyes were on my clothes, and I felt myself turning red with shame as I realized anew how shabby they were. I was wearing a shapeless, patched white yukata with an ugly indigo pattern.

How I hated the teacher then! Why did he have to humiliate me in front of everyone? He was always preaching during our gardening period how we should love what we work to raise, and here he was . . .

When I got home I could not get the incident off my mind. I was afraid, too, that I might have wronged my grandmother in some way by answering like that. The more I thought about it, the more I felt that I had to say something, and finally I told them what had happened.

They were not angry; in fact, they looked almost triumphant. Grandmother simply turned to my aunt and said, "My God, this stupid thing is really the limit. Doesn't even know the difference between what you talk about to outsiders and what you keep quiet about. We'll have to take care in the future not to say what we really mean in front of her; she'll blab about anything."

They had always tried to make me believe that everything they said was absolutely true. I realized now that they often said and did things that were not meant to be repeated. I could never again believe implicitly what they said. From now on I would have to weigh and measure everything.

XIV

With everything taken from me, both school and home were pure hell. But I must have possessed an obstinacy that saved me from being utterly crushed no matter how many times I was struck. Now, too, I was able to discover a world where I could be happy, and when I was alone, this world was all mine. I remember a time, the only time, when I had a taste of joy.

My aunt's family owned a mountain called Dae San, which Uncle had purchased when he worked on the railroad and had planted with chestnut trees. By this time it was bringing in quite a large income to the family. Eulalia and pampas grass grew shoulder high between the chestnut trees, and every fall men were hired to cut the grass. The income from this, too, was considerable.

In the fall when the chestnuts split open and fell to the

ground, someone from the family, usually Uncle, went to gather them. But Uncle was not very strong and sometimes was not up to climbing the mountain; then I would take it upon myself to gather the chestnuts. It was only times like this when I was able to find myself a free person.

That experience of joy occurred in the fall of the year I was stripped of everything. Uncle was in worse health than usual, and I often obtained Grandmother's permission to absent myself from school and go to gather chestnuts. When I went up the mountain I always wore tabi and leggings and tied zori to my feet, for there were vipers, and people were known to have been bitten. Equipped with a scythe, a stick, and a bag to put the chestnuts in, I set out from home in high spirits.

I was not the least bit sorry to be absent from school on days like that. Climbing this mountain all by myself was much more fun than school. Russet-colored chestnuts were already on the point of bursting out of their burry shells. I would twist them off with the forked end of my stick, work them around under my zori, and extract the nuts. If they would not come out with this method, I pried them out with the back of a hoe. After harvesting the chestnuts still on the branches, I went from one tree to the next, searching the ground for nuts that had already fallen out of their burrs.

In some places the ground was all but bare of vegetation, while in others the grass grew deep and thick. A pheasant, startled, suddenly flew up out of the grass, and a rabbit bounded away in fright. I was too startled myself to move at first, but my initial fright soon gave way to a warm sense of intimacy with these creatures. "Oh, you gave me a fright," I murmured. "You don't have to run away like that. After all, we're friends, aren't we?"

Not that the fleeing rabbit and pheasant paid me any heed. I did not care, though. In fact, I smiled to myself at the "funny things" and, leaving some of the chestnuts untouched in the clumps for them, moved on to another spot.

My sack grew heavy and my legs weary. I flung down all my gear and ran straight up to the top of the hill to rest. There was nothing up there you could actually call a tree, but yellow *ominaeishi*, purple bellflowers, and bush clover were in bloom all around. This "mountain" was not very high (in fact, our teacher had once asserted that it was not a mountain at all, only a "hill"), but from the top you could take in the whole of Bugang. To the northwest beyond the fields and rice paddies lay a number of buildings, including the railroad station and the inn. Although Bugang put on airs as a town, it was actually nothing more than a village. The most conspicuous buildings were those of the military police; and from one of these buildings I now saw a policeman in khaki drag a Korean out into the yard, rip off his clothes, and beat his naked buttocks with a whip. I could hear the shrill voice of the policeman counting his strokes: "One, two, three . . ." I almost felt that I heard the groans of the Korean man being whipped.

Not a very nice sight. I turned away and looked toward the south. Beautiful Bu Yong Bong towered off in the distance, and at its base, coursing leisurely from east to west like a silken obi, the Baek Cheon sparkled brilliantly with the reflected rays of the autumn sun. Along its sand banks, a mule plodded along under its burden, and at the foot of the mountain a Korean hamlet of low, thatched-roof houses peeped out here and there from between the trees. The peaceful village dimly emerging out of the mist could have been a scene from a Chinese painting.

As I gazed upon all this beauty, I felt that now, for the first time in my life, I was really alive. Overcome by a feeling of well-being, I dropped to the grass and gazed up at the sky. How deep it was. If only I could penetrate those depths! I closed my eyes and gave myself over to thought. A cool breeze stirred the grass about me, and when I opened my eyes again, there was a dragonfly perched on the end of my nose. My ears were humming with the sounds of crickets and bell-ring insects.

It must have been recess time, for I could hear the loud voices of children at play. I stood up, and there was the school right below me and the children engaged in a game of football.

Every time the ball fell to the ground the children fought over it with great gusto. They seemed to be having so much fun. At school I always had to look on sadly while the others played, but now I felt neither sorrow nor pleasure. It was as if I were merged in the scene. I felt a strength well up from deep inside me and yelled out "Hey!" to no one in particular. No answer came of course, for I was all alone.

The school bell rang and the children returned to the classroom. I descended back down into the grove of chestnut trees. I felt so light-hearted that I broke into a song I had learned at school. There was no one here to find fault with me; I was free as a bird. I sang until I was hoarse, making up my own songs, too. Emotions that I constantly had to repress now rose up freely, uninhibited, and I felt comforted. Thirsty, I picked some pears in the orchard beside the shack where we stored the chestnuts and devoured them, skins and all. Then I tumbled to the ground again to gaze up at the patches of sky and cloud that showed through the trees. I was assailed by the suffocating odor of the grass and the aroma of wild mushroom, and I breathed them in voraciously.

Nature! Nature in which there is no deceit! Simple and free, you do not warp a person's soul as humans do. I wanted to cry out my thanks to the mountain with all my heart . . . until I remembered the way that I lived; then I felt like crying. And cry I did, on and on, until there were no tears left. This day in the mountain was, after all, the only time I had to find myself. This was my one and only day of liberation.

XV

One day in the hottest part of summer, Grandmother's niece, Misao, came to visit. This woman was married to a man named Fukuhara who had his own hospital in Gang Gyeong. She had never been to visit before, and I believe she had hardly ever even corresponded; but she was no vulgar person like me, and the Iwashita family went all out to entertain her.

Misao, a beautiful woman of about twenty-four or twenty-five, brought her child, who was still nursing, with her. She arrived wearing a gauze crepe summer kimono covered with a gaudy flower pattern, and she had girded this with a garish obi heavy with gold and silk thread. In spite of the heat, she wore a silk crepe jacket over this. With a gold necklace at her throat and gold rings on her fingers, her attire was not very harmonious, but it did give the impression of a very well-to-do woman.

The formal greetings upon her arrival were barely spoken when Grandmother noticed that Misao's kimono was drenched with sweat. "Why, Misao, your clothes are positively soaked. Take them off and change into something else."

"So they are. Perhaps I will change," Misao answered. She took off the clothes she was wearing, letting them drop about her. Grandmother herself picked them up and took them outside to dry in the sun, carefully spreading out each garment. She made sure to put them where they could be seen by the poor women of the neighborhood who came by to draw water from the well.

Grandmother was duly impressed when Misao told her of the opulent life she lived at her husband's home. "Oh, my, isn't that just grand. Aren't you the happy one. You'll have to be sure to take good care of that husband of yours."

Grandmother was full of blessings and kind words of

advice for Misao. She kept up her own end, too, boasting to her visitor about her household and the high position it occupied in the Bugang area. They went at it for a day or two without exhausting these topics, and during lulls in the conversation my grandmother or one of the others would escort Misao around the garden or on excursions out to look at their property.

I am sure that I came up in their conversation too. Misao obviously regarded me with disdain and barely even spoke to me. While I did not particularly dislike her, neither did I think her very nice.

Misao had a friend who lived just ten *ri* from Bugang, and she could not seem to make up her mind whether to go to visit her or not. Grandmother encouraged her. "Why don't you go. You can be there in no time on the train."

Misao hesitated. "But I've got this child. It'll be a lot of trouble." It was obvious that she wanted me to go along to take care of the baby. Grandmother picked up the ball. "That's all right. You can have Fumi carry the baby," she said.

Oh, no, I thought. Don't tell me that I'm going to have to lug this brat around in this heat for this woman who thinks she's some sort of queen.

"I guess I could. If she'd be willing, that would be fine, but . . . well, Fumiko, would you?" Misao was trying to get me to agree.

I avoided giving a direct reply, something that any other time would have brought Grandmother's wrath down on me. But for some reason, this time she seemed to humor me. Instead of ordering me to go, as she normally would, Grandmother merely said by way of suggestion, "Oh, why don't you go, Fumi." Then, when Misao was out of the room for a moment, she said softly, "Now if you don't want to, just say so. Nobody's going to make you do something you don't want to."

At the sound of these kind words my heart softened and

all my reserve dropped away. I wanted to cry in my grandmother's lap. I replied with all the simplicity of a child who trusts in its mother's love. "Actually, if it's all right, I don't want to go."

"What!" Grandmother exploded. She grabbed me by the front of my kimono and shook me. Before I knew what had happened I had fallen off the porch and was lying on my back on the ground. Glaring at me and spewing out her usual string of invectives, Grandmother started in.

"What! Don't want to go? Ease up on her the least little bit and this cheek is what you get for it. Well, it's not a question of whether you *want* to go or not: of course you'll go. You used to take care of sniveling little peasant brats, didn't you? But I'm not going to make you go. Oh, no. You don't want to go? Well, that's just fine with me. You've got no more business being in this house, and I'll just thank you to leave. So get out now. Out!"

Grandmother had slipped into the garden clogs and was now beside me starting to stomp and kick away at me for all she was worth. I lay in a daze on the ground while my grandmother left to go to the kitchen. Soon she was back with a chipped wooden bowl the man servant used, which she proceeded to grind into my breast. Then she grabbed me by the hair of the neck and dragged me over the ground to the back gate. By the time I realized that I had been thrown out, she had locked the gate and was clopping briskly back through the yard.

I was so completely exhausted and hurt that I could not move. I think that two or three Koreans passed by and said something, but I did not even make a move to get up. I just lay face down where I was and cried.

But lying there crying was not going to do me any good. No one else went by, and no one was going to come out from the house to call me back in. I had only that chipped bowl Grandmother had ground into my breast, and that was not going to do me much good. I would just have to go back and apologize. Marshalling all my courage, I stood up and groped my way along the wall to the front door and went in. I tied back my sleeves for work and set about carefully scrubbing the dirty porch. As soon as my grandmother saw me she called Kō to do the job. Then I started washing the dishes. But Grandmother pushed me aside and took over the task herself. When I started sweeping the yard, she came over and took the broom away from me without a word. I went to my room like a stray dog returning, dejected, to its lair. Dropping to the floor, I lay there motionless, staring dully at the old newspaper posted on the wall. But then I remembered what had happened and began to cry.

Evening came at last. Grandmother had taken the portable clay cooking stove out under the eaves of the main house and was frying tempura. There was only the garden between her and my room, and the smell of the oil seemed to sear into my empty stomach. I had not eaten a thing since breakfast.

Kō's little boy came up to Grandmother to return a dish his family had probably been given leftovers in. "My, my, what a good boy," Grandmother said, giving him two or three pieces of tempura. Then she looked over in the direction of my room, shrugged her shoulders, and laughed.

I slipped quietly out of the house; but once outside I had no place to go. I went down to the Koreans' communal well on the road just below and gazed aimlessly into its depth. A Korean woman whom I knew came along with a pot of greens to wash. "Have you been scolded by your grandmother again?" she asked in a kindly tone. When I nodded, she said, "Poor thing! Why don't you come over to our house; my daughter is home."

I felt like crying again, but from relief, not sadness. I could have melted in the warmth of her great compassionate heart. "Thank you. I'd like to," I said appreciatively as I followed her.

This woman's house was located on the ridge in back of my aunt's house and gave a clear view of it. I began to worry that perhaps I could be seen from there as well.

"Did you have lunch?" she asked.

"No. Since this morning . . ."

"My goodness, nothing since morning?" the daughter exclaimed in surprise.

"You poor thing." There it was, that phrase again.

"If you don't mind it's being only barley rice, please have some rice. We've got plenty."

I could no longer control my emotions; I broke down and cried. In all the seven long years I had spent in Korea I had never once been touched like this by an act of human kindness. I was so grateful and I wanted to eat so badly that I could have leapt at the food. But I was terrified of the family seeing me, terrified of my grandmother, who would be sure to say that she could not have in her house a beggar who took food from Koreans. I turned down the offer and left the Koreans' house, my stomach as empty as ever. Not wanting to go home, I wandered for a while in the field in back, but finally there was nothing to do but to return home. It was dark by this time, and the lamps in the house were lit. The family were in the living room chatting away over the evening meal. I did what I always did at times like this: I got down on my knees on the verandah outside the living room and apologized.

There was no response. I repeated the apology two or three times, but no one paid any attention. Grandmother finally yelled at me. "Oh, shut up. You do nothing but play all day; and when it gets dark and there's no place to go, you come home, apologize sweet as can be, and turn on the tears. Oh, if that isn't just like you. What's the matter— wasn't there anyone who would even give you a bowl of rice? Well, we're no different. No one is going to put any rice in your bowl here, young lady!"

There was still my aunt. I would throw myself on her

mercy and make her listen to my apology. But she had already joined my grandmother in denouncing me. Misao was there, but of course she would never have interceded on my behalf.

When they were finished, my grandmother and aunt hurriedly cleared away the dishes and then, as was their custom, they took a bench outside to spend the evening in the garden. I was alone in the house now and would use the chance to get something to eat. There was not a single thing to be found, though. Then I remembered the wire box on the girder under the eaves behind Grandmother's room. When I looked inside, however, there was nothing. Then I tried the meat safe in the kitchen corner, carefully opening the door so as not to make a sound. There was usually at least a pot of sugar inside; but now it was empty.

I went back to my room and groped around in the dark for the bedding. After I had laid it out and set up the mosquito net, I dropped down as I was, too exhausted to change into my bed clothes. I could not get to sleep, however, listening to the animated conversation and laughter from the garden and the voices of the Minamis, who lived nearby.

Oh, how I hated them. Yet I would try to think things through: was what I had done actually bad? I really wanted to be able to understand what it was that I had done wrong; but I did not know. It was past one o'clock by the time I finally fell asleep.

When I awoke the next day the sun was already in the sky. Kō was busy sweeping the yard as usual, Grandmother was fixing breakfast in the kitchen, and Aunt, who had taken over my job of cleaning the rooms, was energetically going at the sliding doors and the store room with the feather duster.

This was the moment to make my apology! They might scream and yell at me, but if I went now and plunged into my work, they would have to forgive me. It was now or never!

But completely devoid of strength, physically and emotionally, every time I tried to get up, I fell back down again. I had not eaten, of course, since the evening of two days before, and by now my stomach was so empty that I no longer even felt hungry. I could hardly lift my legs, to say nothing of getting up and working.

In the meantime they had evidently finished their meal. Misao and Uncle had gone out, and Grandmother and Aunt had gone off somewhere, perhaps to the vegetable garden. The house was quiet. I had let my chance slip by. "Well, that's that," I sighed. I did not care any longer; let come what may.

This thought cheered me up a bit. After tossing listlessly for a while, I put my feet up on the quilt I had kicked to the foot of my mattress and spent the next few hours half-asleep, half-awake, gazing up at the ceiling. Then, the sound of dishes clattering aroused me: it must be the family's lunchtime. "This is it," I thought as I forced myself to my feet. Fighting off dizziness, I made my way to where they were eating. Once again I groveled, forehead touching the floor. "I was bad. I will never speak willfully like that again," I apologized in complete sincerity.

No, "sincerity" is not the right word. "Earnestly"—yes, like a convict with the rope around her neck, pleading for her life with every bit of strength that is in her. Not that it was any use. They say that sincerity moves heaven; my grandmother and aunt, however, were not heaven.

"The fish today is nice and fresh, don't you think?" Grandmother addressed her remark to Aunt, pretending she had not heard me. Aunt, however, glared at me and gave me a good scolding. "If you were really sorry, why didn't you get up first thing this morning to make your apology? As long as you keep up that stubbornness, I'm certainly not going to speak to your grandmother for you."

This was more or less what I had expected, but the curtness of this rebuke left me numbed. I dragged myself back to my room, fell face down on the floor, and cried. But I had no more tears to shed. Propping myself against the wall by the window, I gazed absentmindedly at my outstretched legs.

Then, just like that, because I had ceased to resist, it rose up from within and appeared before me in all its simplicity—death. That was it: just die. How simple everything would be. With that thought I felt I had been saved; and indeed I had. I was suddenly flooded with strength, body and soul. My limp limbs tensed, and before I knew it I was on my feet, concerns like my empty stomach left behind forever.

The 12:30 express had not passed yet. Yes, that's what I would do! I would only have to close my eyes and leap.

But not looking like this, not in these rags. I changed my underslip as fast as I could, grabbed a light kimono and narrow muslin obi out of my box in the corner, and folded them into a tiny bundle, which I wrapped in a carrying cloth. I would have to hurry if I was going to make it. Concealing the bundle under my arm, I slipped out the back gate. I ran for all I was worth, radiant at the thought that I was leaving all behind and going to the salvation of death.

I came to the crossing just east of the station. The signal was still up. Good, the train would be coming soon. So as not to be seen from the elevation east of my aunt's house, I changed clothes behind the dike near the crossing. I rolled my old clothes up in the cloth and stuck the bundle in a clump of grass nearby; then, crouching down behind the dike, I waited for the train. It didn't come and didn't come. I realized at last that it had already gone by.

With that I felt a strange fear that I was even now being pursued by someone and was about to be apprehended. Oh dear, I thought, what shall I do? Then my mind became absolutely clear, and I knew in a flash what I would do.

The river, Baek Cheon! Into its bottomless indigo depths . . .

I crossed the tracks and began to run. Sticking to the cover of embankments, trees, and the kaoliang fields, I covered the fourteen or fifteen *chō* over back roads, without a pause, to the place by the old market where the river forms a deep pool. Fortunately there was no one around, and heaving a sigh of relief, I dropped down onto the gravel. I did not even feel the burning heat.

When the throbbing of my heart had subsided, I got up and started filling my sleeves with pebbles. They were soon fairly well loaded down, but then it appeared that the stones might slide out, so I slipped off my underskirt, spread it out on the ground and put more stones inside. I rolled the bundle up and tied it around my waist like an obi.

Everything was ready. I grabbed onto a willow tree by the bank and gazed into the pool. The water was perfectly calm and so dark that it almost looked like oil. There was not even a ripple. But when I stared into the depths I began to imagine that the legendary dragon was down there just waiting for me to fall in, and this thought made me uneasy. My legs felt weak and began to shake. Just then the sound of a cicada pierced the air over my head.

I looked then, once, at all that lay around me. How beautiful it was! I listened intently to the sounds around me, and how peaceful and still they were. This was farewell, farewell to the mountains, to the trees, to stones, to flowers, to animals, to the sound of this cicada, to everything. . . . I was suddenly sad. I could escape in this way the coldness and cruelty of my aunt and grandmother, but there were still so many things, countless things, beautiful things, to love. The world was much vaster than my grandmother's house.

My entire past, mother, father, sister, brother, my friends back home appeared before my mind's eye, filling me with nostalgia. I no longer wanted to die. I leaned against the

willow and thought. If I died here, what would my grandmother and the others say about me, about why I died.
They could say anything they liked, and I would never be
able to deny it, to vindicate myself. I cannot die now, I
thought. No, I have to seek vengeance; together with all the
other people who have been made to suffer, I have to get
back at those who have caused our suffering. No. I must
not die.

I went down again to the rocky riverbank and threw the
stones out of my sleeves and underskirt, one by one.

XVI

What a pathetic babe, determined to die and yet incapable
of carrying out the act! And as if it were not grotesque
enough to seek salvation in death at an age when she
should have been growing and unfolding like the young
grass in spring, what was the one thing she wanted to go
on living for? Revenge. It was horrible, sad.

With one foot over the threshold of the land of death, I
had suddenly turned back. I returned to what was for me
hell on earth, my aunt's house. But now one ray of hope,
albeit a black and gloomy ray, shone for me, and I had the
strength to endure any suffering that lay in store.

I was no longer a child; I had a little horned demon
inside. A tremendous thirst for knowledge grew in me.
What kind of lives were the people in this world living?
What was happening in the world? Not only in the world
of human beings, I wanted to know too about the world of
the insects and animals, the world of the trees and grasses,
the world of the stars and the moon, the whole vast world
of nature. It was not the miserly learning of the school
textbooks that I was after.

Every freedom had been taken from me. At school it was
sports and games, at home—everything. But the life within
me was not so weak as to wither up and die because of

that. Somewhere, somehow, I had to find an outlet for this will to live.

One day I was leaning against the wall of the schoolhouse watching the other children enjoying their games when a friend came up to me with an old magazine, *Young People's World*. "Is it interesting?" I asked.

"Uh-huh, pretty interesting."

I wanted to read it in the worst way. "Let me see it. Could I borrow it?"

She let me have it, and I started in on the first page. While the other children played, I positively devoured that magazine. Every single bit of it was fascinating, and even in class I could not get my mind off it. When school let out I hung back in the classroom to read it. I walked home at a snail's pace reading. At home, I stole every moment I could to read on the sly.

Grandmother caught me at it, of course, and scolded me, but I was not about to give up. I had to stop reading at home after that, but I read on the way to and from school, during recess, and even, unobtrusively, during class. I started borrowing books and magazines of every sort from my friends.

I had a problem when I left school, however, for since I was at home all the time then, I was no longer able to borrow books. I was constantly occupied with the problem of how to find a way to read. The daughter of one of the neighbors happened to bring over *Young Ladies' World* or some such magazine that she received every month. I borrowed it from her and told her that I would like to read any old books that she might have. She brought over a whole year's worth of back numbers and handed them to me right in front of my grandmother. I was beside myself with joy, but I eyed my grandmother and the others nervously. They thanked the girl, however, and accepted the magazines. For a while I was able to read openly and did in fact get through one or two of them without the family saying anything. But Grandmother did not keep silent on the issue for long.

"Why is it that if you let Fumi read she forgets everything else and lets the housework go? We don't say anything about it and it only makes her bolder. Well, we'll just have to stop this reading once and for all. . . ." Naturally my aunt was in complete accord.

"Oh, dear!" I made as if I were about to break into tears. "But suppose I swear never to read in the daytime, only at night?" I pleaded as nicely as I could. But to no avail: they took the magazines and returned them to their owner.

The only reading matter that crossed my eyes after that was the newspaper. Not that I was allowed to read one; newspapers were not for children, in the family's lofty opinion. The only way I could learn what was in them was to listen on the rare occasions when Grandmother read one, for she always read out loud. Occasionally I ventured a furtive glance at the headlines on the news page, or I would skim over the serialized novels when I was supposed to be doing the morning or evening cleaning. I dusted away at the sliding doors and shelves with my right hand, and in my left I held the newspaper. If there was an article that looked particularly interesting I would take it into the privy to read.

There were a few volumes on Uncle's sparse bookshelf that I wanted in the worst way to read. Once when my uncle and aunt went away on a trip, I took one of the books. It was one of Andersen's fairy tales; Uncle did not have much else.

It was not easy to read without being seen by my grandmother. That day and the next passed without my being caught, but on the afternoon of the third day my grandmother came tiptoeing silently up on me, as she was wont to do, while I was absorbed in reading by that outhouse in the corner of the field. She startled me with that shrill voice of hers. "Fumi, would you mind breaking off this branch for me?"

"Oh, oh," I thought, and hurriedly stuck the book in my bosom. It was a bulky four-hundred-page volume, however, and made my kimono bulge. Grandmother immediately noticed this and snatched the book out of my kimono. She called me a "thieving girl" and more.

"What a child! Stealing one of your father's valuable books. What if you had gotten it dirty or ripped it, what ever could you have said in apology? Oh, you're a horrid child, you are!"

To Grandmother and the others, books were not for reading; they were for adorning a room. She took the book back and locked it, together with the rest of Uncle's meager collection, in the closet. All links with books, the last world, the last friend that I had, had now been severed. In the two years between the time I left school and the time I left my aunt's house, I was not able to read a single thing. The only writing that I had access to was that on the pieces of old newspaper that patched my walls, and I had read them over so many times that I knew them all by heart. It was ironic that, what with their lofty rules about children not reading newspapers, Grandmother and the others should stick them up on my walls (something I will go into in more detail later). The reason, however, was simple: it would be sheer stupidity to spend money on a maid's room when old newspapers would suffice. They were quite capable of trampling on their own exalted principles without batting an eyelash if it was to their gain.

XVII

My schooling was over, at only higher primary school, the spring of my fourteenth year. Not only had Grandmother failed to keep her promise to send me to women's college, she had not even sent me to girls' school. I would have been taken out of school even sooner but for the fact that the tuition for higher primary school was the same, forty sen, as for lower primary school. Also, it would not have looked right if they had not sent me to higher primary school.

After graduation my life became unbearable. At least when I was going to school I was out from under the eyes of my grandmother for half of the day; now my whole life, from morning to night, was under her finicky inspection. It was much worse than my life here in jail.

The summer after I got out of school Grandmother made a floor of some pine logs in the storeroom out in back and covered it with three old tatami: from now on this was to be my room. Behind my back this was referred to as the "maid's room"; I had now sunk to the position of maid in name as well as in fact.

The maid's room faced my grandmother's room. It was only part of the storeroom, being separated from the wood shed by a thin wall. Since it was three mats in size, it should have been sufficient for one person, but half the space was still used for storing things. There were buckets, pickle casks, kettles, and the like jammed into the area by the entrance, and on the shelves in the room were washed rice tubs and boxes and other items wrapped in newspaper. My own belongings consisted of a box for my clothes and some faded bedding. Not only was there no desk, I did not have a single cushion to sit on. It was a dark, damp, mildewy, gloomy room, and for a window there was nothing but a hole about half the size of a sliding door hollowed out of the wall that faced my grandmother's room. This is where I had to live, together with all that junk, morning and night. Unless there was work to do in the main house, I spent the day alone in this depressing room, working on the kimonos they gave me to take apart.

It was not the drabness of this storage room that I hated; I was too accustomed to poverty and suffering for that to bother me. What drove me crazy was the meaninglessness of my life in this "maid's room." Some of my schoolmates had gone on to higher studies; others were working to support themselves; still others, though at home, were devoting themselves to preparing for the future that lay ahead of them. And here I was, stuck in the "maid's room," working at ridiculous jobs for my aunt and unable to learn anything that I would need for my life. I cared little about refinements like flower arranging, tea ceremony, or dancing, but I did want to learn basic skills needed for running a household like sewing and ordinary etiquette. I certainly wanted to read. But all of these things were neglected, indeed forbidden. The occasional simple sewing job they gave me did not help me in the least to learn how to sew. (We had not had a good teacher at school and so were taught practically nothing along these lines.) As far as cooking was concerned, the only thing they let me do was to boil the rice and make the miso soup. They were not going to teach me a single thing an adult woman needs to know.

I was young and was aching to grow and expand but did not have a single outlet for my energy. I was a bundle of frustration. Time and again I was obsessed by fears that I would have to spend the rest of my life in this moldy, stifling atmosphere, the "maid's room." I was on the verge of a nervous breakdown.

I was probably suffering from insomnia. I always felt tired and listless and would often doze off while working, yet I could not get to sleep when it was time to go to bed. Most nights I would toss and turn until one, two, or even three o'clock in the morning. Sometimes I would suffer through a whole night without getting a wink of sleep, and the next day I would feel heavy, listless, and headachy. I was often seized by vague anxieties. My life, bleak enough to begin with, had become more dismal than ever.

XVIII

From what I have written, it is clear that I knew nothing but cruel treatment the whole time that I lived in Korea.

But actually, I have recorded only a small fraction of the history of my maltreatment. I deliberately refrained from writing about the most typical, cruelest torment that I suffered, lest the reader think that I was lying, or that I only had my own warped disposition to blame for the way I was treated. I am sure that there are many who, reading even this watered down account, will think so. I cannot say that I was not warped and perverted, for I was. But what made me perverted?

As a child I was a tomboy and enjoyed playing the rambunctious games that boys play. And now, as a grown woman, I do not believe that I am either gloomy or melancholy. But I was the exact opposite during those seven years in Korea. I became warped because, instead of being loved, I was abused. I became perverted because I was repressed and robbed of every freedom. Though not always the case at school, at home I could not open my mouth without first weighing every word. Now I am able to speak with complete candor, but then? Never. I always had to try to guess what my aunt and grandmother would think and then attempt to reply in a way that would not conflict with this. Every action, too, had to be weighed in the same way. I found myself resorting to lies, devious behavior, and out-and-out stealing. What Rousseau said of himself in *Confessions* was true of me as well: abuse warped me to the point where I was even stealing.

As someone seeking after truth, candor, and justice, I personally totally reject the option of taking what belongs to another. Since coming to Tokyo from Korea, as hard up as I have often been, I have never taken so much as a straw for myself dishonestly. And yet in my aunt's house I stole. I would like to speak now of what led me to do such a base thing.

Only poor people, petty officials, and the like gave children money and let them go out and buy things; this was unheard of in the homes of the rich and well-bred. My grandmother's household set great store by this philosophy and prided themselves on its practice. Accordingly, I was never given money to buy what I wanted. Someone else usually got it for me, or I got it on a chit.

But this rule only applied in cases when I had to buy something for myself, not when it came to buying something for Grandmother's household. In fact, after I left school and became the occupant of the "maid's room," I was often given money and sent on errands, and always so on "market day."

In Korea, market is usually held five or six times a month, but in Bugang it was held on the sixteenth day of the month by the old calendar. The Bugang market, which used to be set up along the Baek Cheon, had once been one of the busiest markets in Korea; but after the railroad was completed it declined and was moved to the center of the village, where it now attracted people from a distance of perhaps no more than three or four *ri*. But even so, this meant a good one or two thousand people, and anyone with anything to sell, be they butchers, food vendors, cloth sellers, candy makers, chemists, or green grocers, came from all around to cater to them. Traders in the Japanese community were not about to let such an opportunity pass them by, nor did the Japanese residents spurn the chance to make cheap purchases at the market.

It would of course have been completely beneath my aunt and her household to open a stall at "a place like that," and even to shop there, like "those *okamisan*," would have been a disgrace. Yet being even more fanatic than most about saving a penny, they had to find a way to take advantage of the bargains there, and it was I who was always pulled into service for this job. This is how I came to be placed in a situation where I was forced to resort to stealing.

It was toward the end of the year, and I was fourteen. There was not much fish to be had at that time, and since what was available was quite expensive, the family decided that as far as possible we would prepare egg dishes for the New Year's table. Eggs were about ten for ten sen, and every market day I was sent to buy them.

Before I set out they always told me, "Bargain hard and get them as cheaply as possible. You're not to buy them at a high price, hear?" But how could a child like myself have driven a hard bargain? I did not even know, for that matter, what constituted a cheap, or expensive, price for an item.

One day I came home after buying eggs as I had been told. Grandmother placed one of the eggs in her hand, gauged its weight, and said, "You paid that much for eggs as small as this? Why, Miura's wife just now told me that eggs were dirt cheap today. I'll bet you bought sweet buns with those poor kids. . . ."

How mean of her to suspect me when I had done everything I could to bargain the seller down! In fact I was ashamed of myself because I had haggled so over the price that the seller had actually become annoyed. Even when the purchase had been made I worried and asked the people around if I had not paid too much for the eggs. On the way home I had taken them out of the straw wrapping and weighed them in my hand. What more could I have done to satisfy my grandmother? I was, after all, only a child, and in most cases I simply could not buy things as cheaply as an adult. Pondering what I could do to please my grandmother, I came up with an idea that led to my stealing.

On the days I went to market I would steal seven or eight copper coins out of the change box in the closet. I hid the coins in my obi, and when I got back from the market I handed them over to my grandmother along with the rest of the change from the day's shopping. Naturally, Grandmother would be all smiles; at least she did not get angry. Although I was extremely worried, petrified in fact, that she would find out, I used this scheme for two or three months to win her favor. There was a problem, however. Sometimes there would be only silver coins, no copper ones, in the change box; any silver coins that disappeared would have been noticed immediately. There must be a better way, I thought, and finally I came up with another plan.

I was fifteen by this time, and it was winter. On the morning of market day I found an excuse to go to the rice storehouse at the end of the yard. Sacks of unhulled rice were stacked up high along the left side, and on the right there were five or six boxes of unmilled rice that came up to about my chest. I removed the lid from the box nearest the door and, by the light that came in through the window, carefully observed the surface of the rice. It had been smoothed and traced by finger with the character for *kotobuki*. (Grandmother had done this, I knew, to thwart Kō, who had access to the storeroom and whom she suspected of stealing rice.)

After studying the character in the rice, I practiced writing it the way Grandmother had. When I was satisfied that I could make a reasonable facsimile, I hurriedly scooped up five *shō* of rice and put it in a bag. I hid the bag behind the sacks of rice, smoothed the surface of the rice again, and traced the *"kotobuki"* that I had practiced so many times.

It was time to leave for the market. When I was sure that no one was around, I got the bag of rice that I had hidden and, concealing it under my haori, left by the back gate. I mingled in with the Koreans who were also going to market in hopes that the family would not spot me. At the market, I lost myself in the crowd.

The market was thronged with people milling about. I was familiar with where the various vendors sold and where transactions were carried out. But what would be the best way, I wondered, to dispose of the rice that I had brought? I wanted to change it for money as quickly as possible lest someone I knew see me and become suspicious. My uncle sometimes came by the market, and I knew that if he should ever see me there I would be in real trouble. Should I go to the rice market? But I had so little to sell. (Not that I would have actually had the nerve to go and do business at a place like that.) Several times I ran into people I knew from the neighborhood; they loomed now in my mind's eye as so many spies of my aunt's family. I was reduced to the state of a frightened little mouse and even considered dumping the whole bag of rice in a ditch.

But meanwhile time was flying by. It must surely be close to four o'clock by now, I thought, for the sun was going down. If I did not get home soon they would be sure to scold me and accuse me of having bought something to eat.

The village *okamisan*, I knew, often took things from home to exchange for money with which, in turn, they bought what they needed. Why could I not do the same thing? But no, I could never do that; it would not look right. And besides, someone might see me and report to my grandmother.

But time was running out and I was desperate. Mustering every bit of courage in me, I decided to do what, for the village *okamisan*, was perfectly normal. Before I knew it I found myself standing in front of an eating place run by the wife of a Korean with whom I was acquainted. Here! I would go in this place! I thought. But there were still some customers inside. "If only they would hurry up and leave! If only no more customers come!" I prayed as I circled the area several times. At last, having satisfied myself that there were no customers inside, I entered. Fighting back the guilt and shame that were making my ears burn, I stammered out my purpose in a feeble voice.

"Ah, ah ... Ma'am. Would you buy some rice, please? It's good rice. . . . Whatever you want to give me for it . . ."

When I saw the woman's look of surprise I was more terrified than ever. What if she said no? What if she told my grandmother on me? I wanted to crawl into a hole. But thank goodness! The woman merely answered, "What kind of rice is it? Show it to me, please."

It was going to be all right! I heaved a deep sigh of relief. Though I do not quite remember how, I managed to fetch the sack of rice I had hidden behind the butcher's shack and showed it to the woman. She opened the sack and took a grain in her hand. "It's good rice, all right. How much do you have here?" When I told her I had five *shō*, she said, "Yes, I can see that there's that much. No doubt about that."

There was certainly more than five *shō*. When I filled the sack I put in five full *shō* and then some. But at this point I could not have cared less about how much there was. I wanted to finish the transaction as quickly as possible and get my money—I did not care how much. "Yes, there's plenty. And the price . . . well, any amount will be all right," I said.

At long last the woman bought the rice. I left the shop clutching the money she gave me without even counting it. Then I lost myself once again in the crowd.

How base it all was. But as terrified as it always made me, I did this again and again after that in order to please my grandmother, to cover up for buying things at too high a price. I got bolder and bolder every time, however, until I began to be horrified at the person I was becoming.

If they ever found out! To this day the mere thought makes me shudder. Strangely though, it is the fear that I always think about; I do not believe that what I did in itself was all that wrong. I was forced to do what I did, and I do not think that I should be held entirely to blame. If anything, it is the fact that I had to be sullied in that way because of my grandmother's meanness and miserliness that makes me angry.

XIX

Although I am afraid that I have written at too great length of my life in Korea, this has been necessary in order that the reader understand how, in the course of my seven years there, I developed into a "warped pervert." Now, however, it is time to tell about my departure from that hell on earth, my aunt's house. For the moment had come when I was to escape the grasp of my grandmother and the others, those people who had persecuted and taunted me, taken away my freedom and independence, destroyed everything that was good in me, stunted my development, twisted, warped, and distorted me, and in the end made a thieving woman of me.

One day in the spring of my sixteenth year, my grandmother called me into her room to tell me the following.

"Now, Fumi, tomorrow I have a little errand to do, and I'm going to Dae Jeon. I thought that since I was going anyway I might get you a good outfit. What do you think? Will you go and withdraw your savings from the bank? After all, you don't particularly need the money, and it's not going to do you any good just hanging onto it. I'm not forcing you, but I think it would be for the best. You've gotten to the age, you know, when you ought to have one good outfit."

Although I had never particularly desired fine clothes, I was not unhappy to be told that I was going to be bought something nice to wear. But when Grandmother demanded that I pay for the outfit myself, I was truly disgusted. I may have been young, but I knew that it was for them, not me, to pay for it. For had not Grandmother given that crepe outfit she bought to dupe us with to Sadako without even telling me? And in all my seven years there they had not once made me a proper kimono; the outfit they had given me to wear "for good," a print kimono, had cost all of one and a half or two yen. True, I had been sent to school, but they had certainly worked me hard enough the minute school let out. And the two years after I left school they worked me full time without paying me so much as a single sen. Now here they were, having decided I was old enough to buy a bolt of meisen, demanding that I hand over my savings, or rather, what was left of my savings after various withdrawals for "breakage." They were stingy, to be sure; but this was going too far.

"I don't need a kimono" is what I really wanted to say. Remembering what the consequences could be if I rubbed Grandmother the wrong way, however, I had no choice but to comply; I left on the spot to withdraw my entire savings. It came to ten yen in all: six yen that remained from my original deposit after payment for things damaged had been deducted, plus four yen spending money Mother had sent me in the meantime.

The next day Grandmother bought me a bolt of meisen. It was a dull, checkered pattern on a dark background, the sort of thing a woman well into her thirties would wear. My heart sank when I saw it, but of course I had to make a show of gratitude.

In making up the kimono, material for the skirt flap and lining were needed. Grandmother used an old gray piece of cloth she had around the house for this, and in her munificence, bestowed an old piece of black satin for the lining of the sleeves. What was left from my savings went to buy red cambric for the rest of the lining. This did not matter, however; what I could not understand was why she was going to all of this trouble. I was soon to find out.

Around the third or fourth of April, I returned from an errand to find an old wicker suitcase on the shelf of my room. I cautiously took it down and looked inside. But except for a piece of old wrapping paper sewn with thin white thread over a torn spot on the back, it was empty. "What's this all about? You don't suppose I'm to be ... " I immediately thought. I felt like dancing for joy. But this feeling soon gave way to anxiety and, finally, to hurt pride. "So I'm finally going to be dumped!" I thought. I did not enquire about the suitcase however, and went about my work giving no indication that I had even noticed it. Four or five days later, on the morning of the eleventh, my uncle told me what was in store.

"You've been with us a long time now, and you've finished your higher primary school. You're getting to the age when you should be marrying, so we feel it would be best if you went back to Yamanashi. As it happens, your grandmother is leaving tomorrow to go to Hiroshima, and she can take you with her. Get your things ready."

So that's what it was! I was getting old, and if they kept me much longer they would have to waste money marrying me off. If they were going to send me home, this was the time to do it. They had probably made the decision to send me home as long ago as the end of the previous year.

But I must not go home looking too ragged. My family, the villagers, Mother—everyone would ask me about school and about the clothes I had been promised. If I looked too bad it would be obvious that they had not treated me well; they would have to send me home in a meisen kimono at the very least. No doubt these were Grandmother's calculations when she took my money for the kimono.

I had no sooner finished cleaning up after the meal when Grandmother ordered me to fetch my clothes and the wicker suitcase. When I had brought them, she and my aunt laid out my clothing piece by piece and went over them minutely, looking for things in the bottoms of the sleeves and squeezing the collars, exactly the way things that are brought to an inmate of a prison are examined. Then they put aside all the clothes that were too tight in the sleeves or not right in some other way and packed only those things that looked somewhat decent. But even so, the best of the lot consisted of things like the new meisen haori with its gassed lining and a meisen outfit that was faded and patched and limp from long wear. The muslin summer kimono that had been my favorite they had given to Sadako, and in its place was put a light kimono of Isezaki meisen that Aunt had never worn once in the seven years I had been there because the pattern did not appeal to her. This, evidently, was a tremendous favor and prompted Aunt to remark to Grandmother, "You know, Mother, when you think about it, you really lose out not having your own child. All this worry, and the money you have to spend . . ."

Meanwhile, Grandmother was packing the clothes that I had worn way back when I had come here, things that I no longer had any use for. "You can see for yourself, Fumi, that I'm putting in the muslin haori you wore here, and you can see how I've fixed the hem. The other white summer kimono isn't here because you yourself tore it."

To preempt any grumbling after I got home, she added, "And another thing I want to make clear: you're not to tell them when you get home that I only brought you all those clothes in order to get you to come back with me, hear! If you had been good, all of those things would have been yours. Your heart wasn't in the right place; that's why you didn't get them. You have no one to blame but yourself, see?"

Of course the only thing I could say was "Yes." But in my heart I replied, "I'm not a child anymore, you know."

The next day, after an early lunch, Grandmother and I set out. Grandmother's trip to Hiroshima, planned some time ago, was to arrange for Sadako to be sent to girls' school. Also, she had been invited to the wedding of the eldest son in Misao's family, which was Grandmother's own head house.

As we left, Uncle gave me exactly five yen "spending money." That was it; that was the sum total of what I received from the Iwashita family. Kō had brought our luggage to the station, and Aunt saw us off. Before long the train came and Grandmother and I boarded. Although I had lived in this place for seven whole years, I shed not a single tear on leaving. In fact, this was the prayer that rose out of the depths of my unhappiness at that moment.

"Oh train! Seven years ago you deceived me and brought me to this place, then you went off and left me to face hardship and trials alone. How many hundreds, thousands of times have you passed so nearby, only to throw me a glance and go on your way. But now, at last, you have come for me! You did not forget me. Oh, take me away! Fast! Anywhere! Hurry and take me far from this place!"

Home Again

I ARRIVED at the station of my home town three days later. It was evening, and Chiyo, a young woman two or three years older than me, was at the station to meet me. She had come from Enko Temple, where my father had once been. Chiyo spotted me right away and ran over, taking my hand firmly in hers. "Well, well, Fumi, welcome home."

"Thank you. I'm back at last."

We stood there for a while, hands clasped, without speaking a word. There was nothing that I wanted to say; my heart was too full of happiness, and shame.

"Where's your luggage?"

"I don't have any. There's a wicker suitcase, but it won't arrive today, of course."

"That's true. Well, then, let's head for home."

We left the station and set out immediately for my village. But as it was already evening and we would not have been able to reach home before dark, we stopped to spend the night at my uncle's temple, which was exactly halfway. (I will have more to say about my uncle later.) We reached home at noon the next day.

It was a glorious spring day, and as we approached the village it shimmered in the bright sunlight. The wheat was starting to ripen and the rape blossoms were a bright yellow. A bush warbler sang in the hills and the air was fragrant with the scent of daphnes. Mother's family home was right before me. When I crossed the log bridge over the stream on the east and reached the front of the house, I saw Uncle at work in the vegetable garden.

I had left Korea in such a state of excitement that my only thought had been to get out of that hell as fast as I could. I had implored the train to take me away from Korea—anywhere—and quickly. But where was it supposed to have taken me? This place out in the country in Kōshū was of course where I had to go; but what had ever led me to believe that this could be my real home? When I saw the village, and my uncle standing there, I felt more depressed than ever. Uncle stopped his hoeing when he saw me.

"I'm back, Uncle, finally. Forgive me. I'm no good." By the time I managed to get this out I was in tears.

"Fumi, it's all right. I think I can guess what happened."

My gentle uncle, who normally never said a word and whose face hardly knew what it was to smile, was smiling now and comforting me. He leaned on his hoe and gazed at me fondly. "There's nothing to cry about. Don't see you for a while, and look how big you get! Well, you're grown up now and things will work out. Don't worry."

I had been afraid of what they would say when I got home, but here was Uncle, not only not scolding me, but extending the hand of affection and blessing. I felt the joy of a great burden being lifted from my shoulders. "This really is my home," I thought.

Uncle stopped working to take me into the house. Aunt was in the kitchen preparing the noon meal, and she too had words of welcome. "Goodness, is that you, Fumi? You've come back to us. My, how big you've grown!"

Grandfather was in the garden, and Grandmother was feeding mulberry leaves to the silkworms they kept in their room, but both of them came running when they heard my voice. "Oh, it's Fumi! She's really come home. It's all so sudden, I thought maybe my ears were fooling me. Welcome home," said Grandfather.

"How big you are! Have you been well? We were worried. We didn't hear a thing," Grandmother added.

Chiyo and I washed our feet at the well and then went into the house itself. Although it was what some might call "shabby," I felt immediately at home there.

It was soon lunch time, and everyone gathered around the table. The meal was a simple one, but to me it tasted like a sumptuous feast; if nothing else, I was grateful for the fact that the food went down so effortlessly. I was deluged with questions as we ate, and I told them briefly, in fragments, about Korea, Bugang, Aunt's house, and the school. Of how I had suffered in Korea, however, of how hard it had been, of how I had been abused—of these things I said not a thing. I said nothing, but I could tell that they guessed everything.

As my grandparents took their meals separately, they were not there; so when my uncle went back out to the field I went to my grandparents' room. Again I talked about many things.

My mother had been told of my return and came over first thing the next morning. Mother had aged a lot, but she was well dressed now. "How you've grown!" she said, tears in her eyes. She adjusted the comb in my hair and stroked my back. Then she noticed my arms. "These arms! They're covered with frostbite scars," she exclaimed. "They must have had you out washing from morning 'til night." She suddenly started crying.

I had not forgotten how Mother had once turned a deaf ear to my frantic pleas and gone off and abandoned me, yet I was pleased at the concern she now showed me. The fact that I had just come from Korea where everyone abused me to their heart's content made me all the more grateful.

Mother wanted to know all about my life in Korea, how

far they had sent me to school, and so on. I realized then that I had not written a thing about what it was really like. Every line of the few letters that I did send was censored by Grandmother and the others just the way my letters are censored here in prison. I always had to be sure to include phrases like, "I'm happy and have everything I want. Don't worry about me," so Mother probably thought that I was living the happy existence Grandmother had promised would be mine. I did not go into what it had really been like in Korea. I have no taste for griping, and even if I had told her, I doubt that she would have been able to understand. All I told her was that they had only sent me to upper primary school, that Sadako was to be the Iwashita heiress, and that I was now of no more use to the Iwashita family.

"I thought something was funny. On the first couple of letters it said 'Iwashita Fumiko'; when it changed to 'Kaneko Fumiko' I had a feeling that something must have happened," Mother said.

"I never imagined that they'd just send you home like this without a stitch of clothes and without saying a word," Grandmother joined in the abuse of the Iwashitas. Then the two of them began recalling the things Grandmother had said and done when she had come for me from Korea, cursing the Iwashitas for each and every one of them.

The household had changed a lot in the seven years I had been gone. My grandparents were now completely separated from the main family in their room in the back, and the cypress door separating the two parts of the house had been nailed closed. The water in the pond in back was low and filled with leaves and mud, while the garden my great-grandfather had so lovingly made was overgrown beyond recognition. The two storage sheds to the west of the main house had been torn down, and onions now grew there.

The atmosphere inside the house had changed as well. The two couples, my grandparents and my uncle and his wife, were evidently not able to live in harmony under the same roof, hence the tightly sealed door, and the two generations were living their separate lives. My grandparents eked out a meager living working a field on the premises and raising a few silkworms for cash. My uncle, who had a weak constitution and never had liked farming, supported his family mainly by selling new and used clothes. He had four children by this time, and the eldest daughter, whom I used to carry on my back to school, was now the same age I had been when I lived there before: nine years old.

Mother was married, but it was not the family she had married into in Enzan. Unable to adjust there, she had returned home shortly after I left for Korea and gone to work again at the silk mill. The priest at Enko Temple then arranged a marriage for her with a priest whom he knew, but the man was evidently such a terrible miser that Mother ran away before she had even been there two months. After this she went to work again, for the third time, at the Yamaju-gumi Spinning Mill in Jōshū. This was at the urging of her parents and relatives who were concerned to put a stop to a much talked about affair she was having. The man, who was considered a good-for-nothing, was the second son of a family by the name of Sone, and he had often hung around the Kaneko home back in the days when it was better off. Mother then married a man by the name of Tahara, who had a silk thread business near Enzan station. He had been married before. This was where she was living at the time I came back.

As I recorded earlier in this memoir, my mother had had relations with or lived with a number of men, and after I went to Korea she repeated this pattern again and again. Not that I want to blame her for that now. My mother had, I believe, a very loose sense of virtue, but she was also extremely weak willed and simply could not live on her

own; she needed a man who would support her, or promise to support her. And when men who were well off or
able to give her a comfortable life came along with an offer
of marriage when she was husbandless—and they invariably did—her family would push her into marriage
whether it was for her true happiness or not. For one thing,
her family was anxious to avoid the disgrace of having a
young woman at home whose first marriage had ended in
divorce, and for another, they were eager to have the benefit of connections with a wealthy family.

For a woman like my mother, who had run off with a
man who scarcely knew which end was up only to return
home and go through relationships with a whole series of
men, a real marriage proposal with no strings attached
from a proper family was obviously out of the question. It
is hardly surprising that the only matches she could make
were with men who themselves had a past.

But true as this was, the fact remains that my mother
could never be content with what she had; she always
came running home saying she could not put up with the
man. In the end everyone wrote her off as a woman utterly
lacking in perseverance and began to wonder if even in the
case of her first marriage with Saeki she had not been at
least as much to blame as he. And the repercussions did
not stop at Mother; all the people involved in these
matches, my grandparents, my aunt and uncle, and finally
the priest at Enko Temple, ended up falling out with each
other because of her. In the case of this marriage with
Tahara, too, the household did not turn out to be what the
matchmaker had promised, and whenever Mother returned home she immediately started in on her endless
complaining.

Even now, although at first she listened with indignation
to what I said about Korea, she soon fell into bending my
grandmother's ear with tiresome tales of her own woes. I
felt sorry for her when I heard what she had been through,

but the things she complained of were nothing compared to what I had suffered in Korea. If I had refrained from saying even a single thing about that, why did she have to carry on so like this about herself? To have to listen to these gloomy tales, when at long last I was able to breathe again after my release from that hell, was more than I could bear.

We had only just been reunited, but Mother's griping drove me to the point where I longed to get away from her and my grandmother. But where was I to go? If I stayed at the main house, my uncle's, I would hurt my grandparents' feelings. And it would have been awkward for me to go to Enko Temple, given my mother's relationship with the priest there. Here I was, needing to find myself again after my return from Korea, with no place where I could settle down and live in peace.

And so it was that I found myself wandering aimlessly around the village. Then one day, perhaps four or five days after I had arrived, I was standing around in front of the gate to the house when two or three former school friends, sickles in their hands and baskets on their heads, came up the hill. We exchanged greetings, more in the fashion of adults than of children, and then I asked them where they were going.

"We're going to gather warabi," they said.

I wanted to go along and asked them to wait for me. They gladly complied. I went in the house and got ready without telling anyone, then dashed back out to join them.

The mountain stream we followed was filled with boulders and its waters were crystal clear. Knotwood, raspberry, and mountain *udo* were all growing in profusion among the trees of the thick forest. Many of the plants just sprouting or already putting forth leaves were ones I had never seen before. Warblers in the distant hills and in the nearby valley called to one another in the stillness of the damp forest. And when we emerged from this forest, mountains that almost looked like they were covered with grass towered up all around us enveloped in a soft mist.

The mountains were not of course actually covered with grass. There was a lot of tall brush, but it was too early for any foliage, which would appear in May, so we had no trouble making our way here. The ferns sprouting up all around looked like cheeks covered with floss, and the warabi was curled up as if in a Western-style hairdo. It was the most exquisite pleasure to snap the plants off at their roots and fling them into the baskets.

We went off in different directions to pick, calling out to one another, chatting, and finally singing. When our baskets were filled to the brim we set out for home.

I walked in the house feeling like a conquering hero. "Grandmother, I've been out picking warabi," I said as I set the heavy basket down in front of my grandmother, anticipating a pleased response. She was not pleased, however.

"Warabi? Your grandfather doesn't like warabi," she said, not even bothering to look at it.

"Oh, well, I guess I'll take it to Aunt and Uncle."

But Grandmother did not like this either. These people were her own family and shared the same roof, yet the relationship between the two households had reached such a low point that she could not even begrudge the other this small kindness. "There's no call to give it to the main house. Take it over to Motoei's," she said.

Motoei was the youngest of my uncles. As a child he had been gentle and quiet-natured and was the other uncles' favorite. It seems that the family had even wanted to make him the successor to the headship of the family, since my eldest uncle did not like farming; but from the time he was twelve or thirteen he had expressed a strong desire to be a priest. He had gone to Erin Temple just one *ri* away in the next village to become the disciple of the priest there, who was chief abbot of the Rinzai sect at the time. Uncle was now at the Bogetsuan retreat house of the former chief abbot, now retired, on the premises of Erin Temple.

The day I arrived back from Korea I spent the night at this Bogetsuan with Chiyo, and thus I knew my uncle by sight. The next day, then, I took the warabi to Bogetsuan as Grandmother had suggested. I found Uncle squatting on the front veranda tending the bonsai. He was wearing a solid black kimono tied with a white obi. He looked up at my greeting and a smile spread over his face.

"Oh, Fumi. Good to see you," he said, sitting down on the veranda. "Well, why don't you sit down."

I set the warabi in front of him and told him that it had been Grandmother's idea to bring it. He took the cloth bundle, thanking me. "Well, which do you like better: Korea or here?" he then asked. I did not want to get onto the subject of Korea, however. "I guess they're about the same," I answered. I then asked him, "Don't you get lonesome here all by yourself?"

"Sometimes I do; but I like the freedom." Uncle smiled as he said this.

Though I could not have said why, I felt that Uncle was the most refined person I had ever met. I did not, however, have anything particular to talk to him about, so I took a walk around the grounds.

Unlike the gardens at peasants' homes, this one was swept clean, and the plants and stepping stones were all aesthetically arranged. Although of course I had absolutely no refinement to bring to this scene, I was filled with a sense of its beauty. I circled around the retreat house and found myself in the precincts of the temple in front. It was a rather large temple and had quite a big garden. The trees, too, were large. But it was the peace of the place that attracted me more than anything; my mind was at rest here. There was no depressing talk I had to listen to, and nothing painful weighing me down. I felt that I had found peace for the first time. When I got back to Bogetsuan, Uncle was in the kitchen cooking something. "Fumi," he said when he saw me, "come in and read the newspaper or something; I'm fixing you something to eat."

I was about to enter when I noticed a dog at my side. I love dogs and feel something providential when I encounter one. I started to play with it. "Is this your dog, Uncle?"

"Yes."

"What's its name?"

"Ace."

"Ace? What a funny name. Here, Ace! Here, Ace!"

Ace frisked about and jumped up on me, wagging its head and tail and sniffing. I went off again, with Ace this time, around the place as far as the foot of the mountain and the edge of the rice fields.

There had been a dog at my aunt's house in Korea, and I thought of it now, recalling how they had made it sleep out on the bare ground on freezing winter nights. It used to snuggle up to me, nose running, head drooping, and tail wagging, as if it could understand the sorrow and pain I felt when they drove me out with nothing to eat. I thought of the times I had clung to that dog's neck, crying to myself. I remembered sneaking out at night to put a mat down where the dog slept. I always associated myself with that dog. I felt that we were like sisters, pathetically bound together in our exploitation and suffering. I also recalled the time when I was a small child that my father had stabbed a poor dog to death. Giving Ace a hug, I whispered, as much to myself as to the dog, "Are you happy, Ace?" Just then Uncle called.

"Fumi, come in. Lunch is ready."

Giving the dog another hug, I entered. In the brief time I had been out walking, Uncle had boiled the warabi I had brought and cooked it in an egg dish. There was hot rice, too. It had been a long time since I had had a meal the likes of this. After lunch, a few young priests from Erin Temple dropped by for a visit. They were three or four years older than me, just right to make it fun. We chatted for a while, and before I knew it we were friends. I talked so uninhibitedly with those priests that when I thought about it afterward I felt positively embarrassed. We even played cards like at New Year's; it really felt like New Year's.

When evening fell I went home. Mother was helping Grandmother with the silkworms and, as usual, complaining. "Oh, no; not again," I thought. It only made me miss the fun I had had that afternoon at Uncle's that much more—being able to forget everything, to be liberated, free, relaxed, and, on top of that, to be filled with an energy that coursed through me from head to foot. I was over at my uncle's every chance I got after that.

Into the Tiger's Mouth

ONE of my relatives had informed Father that I was back from Korea, and he came from Hamamatsu to see me. This was the father who had abandoned my mother and me when I was so young. It was at the hands of his family, at the home of my aunt and grandmother in Korea, that I had been treated so badly. That I should feel any affection for him was out of the question. If anything, I felt revulsion. Father, however, still seemed to feel some kind of attachment after all these years, and he even wanted to exercise his authority over me, something I found quite absurd. Father did not stay long at Grandfather's, though. When he learned that my uncle was in the next village he told me to take him there. I complied, not out of obedience, but because I enjoyed visiting Uncle.

Uncle was extremely pleased that Father had come to see him. Father, too, was as genial as could be, quite different from the attitude he had assumed at Grandfather's.

"My, it's been a long time. How good to see you," Uncle said fondly.

"It has been a long time. But you're settled down quite nicely now, aren't you? You've become quite the high-brow, eh?" Father said in a magnanimous, yet half-teasing, tone.

"It was in Okitsu that you put me up that time, wasn't

it?" Uncle said, a wry grin on his face. "I was seventeen then, so I guess it's been six years."

"That's right. You *did* come and see me in my Okitsu days, didn't you? You were just a kid then. . . ."

"Yes, but I was pretty serious, wouldn't you say?" Uncle said with a suggestive laugh.

"Oh, you sure were," Father replied, laughing in the same vein.

They were referring to the time Uncle quit the priesthood temporarily to become a sailor. He had stayed at my father's place for a while, waiting for a job at sea to turn up. But perhaps I had better relate something here of my uncle's past.

As I mentioned before, when he was twelve or thirteen Uncle announced that he wanted to become a priest. My grandfather, who had decided that Uncle was to succeed to the position of head of the family, did everything in his power to dissuade him, but to no avail. Grandmother, however, took her son's part.

"Now, Dad, if he wants it that bad, why not let him? When this child was born his umbilical cord was wrapped over his shoulders and came down his chest just like a priest's stole. That may have been a sign that he was meant to be a priest and make something of himself."

After thinking it over a while, Grandfather gave in. "You might have something there. One thing's for sure: the priesthood is a lot easier life than he'll ever have as a farmer."

Not long after, Uncle became a novice at Erin Temple. Erin Temple is famous for some historical connection with Takeda Shingen, and there were a lot of young priests like Uncle there. Uncle attended primary school while living at the temple and undergoing his priest's training. In the course of his training he was singled out for special attention by the head priest.

Uncle, however, had not been attracted to the priesthood

for religious motivations or because of any spiritual inspiration. He had gone into it for the same superficial reason as the other young priests: it offered a soft, easy life. So when he reached the age of sixteen or seventeen and began to be attacked by the pangs of sex, he started having second thoughts about the religious life.

Religious life appears to be extremely peaceful; but peace does not hold much interest for young people. In fact, young people could not care less about a peaceful life; it is only people who are castrated who want peace. Healthy young people want a more vigorous life; they want a life in which they can stretch their arms, their legs, their desires as far as they will go. Uncle felt this way too, and it was extremely frustrating for him not to be able to do as he wanted.

Finally Uncle came to a decision. He tore his vestments into shreds, threw them under the floor of the priests' quarters, and ran away. This was when he went to stray with my father in Okitsu. As luck would have it, there was an opening in Yokohama for a sailor, and Uncle went to work on a steamer bound for Kyushu.

Life on the sea was quite a change for the farm boy from the remote mountains of Kōshū, and compared to the peaceful temple life it meant a lot of hard work. But there was the boundless sea, the blue sky that stretched out endlessly, the waves, the wind, the clean fresh air, and the raucous ways of the healthy sailors—plenty, in other words, to feed Uncle's youthful spirit. When the ship returned to Yokohama, however, this pleasant life at sea ended; Uncle disembarked to find the family there waiting for him. He was taken home again against his will.

Grandfather and the rest of the family as well as the chief priest at Enko Temple let Uncle know what they thought. "You've got to think about your future; you're not going to get anywhere as a sailor. You're the head priest's favorite student, and the head priest is going to be put in charge of the headquarters in Kyoto. As he moves up, you'll move up too, right? What you've got to think about now is keeping in good with the head priest and building the foundations for your future."

Uncle had little choice but to return to the temple. He no longer had his former pure intentions, however; he was going back to the religious life only because everyone told him to. Eventually he accompanied his master to Kyoto, and there he pursued his general education at Hanazono Academy.

It was in Kyoto that Uncle's priestly degeneration had its modest beginning. While attending the academy he chased after the daughter of a man who had a cigarette shop. When his master became ill and the two of them returned to Bogetsuan, Uncle took up with Chiyo from Enko Temple; he fell in love with her, in fact.

Bogetsuan is where I stayed the night with Chiyo on my return from Korea. The three of us slept together in a storage room in the back. I was exhausted from two days and nights on the train and slept soundly, oblivious of what was going on, but the two of them made the most of the opportunity to enjoy themselves all night long.

Everyone at Enko, the villagers, even my grandparents knew about Uncle's relationship with Chiyo; but no one made a fuss about it. In fact, although they did not say so, they were pleased. It was "the perfect solution," so to speak. I, however, was unaware of my uncle's past at that time. What I myself felt for him was simply a sort of friendly affection.

Knowing how my father liked to drink, Uncle got out the saké and brought something to eat. He and my father passed their cups back and forth, reminisced about old times, and enjoyed themselves to no end gossiping about and showering abuse on the relatives. Then they got around to discussing Uncle's present circumstances and me. Quite a lot of saké had been consumed by this time. Father now looked Uncle straight in the eye and addressed him in a formal tone of voice. "Speaking of Fumiko, actually I came over today because I had a little something I wanted to talk to you about, Motoei. I wonder if we could go into another room. . . ."

"Is that so? Why certainly. Over there . . ." Uncle rose and nodded to Father.

The two of them moved, on very unsteady legs, to another room. They were talking about something not meant for my ears, but with which I was most certainly concerned. I felt uneasy and irked by this uncalled for meddling. I did nothing, however, except sit there, holding my peace. The two of them whispered away for a while, and when the conversation seemed to be finished and it appeared they were ready to leave the other room, Uncle resumed speaking in a normal tone of voice. "If you would do it, that would be fine. And above all, it would be for her own happiness." He and Father then returned to the room where I was and once again took up their cups in high spirits.

What had they talked about in there? I did not ask, and neither of them appeared about to enlighten me. At one point, though, Father turned to address me.

"I haven't done anything for you all these years, but it's not because I didn't care; it just wasn't possible. But now things are going pretty well for me. I'm fairly well known in Hamamatsu, and I want to take you back with me . . . to make up for what I did. How about it, Fumi, will you go?"

I neither liked nor even trusted my father. But since there was nothing for me to do out in the country at Grandfather's place, I thought that I might as well go to the city and have some fun. I agreed to go back to Hamamatsu with my father.

The night I arrived at Father's house in Hamamatsu I found out what he and Uncle had said about me in that room at Uncle's place. Tired from the train ride, I had gone to bed early; but no sooner had I fallen asleep than I was suddenly awakened by the sound of talking from the adjoining room. I strained to hear what was being said. Father and Aunt were evidently talking in bed, and the word "Fumiko" kept coming up in their conversation.

"They're talking about me!" I realized. I suddenly tensed and lifted my head from the pillow to try to make out what they were saying. Father was speaking softly.

"Motoei isn't the chief priest of that temple yet, but if he just settles down there's no question that the position will be his. . . . From what he told me, that temple was built to be the abbot's place of retirement, so there aren't any parishioners. But there's property that belongs to the temple and annual income from rent, so it provides a pretty easy life. . . ."

"Oh, is that all," I thought, laying down again to go back to sleep. But then I heard the word "Fumiko" again and was once more all ears.

"According to the old priest's wife, Fumiko spent the night there with the girl from Enko Temple as soon as she got back. And she says that Fumiko is always over at the temple visiting Motoei. If you ask me, she's soft on him. . . ."

I gave a start when I heard this. Although all alone in the room, I could feel my face go red. "Could it be true?" I asked myself, but I immediately dismissed the idea as absurd. Father went on.

"Well, I didn't beat around the bush. I came right out and put it to him: 'Would you marry Fumiko?' I asked. And him? Didn't hesitate at all; he agreed right off. . . . And so what if people talk a little; if we get Fumiko in that temple, she won't have to worry about eating for the rest of her life. And best of all, think what it'll mean for us."

So Father wanted to marry me off to Uncle! He had even

secured Uncle's word on it. How awful, trying to sell me just like a slave to my uncle! This was a sacrilege. And it was not only my father; here was Uncle, a man who had taken the vows of the priesthood no less, behaving little better than a filthy beast. Even now, the thought of it makes me furious.

Oddly enough, however, at the time I felt neither one way nor the other about the matter. Although I was at the time of life when I was developing an interest in the opposite sex, I had never given a thought to whom I might marry. It was not an issue for me, and, unconcerned, I went right back to sleep.

Later I realized the significance of this incident and was bitterly angry. My father was prepared to sell me, just like an object, to my uncle in order to obtain the Bogetsuan property. And my uncle was ready to buy me to satisfy his lust for the flesh of a virgin. Yes, that was all it was, nothing but lust. This man who had concluded an immoral transaction to take his niece for his wife was in fact a terrible sex fiend. He had supposedly given up all the desires of the flesh in order to dwell in the pure heavenly realms of the priesthood, but he was running after sex like a little beast. He was carrying on with Chiyo at the same time he was trying to get hold of me for his "amusement." And not even a month after he had promised Father to marry me, he was chasing after yet another woman. I heard about this later from Uncle himself.

"It was about two weeks after that [the time Father and I went to visit]. Chiyo brought a friend of hers from Tokyo whose name was Mizushima to visit and they stayed overnight with me. What a gorgeous thing that Mizushima was! She had Chiyo completely outclassed. Why I even went to the station to see her off when she left. And when I heard that she had a younger sister, sixteen or seventeen years old, I could hardly stand it. I guess it was about four or five days later when I slipped away from the temple and went after Mizushima to Sugamo in Tokyo to get a look at the sister. But guess what? The younger sister turns out to be a short, dark, plain kid. I felt like a fool. . . ."

I was still corresponding with Uncle when I heard this story. Our letters were not love letters by any means. I, at least, was only writing to satisfy a kind of vague, unfocused fascination. But even so, I felt no ill will toward Uncle when I heard this. I was not even particularly jealous.

"Why did you go after the younger sister?" I remember asking him. "If this Mizushima was so beautiful, why didn't you love her?"

Uncle laughed.

"Uh-uh. Beautiful she may have been, but she sure wasn't any virgin."

That was it! In those days it was only virgins that Uncle desired. It was because I too was a virgin, and for that reason only, that he had made that ridiculous promise to my foolish father to marry me.

Father lived in Shimotare-chō in Hamamatsu. He had a neat little house set a ways back from the street that he probably rented for about twenty yen. It had all the usual furnishings, including a food safe, hibachi, and chest of drawers, suggesting that Father was much better off now than in the days I was familiar with. My aunt once confided to me that, although Father "put up a good front," given his lazy nature, things were hard for them. Still, their circumstances were so much better than before that there was no comparison.

As in the past, the work Father did now was nothing but a facade. He was ostensibly a reporter, but he worked for a disreputable newspaper that went in for extortion. As all the people in town lived in dread of the newspaper, outwardly they treated Father with great respect. Father was one of those people you gave as wide a berth to as possible.

I was amused to find that my father was still as superstitious as ever. Every morning he prayed to the Inari and Kojin gods who were enshrined on a shelf hung from the ceiling against the wall in the living room. In the alcove of the eight-mat room in which guests were entertained was a calligraphy scroll that Father said had been written by some famous priest. It read: "Thy Will Be Done." (It would not bring anything as long as the priest was alive, mind you, but once he was dead it would command a handsome sum.) Father, the great disciple of fate, still clung to his superstitious beliefs as tenaciously as ever.

On a stand in front of the scroll was a long, narrow box on which were written the words: "Saeki Family Genealogy." Beside this was an old vase that Aunt had bought at a secondhand goods store, but which Father, the connoisseur, insisted was worth a good deal of money. And near the alcove, strategically placed so as to be visible from the entrance, was a desk on which were piled some rough manuscript paper, envelopes, two or three legal books, and an ancient English-Japanese dictionary that looked the worse for long exposure in a stall at some night market. Father hoped that with this front his inferior character and empty head would not be obvious.

Why did Father have to live this life based on lies? Why did he care only about appearances? Although no longer young, he was just as much the good-for-nothing loafer as he had always been. And yet he carried on at home about proper conduct as though he were a paragon of virtue.

If Aunt were working in the kitchen, for instance, and I were in my room reading, Father would yell something, ostensibly a reprimand to me, but actually meant for my aunt's ears. "Fumiko, what do you think you're doing? Here you are letting your mother do all the work while you amuse yourself. Hurry up and get in there and help your mother."

Later, when my aunt was not around, he would sit me down in front of him, work up a few tears, and go to great lengths to explain his true intentions. "Fumiko, I scold you a lot, but you mustn't misunderstand. I don't want to drive you like a slave, but there are appearances to think of. If I'm strict, it's only for your own good. You mustn't forget that you're only a stepchild to your mother."

Oh how pitiful, Father, to have to stoop to such posturing! I knew perfectly well that I had no call to defer to my aunt as a stepmother. Father conveniently forgot what he himself had once done and carried on like the righteous upholder of morals to force me to act like a beholden stepchild, though Aunt herself would have been the last person to have put me in such a position. My aunt in fact truly cared for me, and whenever Father preached at me like this, we would talk about it afterward and have a good laugh.

After two or three weeks of this, I began to realize that I did not fit in with the atmosphere at Father's house, I did not belong here. The hardest thing to put up with was the morning worship. Every morning before breakfast, my father, aunt, and little brother would gather in front of the alcove to offer their pious respects before the "Saeki Family Genealogy." This was done in all seriousness and with absolute propriety. But how was I, who had not once in my life been allowed to bear the Saeki name, to be expected to bow down with them before this Saeki genealogy? Yet Father always kept his eye on me throughout this ceremony. He tried to force on me a respect that simply was not in my heart, and this I could not stand. He must surely have sensed how I felt from my attitude and considered me the most impudent, insincere, arrogant, and "unworthy" child imaginable.

In Hamamatsu I was sent to a practical arts school for girls to study sewing because Uncle had told Father that sewing was the most important thing the priest's wife at

Bogetsuan had to know. But as I have mentioned before, I did not like sewing, or rather, I was not good at it because I had never had a good teacher. The other students at the school were quite advanced, however, and the teacher could not be bothered giving instruction to a beginner like me. Thus, although I had to attend classes, all I did was chat with the other students and idle away the time. Father was of course angry when he found out, which only added to my frustration.

School let out for summer vacation about the middle of July. My uncle Motoei, with whom I had been keeping up a regular correspondence, had invited me to come visit when school was out. Wanting to get away from Hamamatsu, and gravitating naturally to Uncle's, I took the opportunity to go back to Kōshū.

It was about two o'clock in the afternoon, and pouring rain, when I reached Enzan Station. Feeling sick from the trip, I sat on a bench in the waiting room, hoping that my nausea would pass and the rain would stop. When the rain showed no sign of letting up, however, I decided to go to my mother's house to borrow an umbrella.

Mother's house was located in a field about three or four *chō* from the station. I made my way there, taking shelter under trees and the eaves of houses along the way. I could not go up to Mother's house openly, however, for I knew that she had told the family that she had no children. All I could do was wait outside and hope to catch her eye. There was a tall hedge by the house, and I made as if I were taking shelter from the rain there and watched to see what would happen. It must have been tea time, for I could hear mother's shrill voice and laughter and that of the daughters; but although I waited for quite some time, Mother did not appear. I tried to see what was going on inside through an opening in the hedge, but what with the rain, I could glimpse neither Mother nor anyone else.

The rain was coming down harder than ever. I could not

enter, but neither could I go back in all this rain. At last a farmer in trousers torn at the knees and wearing a sedge hat appeared from the mulberry field in front carrying a pail of night soil. Just as he was about to enter the house, I ran up to him and said, "Huh, excuse me. Your wife . . . , I wonder if your wife is at home, Sir?"

"Yes, she's home," he answered, eyeing me somewhat suspiciously. He said no more, however, and quickly disappeared through the back door into the house.

He's probably saying something to them in there, I thought. They would be suspicious and come out, and I hated to think of the fuss that would ensue. There was nothing to do but go back to the waiting room at Enzan Station.

Still nauseous and soaking wet, I felt so bad by the time I got back to the station that I threw up the oranges I had eaten on the train. I lay down for a while on the bench. Then someone came up to me and spoke my name. When I lifted my head, there standing beside me was the uncle from the Komatsuya family (the younger brother of the husband of my Hamamatsu aunt's younger sister).

"Fumiko, what's wrong? Did you get sick from the train? Do you feel bad?"

"Yes. I got train sick, and then I got all soaked in the rain."

"That's too bad. Wait a minute and . . ." Before the words were out of his mouth he had disappeared, but he was soon back with some Jintan for me. Although I do not like Jintan very much, I thanked him and put several of the tiny pellets in my mouth. The man sat down beside me and massaged my shoulders and back. I felt much better after a while, and the rain too seemed to have let up somewhat. "Thank you. I feel much better now. I guess I'll be going home," I said as I started to get my things together.

"Don't you have an umbrella, Fumiko?" the man asked.

I told him that I did not and went on to relate how I had gone to my mother's to borrow one but ended up not even going inside; he was a relative, after all. I even asked him about my mother's present circumstances. "Has my mother settled down there now?"

"Yes. They say she gets along well with them," the man answered. He then told me that he would borrow an umbrella for me from someone nearby, and for me to come with him. I followed him out of the waiting room. He went left in front of the station and stuck his head in the door of a house about one block down the road that looked like an eating place. He had a few words with the "mistress" while I stood impatiently outside.

"Come on in. Come in and rest a bit," the woman called to me. The man removed his shoes and entered the house, going up to the second floor. There was nothing to do but follow. A young girl, her sleeves tied up for work with a red sash, came up after us with two cushions and an ashtray. What's this all about? I wondered.

"Would you please hurry and borrow the umbrella for me? If I don't get home soon, it'll be dark." I tried to hurry the man, but he seemed to have settled in and started taking long drags on his cigarette. "Oh, I'll get the umbrella for you right away. But I thought you'd be hungry, so I ordered some tempura."

"But I'm not hungry. And besides, my stomach isn't settled yet."

"Oh, don't worry. It's still early."

In the meantime, the girl had brought two bowls, which she placed before us, and had gone back downstairs. My stomach really was still upset, but out of politeness I toyed with the tempura with my chopsticks. I soon put them down, however, and waited for the man to finish. At last he was done. I pressed him again to get the umbrella.

"Oh, all right," he said. Picking at his teeth with a toothpick, he stood up and came over to the window behind me.

He opened it slightly and looked out. "What luck! The rain has stopped," he said, more to himself than to me.

Oh, Thank goodness! I thought. "The rain has stopped? Oh, that's wonderful. Let me see . . ."

It happened as I stood up to look out. My head was suddenly spinning. What a devil that man was! I struck out again and again. Then, like a wounded animal, I tore blindly down the narrow flight of stairs.

This was not the man I thought he was! When I got back from Korea, my grandmother had taken me to visit the Komatsuyas, the family my youngest aunt had married into. I had mistaken this man for that aunt's brother-in-law. I realized now that he was one of the men I had seen at the house in the neighborhood of the Komatsuyas where I had gone to bathe.

This is the first time I have ever spoken of this incident to anyone. I may not be on this earth much longer, however, and there is no reason now to conceal it. I must expose to the light of day everything that has had a strong influence on my life, my thought and my character. I write this not to give the judge yet another piece of information on me, but to shed light on a reality that has a much broader significance.

The Vortex of Sex

I WENT BACK to my grandparents' home in Somaguchi, but this was no more my real home than Father's place had been. It seemed that no matter where I stayed I was nothing but a pathetic, homeless hanger-on. And with the constant quarreling, the atmosphere at Grandmother's was suffocating. The only place where I could breathe freely was my Uncle Motoei's temple, and drawn by something I could not have even defined, I found myself hanging around there most of the time.

Chiyo was, of course, another frequent visitor at Uncle's temple. Chiyo truly loved my uncle; but at about this same time she had a proposal of marriage, or rather, her father did. (He was not, strictly speaking, her father, but a brother fifty years or so older than her. There is no need, however, to go into that here.)

One day Chiyo received an urgent telegram summoning her to her married sister's place in a town called Isawa. She changed immediately into her good clothes and set off. It turned out to be nothing of any importance, however. A guest had arrived from Tokyo, and they had only wanted Chiyo there to serve the man tea and run out for cakes and such. At one point during his stay they produced a piece of material for a man's haori and told her to sew it up as quickly as possible. Naturally, she also waited on the guest at meals.

Chiyo was back after only two or three days. Not long afterward the guest concluded marriage negotiations for Chiyo's hand with her sister and her husband. Chiyo herself had absolutely no say in the matter. She already had someone whom she loved, but she was not to be allowed even to choose her own husband. She had been sold like a slave, little better than a piece of merchandise.

Chiyo was crushed. She was so upset that she even began to lose weight. She talked everything over with Uncle and me and asked us if there were not some way she could get out of this marriage. But Uncle, upon whom everything hinged, no longer felt as ardently toward her as he once had. Of course, he had not the slightest intention of marrying her, for Chiyo no longer had the untouched freshness he would have required in a bride. She pleaded with him, but he was unmoved. He could discuss the matter with her perfectly calmly. "Oh, it's really sad. And I'm going to suffer as well as you, you know. But there's really not much we can do about these things. It's fate; and I'm afraid that none of us can live outside the dictates of fate."

Poor Chiyo! She was being forced against her will on a man she did not even know. Yet, when in her distress she had turned to her lover, the man of her own choice, she had found in him a stranger. Oh Chiyo, who was there left for you to turn to?

And yet in spite of all this, the two of them kept up their relationship just as before, Uncle—with the woman he had already abandoned, with the woman who, for reasons of "fate" or whatever, had already made the decision to give herself to another man—and Chiyo—with the man she knew had already thrown her over, already tracing in her heart the image of the man who would be her new lover upon the lifeless corpse of a love that was dead and gone.

I was over at my uncle's temple so much that my relatives were starting to worry; they were afraid that if Uncle's fellow priests found out, it could bring about his ruin. The upshot of the family's deliberations was that I must be kept away from Uncle and someone else found to take my place. The person recommended to him was the second eldest daughter at my mother's present home, a girl by the name of Yoshie. Besides the fact that she came from a good family, Yoshie was also pretty, good at sewing, and just the right age for my uncle.

Uncle had visited my mother's house a number of times, so of course he knew Yoshie. In fact he was already on rather intimate terms with her, emotionally at least. Yoshie, meanwhile, cared enough for my uncle to have fought over him with a classmate, a girl she had introduced to Uncle and who had subsequently sent him a love letter.

My relatives were not the only ones bringing marriage proposals to Uncle. During the period when I frequented his temple, a priest from a country temple near Nara, a man whom Uncle had met when he was in Kyoto, asked Uncle to marry his daughter.

"The daughter is good-looking all right," Uncle had confided to me at the time, "and if it were Kyoto, I wouldn't mind. But way out in the sticks of Nara . . . ?"

Uncle often received letters from women. He never concealed a thing; he always let me read them. I was not jealous, for I thought of Uncle as a close friend about whom it was only natural I should know everything. And yet at the same time there was within me an unsatisfied yearning, born perhaps of the loneliness that came of having to grow up too soon, an indefinable something constantly burning within me, which I felt compelled to pursue.

It was the twenty-sixth or twenty-seventh of August and summer vacation was nearly over. I was visiting at the Komatsuyas, and in the afternoon my grandmother came by to see my aunt about something. That evening Uncle took Grandmother and me to a movie in town.

The movie had already begun when we arrived. After much searching, Uncle and Grandmother found seats in a corner in the back. There was no empty seat for me, however, so I stood and watched from the rear of the theater. When the first part of the movie ended, I became aware of a young man standing immediately to my left. He was dressed in dark blue clothes and wore a student's cap. I glanced at him and then turned back to watch the second part of the movie. After a while the young man spoke to me.

"Excuse me. Is this yours? I thought I felt something at my foot just now, and when I searched I found this." The young man was gingerly holding up a celluloid comb of the type used in chignons. I felt my head, but my comb was still there. "No, it's not mine," I replied.

"Oh, I wonder what I ought to do," he mumbled to himself. He then took the comb over to the window in back and laid it on the sill. When he came back he addressed me in a tone of voice that suggested we were already old friends. "What was the first part of the movie about?"

"I don't know; I just came myself," I answered curtly, gluing my eyes on the screen.

Not in the least put off, the young man kept up a steady stream of talk. Looking back at the incident, I believe I intuited what the young man was after, but I could not simply brush him off because I too was caught in a vortex of desire, although for what, I could not have said. Thus after exchanging only a few words with him, I came to think of this young man as an old friend.

The young man then clasped my hand. This took me quite by surprise, yet I made no move to free myself from his grip. I rationalized that it would have been embarrassing to cause a scene in that crowd, but what I really felt was that it would have been a pity to push him away. I stood there, my hand in his. Then he gave my hand a squeeze and pressed a stiff, square piece of paper in it, which I took without a word and slipped into the sleeve of my kimono. I was dying to find out what it was, so on the way out I took it out of my sleeve and had a look at it under the lamp at the entrance to the movie theater. It was a tiny, flowery, gold-trimmed calling card with the young man's name, "Segawa," and his address written on it.

At the end of summer vacation I went back to Hamamatsu, though it felt more like I was being dragged back by the scruff of the neck. It was night when I reached the house; the garden gate was shut, and it appeared as if the family had gone out somewhere. But I knew the place well enough to reach under the fence, unlatch the gate, and enter the house by the sink near the outhouse.

It was hot, so the first thing I did was to open up the house. Then I took off my clothes, which were drenched in sweat. I had not eaten on the train and was very hungry. I found some food in the kitchen cupboard and was just having a solitary meal of leftovers when I heard the sound of summer clogs in front of the house. It was my aunt.

"Oh, Fumiko, you're back. When I saw the house open, I had a fright there for a moment."

"I just got back. I was hungry, so I thought I'd have something to eat. Do you mind if I have this fish too?"

"No, not at all. How is everyone in Kōshū?"

"Everyone is fine. But . . . where were you, Aunt?"

"Tonight was the fair at Akibasan. It's so hot and all, and we didn't have anything special to do, so we all went."

"Oh. Where are Father and Ken?"

"The two of them stopped off at the Ishibashis'. I didn't want to go looking like this, though, so I came straight home."

As we talked, Aunt changed into a freshly washed and starched yukata, then sat before the hibachi and began poking around for the buried coals to make tea. By this time I had cleared away the dishes and washed up, so now I could relax.

"Fumiko, would you like to see something nice?" Aunt said. Then she rose, went over to the dresser, and removed something wrapped in paper from the top drawer. "I bought these tonight," she said, showing me two gold engraved rings.

I was flabbergasted. "Goodness, did you strike it rich or something?"

"Fumi, are you kidding? This isn't gold," Aunt said with an amused smile. "Why, the two of them only cost me fifty sen. If I wore them every day they would discolor in no time; but if I wear them when I dress up, I think they'd fool anybody."

Aunt put one on each of her ring fingers and looked at them as if to determine if they really did look like gold or not. "Not bad, even if they are fake," she said, as if to convince herself. "You know that watch of your father's, and his glasses? They're fake too. Although it's been two years since he got them, they haven't discolored at all."

Ah! Aunt, too, had at last succumbed to Father's influence. Why did these people have to be so crude and vain? I had only just gotten back, and already I was starting to dislike them. The differences between us were becoming all too painfully clear, and the desire for a life of my own, apart from them, was growing stronger and stronger.

Four or five days after this incident I wrote to the Segawa I had met at the movie. I did not know what to say, though, so I copied down word for word the phrases I remembered reading in the letters Uncle had received from his female admirers. I sent the letter off with a man's name on the return address. Segawa answered immediately with a letter that was full of phrases in broken English and posted in a pink envelope with a woman's name on the return address.

I went back to school, but I hated it more than ever. I was unable to do the wretched sewing, and the school subjects were utterly silly. From despair as much as anything, I went out of my way to clash with the teachers at school. At home, the only thing I did was read—when I could get hold of something, that is. For there was not much at Father's house except insipid, boring story books. I could not buy new books, for Father never gave me spending money. At my wit's end, I asked Father to let me go to Tokyo, but he refused, of course.

"Ridiculous. Remember, you're a woman," he ranted. He then launched into a sermon on his well-worn philosophy. "Do you think I'd let a young girl run off to Tokyo like that? You've got to be kidding. You don't seem to know what people are like. Just let a man come up to a woman on the street to ask directions and people are going to look on it funny. And once a woman gets talk like that started about her, she's finished, she's been branded. And besides, you're not free to go gadding around wherever you please. You're in my care, and as long as I'm responsible, I won't have it."

Father had already forgotten what he himself had done. Whatever he decided, though, was the final word; whether I agreed or not did not matter in the least. But did I have to remain under his tyranny forever? There was nothing at home for me to read, yet he was so strict that I was forbidden even to go to an occasional lecture to relieve my boredom. Young life needs to expand and grow; it cannot help but do so.

I finally decided to quit the hated sewing school. I asked permission of no one, neither my father nor the teacher; I simply left. Father, of course, was livid with rage. But I was not going to obey him any more or, should I say, submit to his tyranny any more. From now on I would have to look after myself. I left Father's and went back to the country.

Grandfather, however, would no longer allow me to frequent Uncle's temple. I had to move to the Komatsuyas', and they then made me go to the sewing school in town. I had escaped from one hell only to be forced into another; but from this one I had no power to escape. I was not yet of age, and I had no money to allow me to pursue the kind of life that I wanted. So here I was, bound fast to a life that was not of my own choosing.

Was I to blame, then, for giving in to despair? Yes, of course I was. I was desecrating my own life by my conduct. But I think that I may be forgiven. I have to be lenient with myself, in fact, for there is no one else who will be, no one who will understand me or sympathize with me. I was too depressed to do anything around the house, and I certainly did not help with the children. I was doing well if I managed to wash my own rice bowl after meals.

Segawa had been a fourth-year student in a local high school but had either dropped out or been forced to leave. By the time I came to the Komatsuyas' he was in Tokyo attending a bookkeeping school. I kept up a correspondence with him, but at the same time I visited Uncle's temple whenever I could. The letters and things that I received from Segawa I stored away in the belongings that I kept in a closet at Uncle's temple.

Chiyo's wedding kept being put off, and she was seeing Uncle the same as always. Once I happened to be at the temple when she was there; she had brought a friend with her that day. It was evening and the sun had already set. Supper was over, but Chiyo still lingered, putting on her hakama only to take it off and fold it up again. I could guess how she felt and I urged her, as I always did, to stay. "Chiyo, it's late; why don't you just stay overnight? If you stay, then I can stay too."

Of course that was exactly what Chiyo wanted to do, but because of the friend, she hesitated. The friend, however, sensed how she felt and encouraged her to stay over with me. "Fumiko will be here too, so they won't think anything of it at Enko Temple. Stay over, why don't you?"

"But you'll have to go home all by yourself," Chiyo said perfunctorily.

"Oh, I'll be all right," the friend said as she left alone, looking ever so slightly put out.

Unlike that first night when I had just gotten back from Korea, this time I could not sleep very soundly. But now I felt nothing but sympathy for Chiyo. Later, as a memento of their parting, Uncle sent Chiyo a pearl ring that she had always wanted. It was a symbol that their relationship was over forever.

Finally, around the middle of November, Chiyo's wedding plans were fixed. The wedding ceremony was to take place in Tokyo, but a simple gathering at which a fish and vegetable stew was served was held at Enko Temple so that she could say good-bye to the village people. Everyone came in good spirits to wish Chiyo the best.

There was much bustling about as the villagers served the meal. The face of the guest of honor, however, wore a look of deep gloom. Chiyo's expression was so cheerless that the chief priest of Enko Temple muttered a comment about it right in front of her. "Funny, I've never seen such a gloomy wedding in my life. This is a temple, but you would think we were holding a funeral, not a wedding."

And truly, if this was not Chiyo's funeral, what was it? That night Chiyo rose without disturbing a soul and wrote a long letter to Uncle. This was to be their final, their eternal parting. When I went to the temple the next day, Chiyo went with me as far as the dark room beside the main hall, then handed me the letter.

"Fumi, take this, will you?" Chiyo's eyes were swollen from crying, and there were still tears streaming down her cheeks. My heart went out to her, and I cried too as I held her tightly. Later that day Chiyo powdered her face, puffy from crying, put on her formal kimono, and, accompanied by four or five friends to the edge of the village, left for her new home.

Two weeks after her wedding, Chiyo sent Uncle a letter. He tore open the envelope and raced through it. "Tsk . . . she's trying to make a fool of me." He had a cynical smile on his face but did not seem particularly angry, nor even sad. He threw the letter in front of me. I do not remember the exact wording, but it spoke about her new life, about how there was a houseboy, a maid, a nurse, lots of patients, about how well off they were, and about how everyone called her *okusan*. Chiyo had completely forgotten her anguish of half a month before and was now evidently perfectly content in her new life.

At the end of the year, Segawa finished his intensive bookkeeping course and came home. His house was only three *chō* from the Komatsuyas', and we saw each other every morning and evening. Segawa could not come to see me openly because, much as I sulked about it, I did have to go to sewing class and to help around the house during the day. Every night he would come and whistle outside the glass door of the Komatsuyas' shop or puff cigarette smoke in the darkness to signal to me; I would then leave the house on some excuse or other to join him. Sometimes I would get permission to leave, but usually I merely snuck out the back door.

The winter cold was enough to freeze our breath. We were young and hot-blooded, though, and did not let the cold bother us in the least. We walked the dark village roads or strolled around the grounds of a nearby temple wrapped in a single cloak. Sometimes we would slip into the large, deserted main hall of the temple to hug and kiss. I slipped out and roamed around until two or three o'clock in the morning with Segawa like this for about two weeks.

But all the while I was leading this aimless, listless life, I never abandoned my true goals and hopes. What were these? To read all kinds of books, to acquire all kinds of knowledge, and to live life to the absolute fullest.

But I was poor. I could not spend long years in school on someone else's money the way the sons and daughters of the rich could. What was I to do? After a lot of thought, I decided that the best solution was to attend a prefectural girls' school and become a teacher. Once I was financially independent, I could, little by little, study the things I was interested in. I could obtain a scholarship to go to normal school, and what little spending money I needed I would get from my family. I decided to ask Uncle to furnish the small amount of school expenses that would not be covered by the scholarship, then devoted myself to preparing for the exam. My nocturnal gallivanting with Segawa cut into my study time somewhat, but I made up for this by using the rest of my time well and studying hard.

The beginning of the school term was drawing near. I sent away for the school's prospectus and filled out the application form. When I took the form over to Uncle's, however, he greeted me with a gloomy expression that was quite unlike him. I dismissed this as loneliness over Chiyo's departure and immediately stated my business. "I brought the application form. Would you please put your seal on it?"

"Application! You mean the application for teachers' school, I suppose," he said, looking gloomier than ever. "Well, look. I've been thinking, and I want you to put all that off for a while. You see, I think you ought to go back to your father's in Hamamatsu."

"Why?" I asked, stunned by this totally unexpected response.

"Oh, nothing special," Uncle said, a little smile playing on his lips. "Anyway, you'll learn the reason soon," he continued, once again adopting a sullen tone. "Right now I'm busy. Why don't you go home."

I was crushed. I did not think he was serious at first; but he had said this so clearly that he could not have been merely joking or threatening me. Was my one hope, my one escape route, to be completely severed like this? By now I was beyond tears. I went home to the Komatsuyas' in a state of despair and lay awake the whole night trying to figure out what it was all about, what Uncle could possibly be thinking of.

The next day Uncle came to the Komatsuyas' with Grandmother from Somaguchi. Then he bought two tickets for Hamamatsu and put Grandmother and me on the train. When we were settled I asked Grandmother what the whole thing was about, but she could tell me nothing. "I don't even know myself. But Genei [Motoei] said he'd come in two or three days, so I guess we'll find out then."

I could not believe that Grandmother was as innocent as she claimed. "Well, then, what did you come with me for?" I asked.

"Oh, no particular reason. I only came because Genei told me to. And besides, it's been a long time since I've seen Takano."

I questioned her no further. I was filled with apprehension, though, and sensed that a terrible danger was closing in on me.

We arrived at Father's house. Having left there after arguing with him, I would probably have not even been let into the house if I had been alone. But as Grandmother was with me, Father said nothing. My aunt was delighted to see Grandmother. I was depressed, however, and had no desire to talk with anyone, neither my father, my aunt, nor my grandmother. I only wanted to be alone and to think, and in fact I went off to another room by myself to read the newspaper and think. Grandmother did not seem to have told them anything about me. I had heard her say only that Uncle would be coming later.

When at last Uncle arrived, he told me nothing to enlighten me and, at least in my presence, said nothing about me to Father or Grandmother. But then Father and Uncle began to drink. Grandmother was with them and I was alone in another room. Uncle was saying something to Father in low tones, but although I strained to hear, I could not catch what it was. Father was obviously furious about something, however. He yelled things like "the little fool" or "Oh, if that guy were here now!" and Uncle tried to hush him. From the fragments that I could pick up, though, I could guess what they were talking about. It made me furious to think of them discussing me like that, and I wanted to rush in there and hurl abuse at them. But I held it all in. What was past, was past. What mattered now was the future.

When their conversation was over, Uncle left immediately for home; he did not even stay the night. I remember his parting words to me at the door: "I've told your father everything, and I want you to listen well to what he has to say to you."

I looked at my father. The glare on his bloated face as much as said he would have liked to have kicked me right then and there.

It was all he could manage to contain himself until Uncle had left. I was kneeling on the tatami at the entrance where I had bid Uncle farewell, and once he was gone, Father turned on me and said in a voice taut with rage, "You animal! You little slut!" He kicked me in the shoulder and I fell over, groaning. My shoulder bone felt like it was broken, but I was too stunned even to attempt to get up.

"Well, well," Father went on, "weren't you the little flirt. Had to go and throw mud in my face, did you? I'll bet this is why they sent you back from Korea. Yeah, I'll bet that's what it was. All right, do as you please; see if I care. . . ."

"What? What did I do?" I retorted angrily, having regained my wits.

"What do you mean: 'What did I do?' You cross your heart and ask me that. Well, do you know now, or not? 'Cause if you don't, I'll tell you good." With this, Father kicked me again, this time on the leg.

"Dad, what are you doing? Stop! Stop it, I say!" Aunt had run in from the kitchen, grabbed Father's arm, and placed herself over me to shield me.

"What do you think you're doing? Why are you standing up for this thing? Get out of the way!" Father screamed. But Aunt did not budge.

"Now, now, that's enough. I'll have a good talk with her later," Grandmother said to soothe Father, although she herself was shaking like a leaf.

"Suit yourself. I've had it." Throwing out these lines of final rejection, Father retired to another room. Aunt rose and picked me up. She rolled up my sleeve and massaged my shoulder. "Are you all right? He didn't hurt you, did he? Dad is too rough."

"No, it's nothing. I'm all right," I answered as I tried moving the arm that had been kicked. Aunt took me into another room, and Grandmother joined us.

"Hey, Takano, bring me some saké!" yelled Father. Aunt, muttering something to herself, went into the room where Father was. Grandmother and I were too engrossed in our own thoughts to speak. Close to half an hour must have passed like this when Father, his face red with intoxication, left for town. Aunt rejoined us and sat down. I was at last able to ask for an explanation. "What did Uncle say about me?"

"Hmph! It's your father who is to blame for all this," Aunt said, looking from me to my grandmother. "Imagine, trying to marry a niece off to her uncle. He only wanted to get hold of the money from Genei's temple. Of course that wasn't going to work out. And when it didn't, he gets mad. Well, it's the one who is so mad now who is to blame."

"What do you mean? What didn't work out?" Although I knew in the main what must have happened, I wanted to make sure.

"You see, your uncle came here to be released from his promise to marry you," Aunt said in a tone that indicated she thought that the whole thing was ridiculous. "Oh, he harped on how you were writing to a no-good young man, going out at night, acting wild . . ."

From the way Aunt related what had been said, it was clear that she was in complete sympathy with me. I had only one comment to make. "If he's so concerned with right conduct, why doesn't he reflect on his own a bit?"

Everything was crystal clear now. There was nothing more for me to ask, and nothing more to say. I had learned about loose sex and been lured into curiosity about unnatural sex at the tender age of four or five. Now that I was sixteen, seventeen years of age and attracted to an indefinable something in sex, my father and uncle would have me believe it harbored a great evil. Well, if it was so bad, the two of them had a little soul-searching of their own to do. I had done no more than they; I had not even carried the act out in fact, merely flirted with it. Father had turned up out of the blue and flaunted his authority over the child he had abandoned ten years before, negotiating to sell her to the "god of fortune" of a little temple. Uncle had treated me no better than a plaything. Now they had discarded me like a used garment, kicked and trampled on me. There was no need for me to defend myself; there was nothing further I wanted to ask. Neither did Grandmother reproach me.

"Well, it's better this way," she merely said, "for both Genei and Fumi. We'd hoped that this would happen for a long time, but there wasn't anything we could do. It's all worked out for the best."

Poor Grandmother. Uncle had only brought her along for security. He knew the family was opposed to throwing us together, and he wanted her here in case Father made a fuss about his backing out on his promise. But as it turned out, she was not needed; Father took all of his anger out on me.

In spite of what happened, I was not driven out of Father's house. Indeed, with no concrete prospects, I was in no position to leave. For the time being at least, my father and I would have to live under the same roof with our radically different ideas. The final blow-up was not long in coming, however. It started with a quite trivial argument about my younger brother Ken. Before going into that, however, I had better take this opportunity to fill in the record about Ken.

As the reader already knows, my parents agreed when they separated that I would be brought up by Mother, and my brother, three years old at the time, by Father. Ken had been taken from his own mother's arms, but waiting to receive him in her place was my aunt. It seems that his early years were spent in great poverty, but as my aunt was a very resourceful woman, he did not have to suffer what I did. My aunt loved Ken very much. Although she used to say that she felt duty bound to take care of the child of the sister she had wronged in the past, from what I observed, there was none of the coldness of the typical stepmother-stepchild relationship between her and Ken. In every respect my aunt loved Ken just as if he were her own child. When the time came for him to start school, and she realized that he would not be able to go because of that business about not being registered, Aunt brushed aside my father's objections and registered him straight away as her own illegitimate child.

But because of Father's mistaken ideas, Ken was not so lucky when it came to the type of education he was to be given. Unlike me, Ken was large; but he was a very gentle, quiet boy by nature and extremely introverted, so much so that he could not even speak to strangers. At school, although he was good at drawing and calligraphy, he did not do well at other subjects. My aunt knew from their long years of poverty that they could not afford a lengthy, drawn out schooling and wanted Ken to go right into business. But my father, who gave not a thought to Ken's nature or to what they were able to afford, foolishly wanted to send him to university to study law and become a distinguished man. My father considered people who knew law to be the greatest people around; anyone less was a nit-wit.

This was Father's plan for Ken, and his educational policy was directed toward its achievement. Although Ken did not have a bent for learning, Father was determined that he acquire one. Sometimes he would sit Ken down in front of him and have him read or do sums. If Ken stumbled over his reading or was unable to solve a problem, Father would tell him how slow he was and give him a sound thrashing on the head.

As if this were not bad enough, Father had to impose his old-fashioned, feudalistic ideas on Ken as well. He would make him do obeisance before that "Saeki Family Tree" and tell him that he must never disgrace the 123 generations of descendants of the Fujiwara minister, Lord So-and-so.

"I was born into this illustrious Saeki family, and no matter how poor I may have been, I have never been made a fool of by others. Why, right here in Hamamatsu there are a lot of people richer than me, but all of them address me 'Saeki-san,' 'Saeki-san,' and treat me as their better. And it's all because of my genealogy. You mustn't make light of a person's breeding. . . ."

Without realizing it, the impressionable young boy had come under Father's influence and was beginning to think like him. I had always considered all of this ridiculous. Now I put into words the critical view I held of Father's treatment of Ken. This was one of the reasons for the estrangement between Father and me.

Just when I was planning to enter the women's teachers' school, Father made Ken take the entrance examination for the prefectural junior high school. Eventually he would send him to university to study law and, if all went well, see him become minister of justice if not prime minister. When Ken actually managed to pass the exam, Father's joy knew no bounds. He praised Ken to the heavens. "Great! Bravo! A chip off the old block. Keep it up, lad. In the West, you know, some people even get their law degree at twenty-two or twenty-three."

Father ordered Aunt to cook the festive red rice dish, and we celebrated the launching of Ken's career. Father consumed even more saké than usual. Then he delivered a sermon in front of the family tree, and he and Ken bowed their heads down to the tatami in reverence to the genealogy. The next day Father pawned some clothes and took Ken to town to buy what he needed for school.

The shoes he had ordered arrived about a week later. Father examined them carefully, then made the following disclosure. "You know, Ken, there were two kinds of shoes. One pair was eight yen and the other, twelve yen. Well, I splurged and bought the twelve-yen pair for you."

Beside himself with joy, Ken put the shoes on and left for school. He returned in the afternoon, however, disappointed and angry. "Father, you lied."

"What do you mean?"

"You know what I mean. When I got to school I found out that my shoes aren't the expensive ones; they're the cheap ones."

"No," Father answered, somewhat flustered, "your father would never lie. Those are the twelve-yen ones."

Ken did not believe him. "But Umeda and Suzuki said theirs were the eight-yen ones, and they look exactly like mine. There were some people with the twelve-yen ones, too, and you could see they were much better made and of better leather."

Father coughed to cover his embarrassment and then answered in a composed air. "No. Your father may be poor, but I would never do anything to make you feel small. Your father paid twelve yen for those, no mistake about it."

Ken still did not believe Father, but it would have been no use arguing further, so he went to his room. He put down his school bag and poured out his anger to Mother and me who were sewing nearby.

Father always judged a thing's value by how much it cost. When he bought something, he would ask the price first and then decide accordingly whether it was any good or not. When he bought something for himself, he would not tell even his wife or child the true price; he would give it as 20 or 30 percent higher, sometimes two or three times the actual price. I had always disliked this base nature of my father, but this time I found it particularly annoying, and I said what I thought in a voice just loud enough for him to hear.

"Have you ever seen anyone with such ridiculous pride? Instead of lying to his own son and telling him he'd bought shoes for twelve yen when he only paid eight, why didn't he tell you that one doesn't measure a person's worth by how much his shoes cost?"

Father leapt to his feet, came over, and kicked me. "Shut up! That's no way to speak to your father. I'm not going to keep a thankless daughter like you in the house. Get out! Now! Get out! This house has had nothing but trouble since you came. My home was perfectly peaceful before you came, and now, damn it, you do nothing but stir up trouble. Get out! Get out this minute!"

Ken was too stunned to react, but Aunt tried to calm Father down. "Stop it, Dad. Don't say things like that."

It had no effect; if anything, Father grew more abusive than ever.

"No wonder they kicked you out of Korea. It wasn't their fault, it was all yours. Who would want a cheeky, willful, stubborn, twisted girl like you? I'm not surprised you were sent away. Look, even your father is fed up with you. Well, I can't have someone who brings nothing but trouble in the house; there's Ken to think of. Go on, get out! This minute!"

Father had grabbed me by the hair and was proceeding to drag me viciously around the room. Aunt grabbed his arm and sobbed, "Stop it, Dad. Stop!"

The incident ended there, but what Father had said was true: there had been nothing but trouble since I came. Father and I could agree on absolutely nothing. In fact, since the incident with my uncle we had become virtual enemies. We were incompatible, and neither could rest until the other had been beaten down. I had meant for some time to leave Father's place and had only been waiting for the moment. Now that moment had come.

Farewell Father!

MY AUNT tried to make me stay. "If you leave now," she said, "the relatives will say I made life miserable for you." But I could endure this life no longer. I had already decided to go to Tokyo, where I would find work and put myself through school. Meanwhile I had to prepare, so I now applied myself to mundane chores like washing and mending my clothes. When the newspaper arrived, I immediately clipped the ads for jobs in Tokyo and for schools that offered English and math, and I tucked these away in my wicker suitcase.

Not that I did not worry. Would things work out, I wondered, when I got to Tokyo? Would there be anyone I could turn to for help? Father's fury subsided, but he would never have offered to help. Even if he had been willing, what could he have done? I would just have to take my chances; for I had to go, no matter what. Then one day I simply decided to leave. I told my father that night: Tomorrow I leave for Tokyo.

Neither my father nor my aunt tried to stop me. The next day I walked away from Father's house, alone. I had in my pocket all of ten yen, and I would have to pay for my ticket out of this amount. I did not possess so much as a single table, not even a quilt to sleep in. Father had not even given me an umbrella to keep off the rain. All right, I would ward off the rain, and the snow, and the cold—everything—with my own body. I was not afraid. My body was tense with excitement, tense to the point of bursting.

In the spring of my seventeenth year, I left this false home to seek the life that truly belonged to me. I was sure that that life awaited me, somewhere. Farewell Father, Aunt, Brother, Grandmother, Grandfather, Uncle—every relationship fate has placed me in. The time has come for us to part.

To Tokyo!

TO SOMEONE set on a goal, determined to carve out a new life, particularly in the academic field, no place could beckon more alluringly than Tokyo. This is true not only for the wealthy youth who have their every expense provided; even for someone like me from the ranks of the dirt poor, barely able to scrape together the train fare, Tokyo exerts an irresistible pull. It may not in fact be as perfect as it seems, but to a young, naive woman it appears a veritable paradise on earth, holding out the promise of everything she desires. Tokyo, city of my dreams! Will you fulfill my one desire and give me a life of my own? Yes, I believe you will, I know you will, in spite of the hardships and trials in store.

I faced unhappiness the moment I emerged from the womb and endured mistreatment thereafter wherever I went, be it Yokohama, Yamanashi, Korea, or Hamamatsu. I had never been able to be "myself." But now I am grateful for everything in my past. Yes, I am grateful for my father, mother, grandparents, uncle, aunt, for a fate that determined I would not be born into a wealthy family, for everything that brought me so much suffering. For if I had been brought up among those people, wanting for nothing, I would only have taken on the ideas, character, and way of life of those people whom I hate and despise so, and I probably would never have found myself. But thanks to a fate that did not bless me, now, at seventeen years of age, I found myself. I had reached the age when I could be independent, could create a life of my own, and Tokyo was to be the vast, untouched ground upon which I would construct this new life of mine. To Tokyo!

Great-Uncle's House

WHEN at last I arrived in Tokyo, I went straight to my great-uncle in Minowa. I had thought of him while still in Hamamatsu but had not written; in fact, I had never written to him in my life. I was confident, however, that he would take me in. It would only be for the short while it took me to get myself set up with a job. As it turned out, when I showed up on his doorstep, Great-Uncle was happy to have me.

Not that the people at Great-Uncle's understood or supported what I wanted to do. Every night after Great-Uncle had had his cup of saké he would have me sit down beside him, and then he would go into a long, rambling speech.

"Now, Fumi, you should give this some thought. You've got your heart set on getting schooling, but even if you do study hard and are able to put yourself through school, you're not going to make more than fifty or sixty yen a month as a school teacher—at the most. Do you think you can live on that? Well, all right, maybe you can as long as you're single. But you're going to get married sometime. You get married and have a child. Well, just see what it's like when you get pregnant; no respectable woman goes off to school with a great big belly. So you're not going to be able to support yourself by teaching after all. Now, what I think you should do is this: stay here for a while, study sewing, and then marry some nice, steady businessman. Say what you like, it's money that counts in this world. A little smattering of learning isn't going to do you any good."

For a person like Great-Uncle, this was a perfectly natural reaction, and I was grateful for his advice. If I had taken it, I am sure he would have been willing to look after me, although I probably would have been treated like a maid. But I could not endure the thought of being dependent on anyone again; I had suffered enough from that already. The desire for an independent life of my own was too deep. "Thank you," I told him, "but a woman like me just couldn't become a merchant's wife."

Great-Uncle persisted. "Everybody thinks like that when they're young. Young people are always full of dreams. But you'd better try to think about this seriously."

Great-Uncle preached this sort of thing at me night after night until it got to be more than I could put up with. "Please let me do what I want," I told him. "I've made up my mind."

"I see," he said, somewhat annoyed. "Well, suit yourself; but don't expect me to take care of you."

"Of course not. I didn't come with the intention of asking you to help me. I'll find a way to put myself through school."

"Hmm. Well, why don't you just do that."

Now I was finally able to go out and start looking for a way to put myself through school. This is how I would build a new life for myself.

Great-Uncle's advice to me was not unreasonable; in fact, it was based on his own experience. He was Grandfather's third younger brother, and when he was young he had married into the family of a small saké dealer in the next village. Not happy there, however, he had taken his family to Tokyo. In the beginning Great-Uncle had hoped to get some schooling; but it did not work out, and he ended up opening a used-clothing shop.

Great-Uncle did not possess any special talent for business, but as the result of many failures he had become extremely tight-fisted. He was so cautious that he never took a step without great deliberation. Through thrift and prudence he had saved money over the years and, little by little, had become a success. He had had a little help from fate too.

Just when Great-Uncle began to start accumulating a little savings, his wife began to "go funny." Being a man, he had his pride to think of, and besides that, his wife's behavior was hard on the family purse. So although they had three children, Great-Uncle decided to divorce her. He remarried, and his second wife turned out to be an extremely capable manager. With this, Great-Uncle's lot improved considerably.

By the time I arrived, the eldest son had already left home and was living with his mother in Nihonzuzumi and running a clothing store. The two younger children were raised by the second wife. She loved them like her own children, and they became so close to their stepmother that they called her "Mama"; when their natural mother came to visit, they called her "Aunt."

The elder of the two was a woman, Hanae. Her brother was still a boy when she married, so her husband was adopted into the family to succeed Great-Uncle as the family head. Hanae's husband was as tight with money as my great-uncle, and the family's fortunes continued to grow.

The story of how this man came into the family is interesting, and I know it is not a lie because I heard it from Hanae herself.

"I was just your age at the time: seventeen. I had finished primary school and was going to a tailor's in the neighborhood for sewing lessons. One day in mid-autumn my stepmother said to me when I came home for lunch,

'We'll be busy today, so you stay home from your afternoon sewing class.' Well, I did stay home, and soon the
hairdresser was over saying that she was going to fix my
hair. I thought it was a bit strange, but I did as I was told,
took out my dressing table, and sat down. The hairdresser
proceeded to take out my red chignon band, undo my hair,
then do it up again in *takashimada* style.

" 'What are you fixing my hair like this for?' I asked, but
she merely replied that this was what my mother had told
her to do. I still was not suspicious, however; I thought
maybe I was going to be taken to a play or something.
After all, I was only a child. Then I noticed that the house
had been cleaned, which was unusual, and that everyone
was terribly busy. The next thing I knew, raw fish and
whole, roasted fish and soup had been brought over from
the fish shop next door. There was enough for ten people,
and four or five of my relatives had now arrived. I wondered what on earth was going on and asked my mother
for an explanation.

" 'Tonight is your wedding. Now hurry up and change,'
she said. Mother got out a formal kimono that she had had
made without my knowledge and an obi and told me to
put them on.

"I was completely flabbergasted; I couldn't imagine
what it all meant and thought that they must be joking.
There was nothing I could do, though, so I put on the
kimono as I had been told and was taken up to the large
room on the second floor. And then, what do you think?
Sure enough, there was the man I had seen talking to my
father around noon, sitting there dressed in a formal kimono. Then my relatives seated me and the man beside
each other, had us exchange the nuptial saké and congratu-
lated us.

"What do you think of that? Really something, isn't it?
That was our wedding. And the bridegroom was my
stepmother's nephew. Well, Fumi, here I am and I've never

once even been in love. Not very exciting, is it?"

The bridegroom, Gen, had been forced into the marriage in much the same way. Gen was a highly skilled tailor of Western-style clothes and had worked for a long time in Nagasaki. One day he was suddenly called home to his parents' and in less than three days' time this is what happened. Here again was a case of parents marrying off their children for their own ends without giving a thought to what the interested parties themselves might feel about it.

As might be expected of someone whom Great-Uncle took a liking to, Gen turned out to be very honest and frugal. He managed his father-in-law's thrift shop and at the same time started up his own tailor shop. When I was there he had three or four apprentices working for him. His dream, he said, was to amass a fortune of ten or twenty thousand yen by the time he was thirty.

It is not surprising that my desire to get an education was not greeted enthusiastically in a household like this.

Newsgirl

I HAD BEEN at my great-uncle's for a little over a month when I found a way to earn a living. One day I was tramping around town wondering how I was going to put myself through school when I came across some handbills posted up on telephone poles. "Welcome, struggling students. Keisetsusha," they said. I had just arrived from the country, you must remember, and when I saw that sign I could have leapt for joy. "Welcome, struggling students!" I tried out the words over and over again. I particularly liked the name of the place, Keisetsusha [evoking an image of study by the glow of fireflies or light reflected from snow] and immediately set off to find it.

This Keisetsusha was down a small back street in Ueno-machi near Ueno Hirokoji. A sign, "Shirahata Newspaper Agency," hung outside. The outer glass door was closed. There were two tables on the dirt floor of the shop, which was only about three *tsubo* in area, and a young man was leaning over one of them checking something in what appeared to be an account book. I opened the door with trepidation and called to the young man. "Excuse me."

He lifted his eyes from the account book and gave me a look that was not very encouraging.

"Umm, I've come about a job. Is the shopkeeper in?"

The young man gave a noncommittal reply and disappeared into the back. At length a large, corpulent, ruddy-complexioned man who turned out to be the shopkeeper emerged. I told him I wanted to put myself through school and asked him for a job. He merely stared at me at first; his reply, when it came, was curt. "It's pretty hard work. A woman couldn't stick it out, I'm afraid."

I felt I could handle it, no matter how hard. Besides, I might never have an opportunity like this again. I simply had to get this job. "I'll stick it out no matter how hard it is. Please give me a chance."

He was not convinced. "I've had two or three women who tried it, but they couldn't keep at it very long. Besides, if a woman comes, there's going to be problems with the men."

"Oh, no," I said as convincingly as I could. "I've had a very hard life. When I think of what I've been through, I know I can do anything. And as you can see for yourself, I'm just like a man. There won't be any trouble between me and the men."

After thinking it over a while, the shopkeeper agreed. "All right. I'll give you a try. You can start anytime." He looked rather cheerful now and even struck me as the chivalrous type.

"Thank you. I'll do my best."

The shopkeeper got right down to business. "There are ten people working for me right now, all men, and they stay in that house in front. You're a woman, so you won't be able to stay there, but you can stay here. I'll take fifteen yen out of your pay for food, rent, and bedding rental, and I'll give you the spot at Sambashi, the best place we've got. It shouldn't be hard to make enough to pay your school expenses there."

I went back in a state of euphoria to my great-uncle's place in Minowa, got my things together, and returned to the Shirahata Newspaper Agency as fast as I could.

I started selling the next evening. The shopkeeper's wife, her child on her back, took me to the spot in Sambashi. She explained procedures like how to wear the carrying basket, fold the papers, and call to the customers. Then she called my attention to a trick of the trade that she considered particularly important.

"Now look, if a customer just says, 'Give me a paper,' you mustn't ask which paper. You've got nine different papers here, right? What you do is you hand him a *Tokyo yūkan*. Most customers will just take it and go on their way. Only if they say that they don't want that one do you ask what they want and give it to them, see? We've got a special contract with *Tokyo yūkan*, so we've got to sell as many as we can."

We had to try to sell the *Tokyo yūkan* because the commission was good; but it wasn't easy. This paper did not sell well to begin with, and since it was an evening paper, unless you got rid of it in quick order while it was still light, you lost what little advantage that was and were out of luck.

When I started in at the Shirahata Newspaper Agency the manager gave me an advance to cover my school entrance fee and other expenses, and I started school. He urged me to enroll in a girls' high school, but I had had my fill of girls' high schools; I was not about to go to all this trouble to put myself through school if it was only going to be for that. I selected three subjects—English, mathematics, and classical Chinese. My goal was to pass the certificate examination for girls' high school graduates and go on to women's medical school. I took out the newspaper clippings I had saved from Hamamatsu and chose Seisoku in Kanda for English, Kensū Gakkan for mathematics, and Nishō Gakusha in Kojimachi for Chinese. Although I paid a month's fee at Nishō, because of a schedule conflict I did not attend even a single class. I entered elementary-level algebra class at Kensū Gakkan and the first-year morning section at Seisoku.

There were hardly any female students at either Seisoku or the mathematics academy. I had purposely chosen schools where I would be studying with boys. Given the life I was leading, I could not be bothered socializing with a bunch of girls at school and having to worry about the competition over clothes and the like. Furthermore, I had learned from experience at the girls' high school in Hamamatsu that girls' schools have a low standard, and that neither the students nor the teachers are very serious. I would only be setting myself back by getting in with that sort. There was vanity too, albeit unconscious, in my motives. I thought that by going to a school with boys I was proving that I was a notch better than other girls. I think, too, that I wanted to get back at men: I would compete with them and show them that I could hold my own.

At the Shirahata Newspaper Agency, the "Keisetsusha," there were other students like myself working their way through school. Two of them, one of whose name was Fujita, went to Tokyo Junior High School. There was a tall, dull boy named Yoshida who attended night school at the Kokumin Eigakkai and a pudgy student named Okayama who stammered and who went to an afternoon course at Denki Gakkō. There were others, too, whose names I do not remember. One went to Kinjō Junior High School, two went to Fukyu Eigo, and one was taking the entrance exam course at the Seisoku cram school. Those who went to school in the daytime hacked the evening edition, and the night school students sold the morning edition. Thus, even though they lived in the same house, three or four days could pass without their saying anything to one another.

Besides these working students, there were three or four regular sellers. One was a man of about thirty-two or thirty-three nicknamed "Armless Kisaburo." He had caught his arm in a machine at a cotton mill where he used to work and had had it wrenched off at the shoulder. There was another man who had a neck swollen with filthy scrofula, was blind in one eye, crippled, and had a left arm that just hung down uselessly; he was pretty retarded as well. As I remember, there was another man with long, bronze-colored hair that he wrapped in a coil on the top of this head; he looked to be in his fifties. "Long-hair," as we called him, always stopped somewhere on his way home to drink cheap saké, and he talked a lot of nonsense; but everyone liked him in spite of his clownish ways because he was very kind and looked out for the young people in a fatherly way.

The students worked on a commission basis. The three men, however, bought the papers themselves, and any papers that were not sold the shop would buy back at the going rate for old papers, two rin per paper. This arrangement was not as good as it sounds, for the three were naturally given the worst selling spots. They really had to hustle to make even enough to feed themselves.

There was one man in this lot who was different from the others; he had evidently graduated from Waseda University, in philosophy I think it was. He said little and was always reading a small book in German, a troubled expression on his face. His name was Hirata, and he was what I suppose you could call our supervisor. When the papers came in, it was his job to skim the front page for something spectacular—"Seven People Murdered in Asakusa!" or "Conflagration in Fukagawa!" for instance—and scrawl that in bold strokes, highlighted with double circles in red, on the papers that hung down from the front of our baskets. When he was done he would go out in his short coat, and with a band tied around his head, to sell in the area from Ikenohata to Yushima. He was always something of an enigma to me.

In the Sambashi area of Ueno where I worked, ringing bells was not allowed, so I had to yell "Evening paper! Evening paper!" at the top of my voice to attract customers. In the beginning the words stuck in my throat and nothing came out. It took a good ten days to get so that I could yell without trouble.

In the morning I went to Seisoku, where I studied until noon. I then went to Kensū Gakkan until three o'clock, when I returned home for a hurried meal of cold rice. By four o'clock I was out on the streets around Sambashi with my basket of newspapers. It was summer then, and I had the hot, late afternoon sun beating down on my head. Covered with dust and sweat and yelling nonstop at the top of my voice, I got unbearably thirsty, but the hope that filled me enabled me to overcome all of these hardships.

One day the girl from the nearby soba shop came to buy a newspaper and asked me to change a bill. Of course I had plenty of small change, so I was glad to oblige. She said sympathetically, "You must be very hot. It's not easy, is it?"

"No," I answered, grateful for her concern, "but it's not only the heat; my throat is so dry that I haven't any voice left."

The girl returned to the shop and a little later came back with an earthen pot and a bowl. The pot contained murky soba water. I drank some and thanked her profusely. It really made me feel much better, and, my strength restored, I went on selling once again. When I got thirsty I fetched the earthen pot from where I had set it at the foot of the bridge and drank more of the soba water. Having the water was a great help, but on the other hand, as soon as I collected three or four yen in change, it seemed the servant girl would be back again asking me to change her money, and of course I would have to oblige.

This went on for about two weeks. Then one night when the manager's wife was checking my sales for the evening she said to me, rather annoyed, "Kaneko, why do you always bring back money in such large denominations?" I told her what had happened, but she was unmoved. "I can't have this kind of thing," she said. "I need this small change, so please don't take it upon yourself to make change for free any more!" The manager's wife made a little money on the side from a commission she got when she took the small change the news sellers collected to a money changer, something I had not known.

We sold for roughly eight hours, from 4:00 in the evening to 12:00 midnight, and had to be on our feet all that time. A lot of people passed by until about 7:00, and this being the time they wanted to read the evening newspaper, we were too busy selling to think about how tired we were. But by 9:00, when things had slowed down, we began to feel bored, the tension let up, and we suddenly realized how exhausted we were. My legs felt weak just standing there for so long, so I often leaned against a telephone pole to rest. Sometimes I would doze off like that, waking up with a start when I fell over.

It was worse on days when there was a sudden rain. Most customers would grab a ride home, so there were few people out on the street; and the people who did come along were in too much of a hurry to bother about a newspaper. Then, too, at such times I could not help noticing people who were in a fix. If the thong of someone's clog was broken, for instance, soft-hearted me would end up ripping up my hand towel to use to fasten it.

People are interesting. I helped not because of any particular quality in my character, but because it was the only thing I could do. Yet people were ridiculously grateful and would go out of their way to throw a bill or something in my basket. They probably also wanted to show their sympathy for a young girl working her way through school, for even at times when there was no special reason for it, many people declined to take the two or three sen change they had coming.

Kizo ["Armless Kisaburo"] had told me privately that we sellers had the right to keep tips like this, and I considered this only proper. When I was hard up for spending money, therefore, I would put this extra money in my own change purse, but otherwise I handed it over to the shop manager without saying anything. When the manager checked the money I brought in against the number of papers and found that there was money like this left over, he gave it back to me. This was not the case with his wife, however. If the intake should ever appear the least bit short, something that happened when there were a lot of three-for-five-sen sales, she would complain; but the times when there was extra money she acted as if she did not notice and put it into her own change box.

Various groups held street meetings in the area where I sold. One of them, the Salvation Army, invariably showed up once a week to deliver sidewalk sermons. Another group consisting of three or four people dressed in formal kimono and wearing student caps often came along at the same time. The big lantern they carried bore the words "Buddhist Salvation Army." They would sing a Buddhist hymn and start preaching in an attempt to drown out the hymns and lively tambourine accompaniment of the Salvation Army. A group of socialists sometimes came along, too. They had no lanterns or such, but as soon as they arrived they would take out handbills and stick them up on the wall beside the sign for the "Chicken Stew" place; then they would take turns making loud speeches accented by energetic gesticulating, frequently brushing their long hair out of their eyes. The three groups occasionally clashed, each one arguing against whatever the one before had said. On nights like this, passers-by became so engrossed with these people that it was very difficult to sell any newspapers.

On one such night I was so disgusted by my poor sales

that I finally gave up and just stood there, my basket hanging down, listening to the speeches. A young man came up to me and said, "You're from Shirahata, aren't you?"

I was a bit startled, but answered, "Yes, I am."

"My name is Haraguchi. I used to be at Shirahata. Say hello to Mr. Shirahata for me, will you?" he said, handing me a leaflet entitled something like "Russian Revolution."

About four or five nights later the same bunch came again to deliver their speeches. When they were finished they tried to sell the five or six pamphlets they had brought—(I think the title was "If Society Were Socialist")—to the people who had congregated. I had no idea what socialism was, but I felt that I should buy one and timidly asked for a copy. "Oh really?" The young man expressed surprise at first but then handed me a pamphlet. "That'll be forty sen."

The man who had previously identified himself as Haraguchi overheard this. "Hey, she ought to be one of us," he said. "Let her have it at cost." The other man then said I could have it for twenty sen.

And indeed, it was not long before I was "one of them." I realized then that the man who had handed me that pamphlet must have been Takao, the Takao [Takao Heibei] who was later killed by Yonemura [Yonemura Kaichirō, leader of a rightist gang]. I found out, too, that this was the group that formed Rōdōsha [Workers' Society] in Sugamo.

Trying to sell the paper on nights when it rained was absolutely miserable. I had an umbrella, but the hem of my kimono was soon splattered with mud, and, more important, the newspapers got so wet that they stuck together and easily tore when I handled them. On fine days I always left the bulk of the papers under the railing of the bridge and just kept a few in my basket at a time. But of course on rainy days this was impossible; I had to bear the weight of the whole lot from the start. And, because of the slow sales, the load did not lighten much as the evening wore on. The heavy basket hurt so at times that I thought my shoulder bone would break. To make matters worse, since one hand was occupied holding the heavy oilcloth umbrella, all transactions, like handing over the papers and making change, had to be executed with just one hand. I would sometimes drop the paper in the mud and become so flustered that the customer, in a hurry to catch the train that had come, would yell at me, "Stop dilly-dallying and get a move on; you'll make me miss my train."

One night I was unfortunate enough to have a downpour for the first hour and made hardly any sales. At ten o'clock I still had more than half of my papers left. The shower was over now, but my customers had long since gone home and would certainly not be going out again at this hour. There was only about a third the usual traffic on the street. I worked up a hoarse yell, "Evening paper! Evening paper!" but the few people about walked right by. I leaned against the wet telephone pole and stared at the hands of the big clock in front of me. The prospects for selling any more papers were pretty dim, and I wanted to go home. That night, however, the hands of the clock seemed to have stopped moving altogether. I called out perfunctorily whenever anyone passed, but of course no one stopped to buy a paper. In fact, when I forgot to yell and just stood there, a couple of people, motivated more by pity than anything else, I think, stopped.

The later it got, the fewer people there were on the street. Discouragement, compounded by exhaustion, finally got the better of me, and I decided that, even though it was still a bit early, I was not going to sell any more papers and might as well go home.

Almost home now, I turned off the main street onto the alley. When I stepped on the boards over the sewer near the house the manager must have heard, for he yelled down from the second floor, "Who's that coming home at this hour?"

"It's me, Kaneko," I answered, looking up. The manager and another person, a guest I suppose, were sitting up there with a bottle of beer between them.

"Kaneko? But it's still early. It's not even eleven o'clock yet, is it?" His tone, though not angry, did not suggest that he was about to give in. "Nobody else has returned, you know. You have such a good spot, and here you are back before anyone else."

"Yes, but I wasn't selling at all. What with the evening shower, all the customers dropped off."

The manager was not the least bit sympathetic. "You're bound to have a bad night once in a while. But you've got to stick it out until the time is up; otherwise the spot will go bad."

I dragged myself back to my post, but by this time there were hardly any passers-by at all. I was in no mood to yell "Evening paper" anymore, and the few times that I did, the plaintive echo that reverberated back from the woods in Ueno only underscored my own desolate state of mind. I leaned against the railing of the bridge and waited, tears rolling down my cheeks, for the time to pass. Above the big clock, two or three stars shown in the clear night sky.

Then an empty rickshaw approached from the direction of the main street and stopped in front of me. The young man pulling it quietly set down the shafts. "Excuse me. Could I have two or three papers?" he said.

"Of course. Which ones would you like?"

"Oh any, whatever you have left over."

I could tell that he only wanted to buy the papers because he felt sorry for me, and I did not give him one. But I could not take my eyes off him. He was wearing a student's cap, but the insignia had been covered with a piece of paper. I was sure he was a student working to put himself through school like me. The recollection that I was doing all this to be able to go to school filled me with pride, and I suddenly felt much better.

"You're going to school, aren't you?" I asked. "What's your school?"

He smiled but did not reply. I repeated the question two or three times. "The same school as you," he finally answered. "We're in the same class."

"What! The same school, the same class?"

"That's right. I don't suppose you noticed me, but I've known you for a long time. You fall asleep in class a lot, so I was sure you were working your way through school. And I've seen you selling papers here lots of times."

We stood there talking for a while, and in the course of the conversation he told me that his name was Itoh and that he belonged to the local Salvation Army; he was a Christian, in other words. He had been a student at a veterinary school in Azabu but had been unable to pay the fees. He had gotten sick and eventually left school. Now he was taking algebra at Kensū Gakkan with a view to returning to school the following semester. Being the only girl at school, I had stood out, and he had had no trouble recognizing me when he had come to this spot with the Salvation Army group. Itoh had evidently been keeping his eye on me for some time.

Only a week after I started selling the evening paper, I came close to being taken in by a man who specialized in luring poor students. The manager had told me to be careful, and after that I watched out for men. But I could tell at a glance that Itoh was not that sort. I felt lucky, in fact, to have met someone like him. Before leaving he gave me some advice.

"You're going to get tired from this work. It might not matter to you now, but gradually it will harden you. You should try to find something else. If you've got anything on your mind, please feel free to talk it over with me. As you can see, I'm just a nobody myself, but I'll be glad to do anything that I can to help."

At that point I was so happy to hear this that I could

have cried. When we parted my heart was filled with gratitude.

The Shirahata Newspaper Agency had advertised that it would make it possible for working students to get an education. And indeed there was a whole group of students there going to school thanks to the jobs provided by the agency, people like me who would never have been able to go on their own. I knew I should be grateful to Mr. Shirahata for giving me the chance to go to school. But I don't think Mr. Shirahata could claim to be "saving" us students, thus putting us in his debt. For while it is true that Mr. Shirahata made it possible for us to study, it is also true that he supported himself thanks to us students. And from what I could tell, Mr. Shirahata was getting a lot more than he was giving.

Although I did not notice in the beginning, after I had been there for ten or twelve days I realized that Mr. Shirahata was very much like my father in character, and his household was much like my own had been. But it was not only character that was to blame for his doings; Mr. Shirahata was able to carry on as he did because he was keeping for himself the lion's share of the money we students were bringing in.

Mr. Shirahata had two wives, the woman who was living with him at that time and the woman she had driven out—his former wife, in other words. You would suppose that he no longer saw this "former" wife, but not so. He was still looking after her, so that you could in truth say that he had two wives.

The story I heard had it that he met his present wife in a teahouse in Asakusa. The fact that she had kicked the former wife out would suggest that she was a pretty confident person. This was not the case, however. She was an extremely nervous, vicious woman and was given to uncontrollable fits of hysteria.

As if two were not enough, Mr. Shirahata had still another woman in Funabashi, and at least once every three days he would douse himself with cologne and go to see her. To get back at her husband, his present wife would lift twenty or thirty yen from what we sellers had brought in and go out and buy a kimono or obi for herself. This actually happened once while I was there. Mr. Shirahata got angry, and his wife threw the business of the other woman up at him. They had a big fight, after which his wife went berserk, let herself down onto the main street in front by a brocade obi that she tied to the second-story banister, and went off in a rickshaw. She spent the whole night wandering around Mukōjima and ended up stumbling into a friend's place in Honjo where she sat for two days and nights in a daze, eating and drinking nothing and mumbling to herself as if she were counting money. When that happened I had to do all the household work, from getting the meals to taking care of the three children.

While the one wife carried on like this, the other lived in a backstreet tenement in Shitayazaka Moto-chō. Although the rent was paid by Mr. Shirahata, she had to eke out a living for herself and her two children from the sale of the hundred or so newspapers she got from the shop. She was not given a very good place to sell and made only two yen even if she managed to sell all her papers. The other wife was always finding fault and harassing her in petty ways like getting the papers to her late. She treated her no better than a beggar.

It was sad to have to watch a situation here that was so like that of my own family. But in this case there was money, and money wrung from the sweat of impoverished students at that, and this somehow made it worse.

What was my own life like at the Shirahata News Agency? At four o'clock in the afternoon I went out to sell papers, and I got back at twelve. But I was not able to go right to bed because all the sales were checked in my room. This was not a problem when Mr. Shirahata did the checking, for he kept the work to one side of the room. But when his wife did it, the whole room was littered with papers, and she made such a racket that getting to sleep was out of the question. I usually did not even try and instead, to shake off my drowsiness, would go to the kitchen to wash the dishes that had been left from the meal that morning or wash the rice for the next day's breakfast. The wife, however, soon took advantage and had me doing this work all the time; it was thus always one or two o'clock by the time my work was finished. Nevertheless, I had to get up the next day at seven o'clock.

Although I rose at seven, it was eight o'clock by the time I cleaned the room and prepared breakfast. My classes started at eight o'clock sharp. I had a thirty-minute train ride to the school, however, so that even if I could get away from the house by eight I could never catch all of the first-period class. On top of this, the wife ordered me to take two of the children to kindergarten, and when they gave me a hard time I did not get to school until the end of the second period.

I was at Seisoku until noon and Kensū Gakkan until three o'clock, and as soon as I got home from the latter I had to leave right away for work. When I got home at midnight I was covered with grime and sweat, but it was too late to go to the public bath. I would have liked to have had a little time to myself on Sundays at least, but just getting myself and my clothes with their load of dirt cleaned up took up most of the day, leaving me virtually no time for rest.

I was so tired from overwork and lack of sleep night after night that when I got to school and leaned on my desk I immediately fell asleep. Try as I might to stay awake, exhaustion got the better of me. I of course had no idea what the teacher was saying. I did not even know

what I had written with the pen that was in my hand. I had
told Mr. Shirahata that first day that I could handle anything and put up with anything, and I was truly trying my
best. But no matter how willing the spirit, the flesh simply
could not comply. I finally realized that no matter how
hard I tried, it was impossible. I could go on with this life
no longer.

I decided to leave the Shirahata News Agency, but I
could not do so until I had paid back the twelve or thirteen
yen I had borrowed for school fees and clothes. I did not
have the money. Itoh, the rickshaw man, wanted to help
me pay off the debt and find me a good job. "Being tied to
them like that," he said, "you're not going to be able to
study, and you'll only end up going bad. You should get
out of there as soon as you can and find something that
will give you some independence."

It did not sound very realistic. How could Itoh be of any
help when he himself was having such a hard time getting
by? I therefore went next to Haraguchi, the man I had gotten to know through the talks on socialism, and asked his
help in getting some money. He did not want to get involved, however, and told me flatly that he could be of no
help.

I would just have to bide my time until something
turned up. In the meantime, someone heard that I wanted
to leave (I probably had complained to one of the others
about what a hard time I was having and mentioned wanting to find other work), for one day Mr. Shirahata, sullen
faced, took me aside for a grilling.

"Kaneko, I hear you're laying plans to leave. Is it
true?"

I had planned to keep quiet about leaving until I could
repay the money, but when he came right out and asked
me like that, I could not very well lie. "Yes. You see, I'm
too tired to study, so I thought that after I paid back what I
owe you, I'd ask you to let me go."

"I might have known. I told you right from the start that this would happen," he said, his expression hardening. "All right, if you want to leave, go ahead. In fact, I'll thank you to be out of here tomorrow."

I had to assent, for there was no hope of staying on after this. But what was I going to do? I was flat broke, out of work, and without any prospects for the future.

Here I was, having to leave the next day, and what did Mr. Shirahata do that last night but change me to Hongō San-chōme, one of the worst spots. I thus managed in the course of that night to increase my debt by fifty sen. Since I was being let go, I naturally assumed that the manager would write off what I owed him. I heard later, however, that right after I left, Mr. Shirahata took a rickshaw to Minowa, bad-mouthed me at great length to my great-uncle, and produced a detailed account of all that I owed him. It seems that he took a big box of fancy cake, putting Uncle in a position where he felt obliged to hand the money over then and there. My great-aunt really let me have it afterward and made me apologize to Uncle.

Street Vendor

IT WAS evening when I left the Shirahata News Agency. I had nowhere to go, not having had time to make any arrangements. And now, as luck would have it, it was pouring rain. I stood on the stone pavement in front of Matsuzakaya department store at a complete loss for what to do. After pondering my predicament without much result, I finally remembered a certain Akibara, a Salvation Army platoon leader in Kuromon-chō whom I had met once or twice through Itoh. I would go and ask Akibara to put me up for the night.

As I had no umbrella, I turned up the hem of my kimono and slopped through the mud in my low clogs from the shelter of one house to the next until I reached the platoon headquarters. It was Wednesday or Thursday and the place would normally have been closed, but the lamps were blazing away as if a meeting were in progress, and there seemed to be people inside. I hesitated to go in at first; but I could not stand outside forever, so I gathered up my courage, opened the door, and entered. There were about thirty people seated on benches; I could see Itoh in the second or third row from the front. He spotted me right away and came over. "I've finally been fired," I blurted out.

Itoh took me over to the corner. "Let's talk it all over later. We're having a special meeting, and Major K from the Kanda headquarters is here to give an address. You came just in time; we're about to start. Why don't you sit down."

Itoh directed me to the women's section where I sat down. He brought me a hymnal and small Bible, which he opened to the place that would be discoursed upon that evening and then returned to his place. But I was hardly in a frame of mind for reading the Bible. I was filled with disquieting thoughts and felt as though I was going to be pulled down into a deep pit.

Presently the meeting started. There must have been prayers and hymns, but none of it sunk in. I merely did what everyone else did. When they bowed their heads, I bowed mine; when they stood up, I did too. Even Major K's sermon failed to penetrate. After a while, however, the mood must have affected me, or perhaps I had begun to calm down, for a bit of what the Major was saying began to get through. But by this time he was at the end.

When the sermon was over the hymns began. How powerful the rhythm was, like enormous, all-encompassing waves! I was seized by a sensation as of being lifted up on those waves and carried off to some great, vast place. The Major went on praying, so moved by what he was saying that he practically choked on his own words. He had so completely taken on the suffering of the soul whose salvation he was praying for that one felt his prayer could not help but be heard. Then, his prayer ended, the "witness" of the faithful began. A young man who looked like he might have been a clerk in a store got up and gave witness of how faith had saved him from an utterly hopeless condition of suffering. The old lady beside me said, "I'm so happy 'cause the Lord Jesus has saved me," and everyone responded with shouts of "Amen!" and "Hallelujah!" Some people, overcome with emotion, yelled out, "Oh yes, Lord!" Then Itoh went up to the front, knelt down at the table, and prayed. He seemed to be praying mainly for me, for my salvation.

I could not remain where I was. I felt that there was something out there, something that I should put my trust in, that was beckoning to me. I was being drawn by some force that I did not understand, and before I knew it I found myself at the feet of the platoon leader, head bowed down to the floor, crying. The platoon leader shouted "Amen!" and lifted me to my feet. He then began to ask me all sorts of questions, which I answered candidly through my sobs. The platoon leader wrote everything down in a notebook, then knelt and prayed in a voice that trembled with fervor "for our sister who has been saved." Itoh and a few others added their prayers of thanks. Intoxicated with emotion, I forgot every care and joined with all the others in praising God. Before I realized it, I had become a member of the Christian community.

Itoh rented a room for me in Shimbana-chō in Yushima and then stocked me with three or four yen worth of soap from a dealer he knew. I was now a soap powder vendor. I sold at Nabe-chō in Kanda. At four or five o'clock in the afternoon, just when the tōfu vendor's horn began sounding in the streets and people were starting to think about fixing supper, I would put the thirty or so bags of soap powder, five or six old newspapers, and a double-wick lamp into a tin wash basin that Itoh had gotten for me, wrap the whole thing up in a striped cotton carrying cloth, and set out for my new business.

My new stand was located on the corner of the T-shaped juncture of the street that runs from Nabe-chō and the railroad tracks. Next to me was a used-book vendor who sold *Kōdan kurabu*, children's magazines, and ukiyoe; and next to him was an old lady who sold roast corn on the cob. She had a clay charcoal stove set up on a platform, and she sat behind this on a box, fanning away at the embers under her corn. Just opposite me on the other side of the street was a used-clothing dealer. Beside him was an old man, mustached and wearing a hakama, who had a number of dubious items on his stand that he claimed were roast seal, cycad seeds, and the like, the virtues of which he expounded much as if he were delivering a lecture. Along the crossbar of the T there were a number of stalls that sold things like fountain pens, potted plants, and toys.

The first evening I introduced myself straightaway to the used-clothing dealer across the way and to the used-book man next to me. The clothes vendor looked pretty slippery, but the book seller seemed a likable enough old man. "Well, well, and just what are you selling?" he asked, eyeing me doubtfully, a smile playing about his lips.

"Soap powder," I answered.

"Oh, a soap peddler, eh? Well, good luck." The old man watched, amused, as I set up shop. When he could no longer bear to watch the inept way I was going about it, he came over and showed me how to arrange things and gave me some tips on how to do business.

The people here all earned their living from these night stalls, so naturally they did not have it easy. But they at least had stalls that really looked like places of business. But me? I did not even have a platform on which to display my merchandise; it was set out on four or five pieces of newspaper that I spread out on the bare ground. It all came to fewer than thirty bags of soap, with a tiny, dim excuse for a lamp set in the middle. It was a miserable stand, and it looked it. There I sat behind the goods, also on a piece of newspaper, a reader opened on my lap, waiting forlornly for a customer to come along.

The man who sold next to me was a kind, engaging sort. His face was perpetually flushed from saké, and whenever he felt the effects wearing off he would turn his stall over to me with a "Look after things for a minute, will you, Lass" and disappear off to the nearby liquor store for a swig. As the night wore on and fewer and fewer customers came, he would take out a jōruri book or some other item from his stock and, his old, wrinkled eyes blinking behind his glasses, chant away in a melancholy tone. When he got bored with this, he would turn to me.

"Lass, that stall you've got there looks so gloomy you'd half expect to see a ghost or two pop out. Here, why don't you give it a little dusting," he would say, throwing me his feather duster, a good-natured grin on his face.

With no customers, I was always bored, so I would naturally get into conversation with him. "That won't help, Uncle. No amount of dusting is going to make up for not having a platform. All the dust people stir up when they pass falls directly on the merchandise. But today I really had it bad. When I got here the ground was so wet it looked like somebody had sprinkled water all over, and so I had to wait for it to dry. But even so, just look at the soap and newspapers—practically dripping wet."

"Hmm. It's damp all right. Not so good, eh?"

"Of course not, Uncle. It says right on the back of the sacks that you mustn't let them get wet."

"Well, then, you ought to set up a platform."

"I don't need anybody to tell me that. The problem is that I haven't got any money. But say, Uncle, how about that?" I said, nodding toward the empty box he was sitting on. "Would you lend me that empty box you're sitting on? It's perfect for a platform."

"What! This box?" His eyes widened as if he were shocked at the very idea. "Oh, I couldn't do that. It might solve your problems, but then I'd be in a fix. I'd be wiped out. An old man like me having to stand all night? Goodness, gracious," he laughed.

We thus became good friends and good neighbors. But this in turn held a sadness for me: Why, I thought, could I not have had a father, or a grandfather, like this man?

My setup was so dreary looking that most people passed by without even noticing it. If they did notice, it was usually merely to glance over before going on their way. Occasionally a young man might make as if he were trying to decide what to buy from my wide selection, to tease me no doubt, and then perhaps buy one or two sacks for a lark. I would usually be given a fifty-sen or one-yen bill to pay for the ten-sen soap, and then my good relations with the old man would come in handy. Asking the customer to wait, I would hand the bill to the old man to change. I kept ten sen back from the change I gave the customer.

My sales for an evening only came to fifty or seventy sen at best. I was operating on a 30 percent commission, so it is little wonder that I could not make enough to eat. There were days when, even if I used all of the money from my sales, I did not have enough to pay for my keep. My stock gradually dwindled, and my stall looked more and more forlorn with each passing night. The old man next to me noticed this and spoke to me about it.

"This is no good, Lass. You know, people are funny. Even if they're only going to buy one pad of paper, they'd like to buy it in a fancy store if they can. So a shop that's doing badly is just going to do worse and worse, while a shop that's thriving is going to do better and better business all the time. If you want to sell, you've got to make your place look good."

He was absolutely right. As the days passed and the merchandise diminished I sold less and less, and all the while the state of my pocketbook steadily declined. I was always fantasizing: Oh how I wish I had twenty yen! If I had twenty yen I could run this stall right and really put myself through school! Yet this work was much easier than selling the evening paper and being on my feet constantly. Thus, in spite of the fact that I sold practically nothing, I stuck it out in the damp air, on the bare ground by the side of the road, until everyone else folded up for the night.

I generally closed up shop at about ten o'clock and, covering the twelve or so *chō* to Yushima at a brisk clip, arrived home at eleven. By this time the door was usually locked and everyone in bed. Clutching my cloth bundle in one hand, I rattled the door with the other and yelled to try to rouse the woman of the house. But not having the heart (or the nerve!) to keep it up for long, I would then go over to the grounds of Kanda Myōjin Temple, abandoned for the night by the cider and sweet ice vendors, and lie down on one of the benches under the wisteria trellises. Although it was summer, the nights were cool enough; but I was so mercilessly attacked by mosquitoes that sleep was impossible. I finally hit on the trick of covering my head with the cloth I wrapped my goods in, letting the sleeves of my kimono down, and sleeping scrunched up in a ball. I was usually so tired that I slept like a log, but sometimes I was awakened in the middle of the night by rain beating down on me . . . or by a policeman. I would then have to accompany him to the police box.

I could not keep this up forever. When it rained four or five days straight I did not earn even a sen. I could not afford one meal, to say nothing of three. Finally, with the little stock I had left, I started trying to peddle house to house.

For a novice like me this was about the most difficult job I could have chosen. Every day I would go home from school, change from my hakama into a kimono, and set out with my goods. But do you think I could get up the nerve to actually go into anyone's house? Every time I went up to a house I would say to myself, "Oh, they wouldn't want this soap; if I went in they'd only bite my head off. . . ." I could never bring myself to take the plunge and go in, so the whole day would be wasted walking around aimlessly like a stray dog, wearing down my board-stiff legs. Then I would upbraid myself for being so cowardly or try to justify myself with the thought that my hesitation was only because I had not completely lost my pride; but neither had the least effect. When evening came and I was desperate beyond caring, I would knock on one door of the one hundred or so that I had passed during the day; but I would almost always be turned away.

One hot day in late afternoon I was wandering around the Yaegaki-chō area of Nezu, my dirty striped cotton bundle in my hand, unprotected by any parasol from the scorching rays of the sun. I had no money, for I had hardly done any business to speak of for four or five days, and was almost fainting from hunger and the heat. I had reached the point where I could no longer afford to be embarrassed or held back by my feeble-heartedness. Cutting into a narrow side street, I walked past seven or eight houses and came to a neat-looking house with a little garden. Inside I could see a woman who appeared to be the mistress of the house sitting in front of a dresser by the window in the room off the entrance, having her hair done up by a hairdresser. This is it; this is the house! I would go in. But then—wouldn't you know it!—I got cold feet again and just stood there in a state of indecision in the entrance. After giving myself another talking to, however, I at last opened the glass door and went in. "Excuse me," I said, shaking like a leaf.

"Yes?" came the reply from the other side of the sliding door.

"Ma'am, I wonder if you'd care to buy some soap powder; it's cheap and it really gets things clean. . . ."

I was about to take the goods out of the cloth, but the woman gave me a prompt rebuff before I had the chance. "Sorry, but I'm busy now."

"Busy" . . . ? She thought that I was a beggar! I felt as if I were reeling from a blow on the head. I tied up the bundle I had begun to undo and left the house like a dog that has been caught stealing. On the way out I overheard them talking.

"Oh, what a nuisance. Those beggar kids come around every day now. I felt sorry for them at first and would give them five or six sen, but there's just no end to it. I've decided lately just to turn them down flat."

"Yes, Ma'am. That's the best way. You keep feeling sorry for them and end up with your own pocketbook empty."

"Isn't it the truth." Then laughter.

My hard-won courage shattered, my legs felt more leaden than ever. The sun was going down as I resumed my wandering, and my one thought was of getting something to eat. Just then I noticed a woman at the end of a lane, her hair caught up hastily by a comb, washing clothes, a boy of seven or eight who appeared to be her son beside her. She had a light kimono on the scrub board, and as she scrubbed away at it she scolded the little boy. "Oh, what a naughty boy. Look at this new kimono; I'll never get the grease out of it."

I went straight over. When I sold at the night stall I used to put machine oil on a white cloth and then demonstrate how clean I could get it. I recommended the soap to the woman with complete confidence. "The spot will come right out. Shall I show you?"

"Well, why don't you leave me a bag," the woman said, taking her purse out of her pocket and giving me twenty whole sen. I thanked her, and as soon as I had the money in hand I all but ran out of that alley to the main street. I flew into a sweet shop I had eyed from the outside and ate two dishes of rice cakes. As I had not eaten all day, this was not enough to satisfy my hunger, but at least it made me feel a little better.

I was beginning to get used to peddling. But while going up to peoples' houses was not the traumatic experience it had been at first, I still was not selling very much. If I sold thirty sen worth a day, that was really an accomplishment. But thirty sen on a 30 percent commission meant only nine sen for me, not enough to keep body and soul together for a day. When my initial stock was sold up, therefore, I was not even able to restock. Since I was walking constantly, my clogs were worn practically down to the ground. I could not afford new ones however, so I often wore clogs picked off the rubbish piles of the big houses on the outskirts of the city. I wore men's clogs, girl's clogs, any kind I could find.

I had time for school now, but I only attended Seisoku as I could not manage to pay the fees for the other schools. I was in the second year. There was a special summer course, and I had to leave the house at seven o'clock to make it. I got up early, read a passage from the Bible, prayed for a while on my knees by the wall, and then left for school. I could not wash my face before leaving, as I had sold my wash basin, so I washed it on the way to school at the wash stand at the entrance to the restroom in Yushima Park. The times when I had money I would go around by Shōhei Bridge and get some breakfast at a cheap eating place below the railroad bridge; when I did not, I would take the shortcut to school from Juntendō past Ochanomizu.

One good thing befell me at this special course. One of the two or three women in the class, Kawada, brought a big lunch with lots of rice for me every day. Kawada was the younger sister of a socialist and lived in Totsuka.

Nevertheless, I was at the end of my rope. Then I had an idea. I bundled up two or three pieces of winter clothing and went to a pawn shop. The shopkeeper looked up from his abacus and greeted me when I entered the dark shop. One look at my shabby appearance, however, evidently convinced him that I was not a promising client, and he immediately turned back to his abacus and account book. Timidly I took out what I had brought and asked the shopkeeper to give me some cash for it.

"Who told you about this place?" he said peevishly. "I don't do business with people like you who just pop in out of the blue."

"No one told me about it. I live nearby, over there. You can check for yourself if you like."

But the man would have nothing to do with me. He kept his gaze fixed on his account book as much as to say that I was bothering him terribly. "That's all well and good, but I have a rule not to do business with people without an introduction from someone."

I went home and turned out the contents of my wicker suitcase to see if there were not something I could sell. The only things that held any promise of bringing some cash were an algebra reference book I had bought at a secondhand bookstore for one yen, fifty sen when I was working at the news agency and an English-Japanese dictionary I had paid about three yen for. I would not be needing the algebra book for a while, so I took it to a secondhand bookstore. I thought that I would get at least seventy or eighty sen for it, but I got only twenty. Later when I saw a price tag of one yen, twenty sen on it at the same shop, I was angry.

Nevertheless, twenty sen looked pretty good to me at that point. As soon as I had the money in my hand, I ran off to a cheap eating place and ate until the pangs of hunger had been stilled. Occasionally I ran into Itoh at this eating place. He himself did not make much at his nighttime rickshaw work, but when I was really hard up he would stint on his own meals and bring me twenty or thirty sen. If I chanced to meet him on my way home from school, we would often go together to "the eatery."

But the only thing Itoh talked about at such times was faith. "How is the state of your faith these days?" was the first thing he said when we met. And if we had a problem to talk about, regardless of whether we happened to be on the street or right in front of a house, Itoh would first kneel down and pray in great earnest.

Itoh told me that I absolutely had to go to worship service on Sunday morning, and that I should pray whenever I was suffering or in trouble. "Prayer will give you strength," he would always say enthusiastically. His words did not carry much weight with me, though; after all, what good was a little strength going to do me? Nevertheless, I went to church and prayed as I was told.

I did not believe in miracles, and I told this to Itoh and Akibara. I had to have faith, they said; if I had faith, understanding would come. Although I did not believe this, I trusted Itoh. I went to church on Sunday, I prayed, I even got up early in the morning to clean the toilet at my lodging house without telling anyone, "to serve others," all because Itoh told me to. I was serving God and my fellow human beings, but where was my reward? I had not eaten for three days. I looked for a new job, but even this was not granted me. On top of all this, my rent at the lodging house was due, and the landlord had come around demanding to be paid. Of course I had no money.

I finally decided to take the advice Akibara had once given me and work as a maid. I got together what belongings had not yet been sold off and left the house. On the way out I set my things down in the entrance and, bowing deeply, said good-bye. "Thank you for all that you've done for me."

The wife, who was eating with her husband in the room off the entrance, did not even bother to put down her chopsticks, but merely replied curtly, "Don't mention it. Good-bye."

Although my room was paid for, I had slept out on a wooden platform rather than interrupt her sleep. I had cleaned the toilet when I did not have to, when I myself was so busy that I did not even have a chance to use it. But all that meant nothing to her. Was what Christianity taught really true? Was it not just something to anesthetize people's hearts? If sincerity and love were unable to change people and make the world a better place to live, that kind of teaching was only deception.

Maid

AKIBARA helped me to get work as a maid in the house of a sugar merchant named Nakagi in Asakusa Shōten-chō. There were eleven people in the household: the older couple who were in their mid-fifties, their eldest son, his wife and their two young children, two younger sons, a clerk from the store, a maid, and myself. The elderly master had turned the business over to his son and no longer had anything to do at home. He was away most of the time, returning only once every four or five days. I learned later that he frequented a place near Asakusa Park where he passed whole days and nights drinking and gambling with other men of his ilk. He also kept a mistress near the park, and that was where he spent most of his time.

I had been at this home about a month when a woman who looked twenty-five or so came over. "I was visiting Shōten Shrine and just thought I'd drop by," she said. The wife later told me that the woman was her husband's mistress. With her wide-striped haori thrown over her shoulders and her swept-back hairdo, she was quite the smart woman of the world.

The master's wife was almost fanatic about cleanliness. But although she made everyone wear slippers even on the tatami, she thought nothing of stepping directly on the floor of the privy in those same slippers. She must have had a fine complexion when she was young, for it was quite fresh even then. She took so much care over her looks that she was always a good two hours in the bath.

On the occasions when the old master came home, the two of them would face each other across the long hibachi and she would harangue at great length, evidently about the mistress. A number of times I saw him get angry and tell her to "shut up." He would then get up and leave, although he had only just gotten back.

The young master, meanwhile, was an ordinary, nondescript man whose conduct was above reproach. His wife was a very attractive woman. There was nothing wrong with their relationship; in fact, they were an unusually close couple.

But it seems that things were not very smooth between mother-in-law and daughter-in-law, the latter being thoroughly intimidated by the former. The son invariably took his wife's part, even in front of others, something that upset the older woman to no end. She was always complaining about this and occasionally even collapsed in fits of hysteria over the long hibachi.

The younger brother, Gin, twenty-four or so, was the most punctilious and at the same time the most tight-fisted member of the family. He was still a bachelor and spent a lot of time hanging around the house. When no one else was around, he would hug and kiss his sister-in-law, much to the timid woman's consternation. He would not settle for a wife, he said, that was not at least as good-looking as his sister-in-law; and although he had no concrete prospect to give them to, he had bought a woman's umbrella and had had dainty, gold-trimmed calling cards printed up with just the "Nakagi" on them, which he kept in anticipation in his dresser drawer.

The youngest brother, Shin, went to a private junior high school in Kanda. He was a rather different type from his older brothers. Tall, thin, silent, with stern but handsome features, he had a somber air about him. He was not much of a student, and the gossip among the clerks was that he was unable to pass his courses even though he had taken a sack of sugar to the home of his teacher.

I do not know how much this family's wealth came to, but it had already been divided among the members, and the only communal funds were what the family spent every day for their meals.

I now had a place to live, but I was sick at heart that I had given up school, the sole object of my coming to Tokyo, to work as a maid. Knowing that I could never feel at home there made me doubly depressed. I needed to unburden myself to someone, and although I had no particular idea to propose, I wrote to Kawada after I had been there a little while. She came to visit the very next day. I was so happy to see her that I could have danced for joy. I asked for a little time off, and the two of us went out for a walk. When I had told her all the things I could not write in the letter, she was more sympathetic than ever.

"You know, my brother's going to be starting up a printing shop in the city soon. How about working there? Then you'd be able to go to school."

If it had been possible, I would of course have wanted to do this. But it would have meant joining the socialists, and I felt that this would have been a betrayal of Itoh and all that he had done for me. "Thank you. I couldn't ask for anything better, but . . ." I told her about Itoh. "It would mean going against Itoh, and I just couldn't do that."

"I see what you mean," Kawada said. She fell silent, but then her face brightened. "You know, I think it'd be all right. You can pay back the favors that this Itoh did for you. Of course, not the spiritual ones, but the material ones. If that's what's standing in your way, I think I can manage to get some money."

I had been wanting to make the break with Christianity;

also, a chance like this might never come along again. Presumptuous as it may have been, therefore, I decided to take Kawada up on her offer.

Two days later, a money order arrived from Kawada for twenty-five yen. Filled with gratitude, I went to the post office to pick up the money. Then, after thanking the matron of the house for what she had done for me, I asked to be let go. As it happened, however, the matron had just had an abscess on her hand incised. She contemplated the bandaged hand with a look of dismay and turned the request around on me.

"O-Fumi, if you leave us now, I just don't know what I'll do. What with the young wife being so weak and now pregnant on top of it, and Kiyo [the other maid] not able to hold her own . . . and just look at what's happened to my hand. . . ."

She had put me on the spot, but I felt that I could not go back on Kawada. "Yes, I understand. But I'm afraid that I may never have an opportunity like this again."

But she would not let me go. "Please help us out until my hand is better."

I could not just turn a deaf ear and walk out. My plans would have to be abandoned. I agreed to stick it out for the rest of the year. It gave me great pain to have to betray Kawada's kindness, but I had no choice. I would return the money, though. Kawada, however, would not take the money back.

Itoh came around at least once every three days to talk religion with one of the clerks, Yamamoto, and the others in the family who were co-believers. Exams were approaching, however, and he was so busy trying to earn a living that he was having a hard time finding any time to study. I wanted to give the lump sum I had received from Kawada to him. I would avoid pompous statements about paying him back for what he had done and would simply tell him I wanted him to use the money so that he could study. This decided, I waited for his next visit. He did not come, however.

I waited and waited, but when he still did not show up I made out a money order and sent it along with a letter that went something like this: "I'll write later to explain. I'm sending you some extra money that I happen to have. I think it should at least tide you over for a month. Please take a rest from work for a while and devote yourself to studying for your exams." Naturally, I signed the "Kaneko" on the return address so that it would appear as if the letter were from a man.

Itoh came over two or three days later. When he left I saw him off, as always, to the tram stop. When the two of us were alone he brought up the letter. "Thank you for the money. But your letter really gave me a jolt. From now on, if there's something you want to talk to me about, wait for me to come. Please don't ever send me any more letters. If people thought I was getting letters from a woman, they would lose their trust in me."

"I realize that. But I couldn't wait any more. And I purposely wrote a masculine signature on the envelope."

"I'm grateful for your thoughtfulness, but please don't send me any letters."

Deflated, I apologized. He then left. I could not blame him; if anything, this incident made me trust him more than ever. The times Itoh paid a visit I always saw him off when he left. At night it might be "as far as that lamppost" or "up to that pole" until we ended up walking along and talking for quite a distance. The people in the house were not the least bit suspicious, however, for they trusted both of us.

Life was a little easier now that I no longer had the burden of school; it was thus my turn to help out Itoh. If I saved up one or two yen from tips, I would give the money to him. Though they had nothing in particular to do at that hour, the family was in the habit of staying up until twelve or one o'clock; I used this free time to make things for Itoh.

One night after a visit I went out, as usual, to see him off. I left by the back door with a big bundle. "Hey, what's that?" he asked suspiciously.

"This? Well, it's getting cold, you know, so I thought I'd make you a cushion . . . and, well, a pillow too. You don't have a cushion, do you? And I guess your pillow is pretty filthy."

"How did you know my pillow was dirty?" Itoh asked with surprise.

"Don't you remember? Yamamoto from the shop had a nap when he was at your place not long ago, and when he got back he said that your pillow was dirtier than the bedding in a pig pen. That's how I know. And that's how I knew that you didn't have a cushion to sit on."

"And so you made these for me?"

"That's right. I was going to use the muslin from the sleeves of my undergarment; but it had some red in it, and I didn't think it would look right. I bought some cotton print cloth, not very good, I'm afraid, and made it out of that. It's bigger and thicker than the normal size, so it should be comfortable. I just guessed with the pillow size, so if you don't like it, please tell me and I'll do it over again."

Itoh thanked me profusely, which filled me with joy.

I will never forget the night of November 30. Itoh, who had not been over for a while, turned up that night suddenly. He was pale and sickly looking, not like himself at all. I hurried through my work, wondering what could have happened. When he left, I got permission from the master to see him off.

Itoh kept to himself for seven or eight blocks, speaking only to respond mechanically to what I said. When we reached a rather dark place where there were not many people, however, he stopped abruptly and began to speak in a confidential tone.

"Fumiko, I have a confession to make. I misjudged you. I mean . . . well, I thought you were a bad girl. But recently I've begun to understand that you're really a truly loving person. I've known the platoon leader for a long time, and quite a lot of other women believers, too; but you're the first one who has been so warm, gentle . . . womanly. I apologize for not having realized it before."

His words stunned me. And I could tell from the expression on his face that he was absolutely serious. Those words, "bad girl," hurt and made me feel like I had been pierced with a sharp needle. But the "first warm woman" that followed embarrassed me. I was both pleased and saddened at the same time.

I had listened to all this in silence. Then I suddenly realized that we had passed Kaminarimon and were at Kikuya Bridge. When I saw by the clock at the tram stop that it was past eleven and noticed that the shops around were starting to close up, I stopped in my tracks. "It's past eleven. I guess we should say goodnight."

"Yes, it is pretty late," Itoh said, though not with much conviction. It was usually he who urged me to go home, but tonight he did not seem able to say good-bye. "Actually, I've got a little bit more I'd like to say. Would you walk with me as far as Ueno? You can take the train home."

My heart had gotten the better of my reason and I agreed. We started walking again, both preoccupied with our own thoughts. When we reached Shinobazu Pond in Ueno we stopped. The evening was quite still and there was no one around. Itoh squatted under a willow at the side of the pond and started writing with a twig on the ground.

"As I said, ever since you came to Yushima, I've had a terrible time trying to keep my emotions under control; but lately it's gotten to the point where I can't go on any more. I can no longer think of you only as a neighbor. I think you know what I mean. . . . Even at home when I'm reading a book, my thoughts fly to you. I'm so lonely if I don't see you even for a day that I can't stand it. With things like this, I'm not getting on at all with my studies, and my faith is starting to waver. This past month I've been so miserable I could die. . . ."

This is what I had secretly hoped would happen. It was all I could do to keep my heart from leaping out of my breast. But I contained myself and listened in silence to what followed.

"I've thought it over and decided that I have to forget you and go back to being the person I was before we met. It's the best thing for both of us. To do something foolish when we don't have any prospects of living together would be a great sin. We'd be ruining our lives, don't you see? And that certainly wouldn't be good. . . ."

Why does he have to think like that? I wondered, disappointed. But he went on, raising his voice as if to strengthen his resolve. "So I've decided that tonight will absolutely be the last time I see you. From now on I will never meet you or think of you again. Today is the last day of November; I came to see you today because this is to be the day of our parting. You understand what I feel, don't you? I won't ever go to your house again. I'm going to get the better of myself. . . . Let's say good-bye now. I will pray for your happiness." This speech over, he rose to his feet.

It was quite a letdown. What a cowardly disciple of love! I wanted to say something, but Itoh looked like he was about to leave, so I merely replied, "I see; well, good-bye." He walked briskly away without turning back, as if he were trying to give someone the slip. I followed his departing figure with my gaze until he passed out of sight. I felt lonely, sad, and . . . amused.

The family at the Nakagi Sugar Store led a very unorganized existence. Shin attended school and thus had to leave the house at seven, which meant we had to get up at five o'clock to get him his breakfast. Barely an hour later the young couple would get up, followed by Gin at around ten o'clock. Finally, at around eleven, the matron would rise and block the tiny kitchen for the better part of half an hour washing her face. The miso soup would go cold and have to be reheated three or four times. Then, when the matron had finished her breakfast and gone off with a daikon offering to Shōten Shrine, it would be time to start preparing lunch for the young couple. We thus spent the whole day in the kitchen. Actually, though, the morning and noon meals were not the worst of it. At night we would be sent out for food and have to fetch Western-style food, donburi, sushi, casserole dishes, or whatever the family fancied. Since they rose so late, we would be running out for these orders at nine or ten, sometimes even eleven or twelve o'clock at night.

It was really a very grueling schedule; in terms of hard work and lack of sleep, it was as bad as any job I had had. Yet I had a great desire to serve the family faithfully. No. To be honest, I did not really want to serve them; I wanted them to like me. I would rise early, for instance, so as to be busily at work fixing breakfast when the other maid, O-Kiyo, got up. And when Shin's friends came over I went out of my way to talk to them about school, to look at their notebooks and show off by pointing out mistakes—all so that they would not think of me merely as a maid. I was trying, in fact, to elbow out my fellow worker and shine all by myself. I even carried my efforts to exhibit my superiority to the point of wounding Shin's pride. Looking back on all the things I have done in my life, there is nothing I reproach myself with as much as this. How mean and base I was! Every time I think of it I shudder.

The long-awaited day, December 31, arrived at last. I managed to finish my work a little after midnight, and after getting my things together and fixing my hair, I went before the family to say good-bye.

"Thank you," the older woman said, "you've been a great help. This is your payment from the master. We would have liked to have given you more, but since Kiyo, who is older than you and who has been here all along, is staying on, it wouldn't have been right. I hope you'll understand." My payment was wrapped in a piece of paper and tied with red and white cord. She presented it to me on a tray.

Free at last, I took my bundle of things and left by the kitchen door. Luckily, the last streetcar came along just as I got to the stop. It was going to Koishikawa, where Kawada lived. There were only thirteen or fourteen people in the coach, and I settled down on a long, empty seat near the door and took out the pay packet the Nakagis had given me. I was dumbfounded to find only three five-yen bills inside. This for three months and one week of hard labor with scarcely any time to sleep or rest! I could not have been more taken aback. I felt like screaming curses at myself for my stupidity. Of course it was my own fault for not making them specify my wage at the start. But in this I had only done as Akibara had advised. "Don't talk about money with them," she had told me, "it's not nice. You don't have to say anything. The Nakagis are an upstanding merchant house, and they would never do wrong by you."

What would she call this? I wondered. I had wanted to go to school so badly; I had had such a good offer from Kawada, and I had thrown it all away for them, for the Nakagis, because they had needed me. What did they give me in compensation? It did not even come to five yen a month. These were people who lived in the lap of luxury; here was an old man who kept a mistress and spent his days at houses of assignation and at gambling; here was an old woman who took two hours over her toilet; people who stayed up until all hours and slept in as late as they liked, all the while working their maids without a break and allowing them only four or five hours of sleep at night. . . . What an injustice! How selfish!

But I was more furious with myself than with them. I crushed the bills and paper in my fist and stuffed them into my sleeve.

Drifter

AFTER LEAVING the sugar merchant's I stayed with several "leftists." In the end, however, I went back to my great-uncle's in Minowa. "Didn't I tell you this would happen?" he scolded. "How did you expect to put yourself through school hawking newspapers and selling at a night stall? Even a man couldn't do it, much less a woman. You'd better just give up this idea of school."

Yet Great-Uncle did not force me to abandon the hope I had clung to so tenaciously; he realized, I suppose, that it would have been impossible. I started attending school again and helped with the housework at Great-Uncle's.

I got up at five o'clock and lowered the electric light so that I could study while cooking the rice and making the miso soup. When everything was all laid out for the others, who were still asleep, I had my own meal and left for school. When I got back in the afternoon, I was immediately swamped with the washing, cleaning, and preparation of the evening meal.

Although I was just as busy here as at the sugar merchant's, these were my own relatives, so I had a little bit of flexibility as far as hours went. I was given five yen spending money each month, out of which I paid two yen for school fees and two yen, thirty sen for car fare. The seventy sen left gave me just enough to buy pen and ink. I had an avaricious desire to read at that time, and it was hard for me not to have enough money to buy even a single book.

While at school I got to know two socialists. One was a Korean named Seo, a man who seldom spoke yet who always wore a look of suffering on his face. He sat at the desk directly to my left, and in every spare moment he was engrossed in a copy of *Kaizō* magazine.

Seo was not there because his family was rich. Like me, he was barely able to keep the wolf from the door. I think he must have gotten to the point where he could not afford to go to school any more, for after a while he no longer came to class. About a year later, when Pak and I were living together, Seo joined our group and helped put out our paper. Seo had a weak constitution, however, and was often sick. He subsequently went back to his home, and our first winter in prison I heard that he had died of pleurisy in a hospital in Seoul.

The other socialist was a man named Ōnobō. I think he had been fired the previous year at the time of the Tokyo streetcar employee's strike. His desk was right in front of me, and he used to read in a squeaky voice. He belonged to a labor union at the time, "Shinyūkai" [Fraternal Society] or some such name, but he was not very serious; he was one of those "more-or-less" socialists. However, he often brought union papers, pamphlets, and leaflets to school, and thanks to the reading material I got or borrowed from him, I began to get a grasp of the ideology and spirit of socialism.

Socialism did not have anything particularly new to teach me; however, it provided me with the theory to verify what I already knew emotionally from my own past. I was poor then; I am poor now. Because of this I have been overworked, mistreated, tormented, oppressed, deprived of my freedom, exploited, and ruled by people with money. I had always harbored a deep antagonism toward people with that kind of power and a deep sympathy for people from backgrounds like mine. The sympathy I felt for Kō, the menial at my grandmother's in Korea; the feeling, almost as for a comrade, toward the poor dog they kept; and the boundless sympathy I felt for all the oppressed, maltreated, exploited Koreans I have not written about here but whom I saw while at my grandmother's—all were expressions of this. Socialist ideology merely provided the flame that ignited this antagonism and this sympathy, long smoldering in my heart.

Oh how I want to . . . to give my life, to give everything, in the struggle for this wretched class of mine!

But I did not know what to do with these feelings. I was powerless. Though I wanted to do something, I was not ready; I did not know how to proceed. After all, what was I but a lone, directionless, rebellious youngster, seething with discontent and revolt?

One day at this restless, tormented period of my life, I had the following encounter. I was coming home from school and had just turned the corner from the path beside my great-uncle's shop toward the back door when someone called out to me: "Fumiko, Fumiko." I turned around to see who could be calling me to find Segawa. What a surprise! I could feel my heart pounding in my breast.

"Goodness! Don't tell me it's you, Segawa! What's this all about?"

"I've been waiting around here for ages," he said, smiling.

"You've been waiting here? But how did you know . . . I mean, that I was here?"

"Oh, I knew. I looked all over for you. But that doesn't matter. Come here. I've got something to tell you." Segawa drew me back in the direction I had come from, and the two of us stood there talking for a while, hidden from the house by a wooden fence.

It turned out that he had not come with any purpose in mind; he had just wanted to see me and to have me come visit him at his lodgings. He had heard that I was here from my uncle, the priest, whom he had met at a night school course at some private university. Segawa evidently had a job now at a public office. Although he had never once so much as crossed my mind since I had come to Tokyo, running into him like this, I felt attracted again. We parted after I promised to visit him.

Summer vacation was approaching and my father sent me a few yen to come home during the holidays. I had no particular desire to see my father, but I went because I thought this would be a good chance to give my body, exhausted from life in Tokyo, a rest.

The visit did give my tired flesh a needed rest. The town was quiet, almost asleep, compared to the hustle and bustle of Tokyo. While I was there I rose early and walked by the sea, or among the rice paddies and fields wet with the morning mist. I felt like I was strolling in a free land here and, one with nature, would throw out my chest, open my mouth wide, and breathe in great lung-fulls of clean, fresh air.

The atmosphere at Father's house, however, was just the same as it had been two or three years before. If anything, the smugness, vanity, base posturing, and cheapness that I found so depressing were worse than ever. There was nothing but friction, quarreling, and discord between the two of us.

When I could stand it no longer at my father's, I went to Kōshū. But here, too, it was just more of the same thing. Mother had left the Tawaras' and was working at the spinning mill. My grandmother and aunt were pleased that I was putting myself through school, but they kept lecturing me about taking care of my mother when I finished school and got a teaching job. Here I was practically killing myself trying to work and study at the same time, with absolutely no idea of what lay ahead of me, and they were going to burden me with my duty toward my mother, the mother who had abandoned her child in order to pursue her own happiness.

I was unable to stay there any longer either. I had to get back to Tokyo.

I returned to Tokyo the end of August. Four or five days after I got back, I was in town one evening on an errand when I got caught in the rain while changing streetcars in Kasuga-chō. Segawa's place was in the neighborhood, and as I had not seen him for a while, I decided to go there. I ran up the stairs and, unannounced of course, opened the sliding door to Segawa's room. He was at his desk writing a letter or something, but he smiled when he saw me.

"Oh, it's you, Fumi. You gave me a start."

"I got caught in this awful rain. Look at me! My hair, my clothes . . . absolutely drenched." I stood there behind him and spread out the skirt of my kimono. "What are you doing?" I asked, looking in the direction of his desk.

Segawa hurriedly covered the letter and put it away in the desk drawer. He then leaned casually against the desk. "Well, why don't you sit down?"

I was, of course, hardly the well-mannered young lady; "uncouth delinquent" would have better described me. I sat down cross-legged, my wet kimono skirt spread out over my knees.

"And just when did you get back?"

"Four or five days ago."

"That was quite a long trip. Where were you traipsing around those fifty, sixty days? I wanted to write, but I didn't know where to send a letter. You might have let me hear from you at least once."

"But I didn't have anything to write about."

"Oh, I see. You don't write unless you've got something

to write about. Hmm. And I'll bet when you're away from me you forget about me completely, don't you?"

"Well . . . maybe I do. I'll bet that's just what you do too. . . . But, I'm hungry. How about ordering some food?"

The lodgers had already had their meal, so Segawa ordered out for some soba for me. By the time the street lights went on it had stopped raining; but I had already decided not to go home and was settled down to stay. Segawa and I were sitting there talking when two men dropped by. They looked about twenty-three or twenty-four. One was light complexioned and tall; the other was of medium build, had a narrow face, long hair combed straight back, and wore black, horn-rimmed glasses.

Segawa introduced them to me. The one with the long hair was a Korean socialist Segawa had already spoken to me about. His name was Hyeon, although he usually went by the Japanese name of Matsumoto. The tall one was a friend of Hyeon's named Cho. Segawa had once told me that Hyeon lived in the boarding house and "always had two cops tailing him, a real big-shot." I was thus particularly interested in him. There was nothing out of the ordinary about him, however, nor did he say anything to indicate that he was a socialist. The two of them left after only a brief chat, apparently not wanting to intrude while I was there.

That night I slept with Segawa, as always, in his one and only set of quilts. Next morning the rooming house maid brought a tray with breakfast, for one. Segawa did not ask her to bring anything for me, and he himself took up the one set of chopsticks. "Fumi, do you want to eat? I could leave you some from my portion. . . ."

"It's all right," I said, suppressing my true feelings, "I'll eat when I get home." I leaned against the desk and opened a magazine. When Segawa had finished eating, he went to the window.

"Fumi, come here. It's really nice outside."

I responded indifferently and then broached a subject that I had been thinking about. "Hiroshi, here we are carrying on like this, but what'll we do if I get pregnant?" I had been worrying about this for some time. I was terrified at the thought, and yet I also fantasized that I was already a mother and hugging the unseen child in my heart. But Segawa merely turned ever so slightly toward me, stretched, yawned, then replied as if he could not have been less concerned.

"What do you mean, 'what'll we do'? What have I got to do with it?"

I felt totally deserted. But Segawa surely was only saying this; he was really thinking seriously about what I had said and would now tell me what he thought. He said nothing, however. Taking his violin down from the wall by the window, he sat down on the low window frame and began to play as if he had not a care in the world.

I knew that we did not love each other, so I cannot entirely blame Segawa. Nevertheless, I think that in a situation like this he should have done the right thing. But no, he completely shirked all responsibility. I realized then, all too painfully, that I had been nothing but a plaything to him.

Lonely and livid with anger, I abruptly rose and left the room. Segawa said something to try to stop me, but I ignored him and went down to the sink at the bottom of the back stairs. In a room nearby I caught sight of Hyeon, the man I had been introduced to the night before. He was wearing a bold-striped yukata and was reading a book at a table by the window. I wanted to go into his room, but I felt that as I had only just met him it would not be right. I turned on the faucet and went about washing my face. As I was drying it with the towel, I looked again in the direction of Hyeon's room. He had put down his book and was looking at me.

"Good morning. I'm sorry for intruding last night," I said.

"Oh, no. I'm the one who intruded. It was raining last night, but it certainly is nice today, isn't it?"

I went over to his room and looked from the doorway at the shrubbery in the garden beyond. "You have a nice room and a view of the garden."

"Why don't you come in? I'm not busy." Hyeon moved a chair over beside the table, and I went in and sat down. I then began looking around the room with great interest. The walls were covered with photographs and portraits of famous revolutionaries and papers that appeared to be political handbills. I got up and looked them over carefully; one of the photos particularly drew my attention.

"Hey, aren't these people the G group?"

"Yes. Do you know them?" Hyeon asked as he took the photo down and put it on the table.

"Uh-huh, three or four of them," I said, bending over the picture. "This is T," I said, pointing, "and this one is H. This one is S. And this one is you, isn't it?"

Hyeon leaned over the picture, too, so that our faces were practically touching. "You're right. That's me."

"I thought so. When I saw you last night I thought that's who you were, but it would have sounded funny asking you, so I didn't say anything."

He seemed pleased to be able to regard me as a comrade, and now that the ice was broken, he immediately let down his reserve. I too felt a familiarity, particularly since he was Korean. It was like the happiness of meeting an old friend after a long absence.

We could now be perfectly candid. I told him about how I had lived for seven years in Korea, and he told me about his home there. He said he came from Seoul, where he was the only son in a wealthy family of high social standing. He was now enrolled in the philosophy course at Tōyō University, but he hardly ever went to classes, spending his days instead with his friends.

"Oh, so you work in the movement all the time?" I asked.

"Oh, no," he answered with a sad smile. "You see, I'm a 'petty bourgeois,' an 'intellectual.' They wouldn't have someone like me in the movement."

I was not seriously involved in the movement, nor did I belong to any particular group at the time. There was thus no need for me to look down on Hyeon or ostracize him. I was simply glad that I had found in him a friend, someone who felt as I did.

Just then, however, I heard the sound of slippered footsteps hurrying down the hall. When I turned around to see who it was, there, standing in the doorway, was Segawa. "Fumi, you can't just go barging into people's rooms like this. Come on."

"What!" All my bottled-up anger exploded. "This is none of your business," I shouted. "I can take care of myself, thank you. I'll do as I please, so shut up!"

"But look, you're bothering Hyeon. It's still the crack of dawn, and you're already in here making a nuisance of yourself."

"Shut up!" I yelled, louder than ever. "If Hyeon doesn't object, what right have you got to say anything? Stop butting into other people's business. Take your lunch box and get going!"

"I'll remember that!" Segawa fumed as he stalked out. But I don't think he went to work that day feeling very hurt. In any case, he never came over after that.

The servant girl had stood by listening to all this in stunned disbelief. This did not bother me in the least, though, for at that time I was a firm believer in doing what you liked regardless of what others thought. I went on talking with Hyeon for almost an hour after that, chatting away in high spirits, excited, I suppose, from the sheer pleasure of having told Segawa off.

It was half past nine when I left. I had gone one or two blocks when I heard someone calling me from behind. It was Hyeon. He was running after me, dressed in a suit and wearing a Bohemian necktie. I waited for him to catch up with me.

"Have you eaten?" he asked. "I haven't had anything myself yet. The food at the rooming house is pretty bad, so I thought I'd go out and eat. Would you mind coming along? I won't take up much of your time."

"Oh, I'd be glad to. I haven't eaten yet either."

"Perfect. Let's go."

We climbed the road up from the tracks until we came to a post office. I waited while Hyeon went in. He went up to the money order window, to pick up his money, I suppose. He was soon back, putting something in the inner pocket of his suit. We then went up to the second floor of a cozy Western-style restaurant beside Tenjin Shrine. It was still early, so there were no other customers. Hyeon and I were already just like two old friends.

When I got home from school the next day, there was a letter for me from Hyeon. "Special Delivery" was written in red on the small, white, Western-style envelope. The letter itself, on good-quality stationery, said that Hyeon wanted me to come that evening to the Kangetsu Bridge in Ueno.

It was one of those unbearably hot late summer days, and the bridge was covered with people trying to catch a bit of breeze. I crossed slowly, scrutinizing every face, but there was no sign of Hyeon. Surely he could not have been deceiving me. . . . Ah! There he was, waiting for me on the other side! He immediately took my hand.

"Fumiko, thank you for coming. You know," he said as we walked through the park, "you've completely capti-vated me."

I too spoke frankly of my fondness for him. We again went into a small restaurant and I told him everything, both my present circumstances and my dreams for the future. Hyeon then made me a promise. He said he would find a place where we could live together.

I was infatuated. If even a few days passed without my seeing Hyeon, I was miserable and would go looking for him. My searches were usually fruitless, and I would return home exhausted.

The family at Great-Uncle's began to keep a close watch on my movements, and it became harder to get away. Every time I met Hyeon I asked him about the house. He would take out the rental ads from his pocket as proof that he was "looking every day." I was desperate for a place of my own so that I would be able to get away from my great-uncle's.

One night, well past nine o'clock, I was sitting in the living room sewing some things for winter when Hyeon phoned. "Fumi, is that you? Did you know that Kunō was quite sick? . . . You didn't? Actually, I only just found out myself. It seems she's in serious condition. I thought I'd go and see her. Why don't you come too?"

Kunō was a socialist, a woman of about thirty-five. She had two children by a certain intellectual, so I heard, but had left her husband to devote herself completely to the movement. I had met her a number of times. She was living a hand-to-mouth existence with a young socialist and carrying on a militant struggle. I had not known that she was sick. I of course had to go and see her. "Yes, I'll go. Wait for me. I'll leave right away."

"I'll be waiting. Get here as soon as you can."

I got permission to go out; but as I was getting ready to leave, I overheard a comment by Hanae that was obviously meant for my ears. "It's just a lie. She wants to see that guy—What's his name?—so she has him call her up."

Although I was glad to be on my way to see Hyeon, I was honestly thinking only of Kunō at the time and so was not offended by Hanae's remarks.

About thirty minutes later I arrived at the lodging house

where Hyeon had said he would be waiting. I was shown to the friend's room where I found three or four men sprawled out talking. "Good evening," I said. "I'm sorry to have kept you waiting. Well, Matsumoto, shall we go?" I was standing in the open doorway and trying to hurry Hyeon. He made no move to rise, however, and just lay there laughing. One of his friends stood up and took my hand to pull me in.

"Hey, that was all just a lie," he said. "But now that you're here, come on in."

"What! A lie?" I made as if I were angry, but I was in fact pleased. "Come on. What's all this about, calling me up and everything? What's going on?"

"Fumi, it's like this," Hyeon said. "There was a blind flute player here a while ago, and we got so sad and carried away by the music that I even cried. But come on in. We just got lonely, that's all." Hyeon did seem rather sad; his voice was actually quivering with emotion.

"What am I going to do with you spoiled boys?"

They seemed tremendously pleased to have me join them. "It really was a lonely night," said the friend whose room it was. "But now that you're here, things have brightened up a bit." He sent out for a whole variety of Western- and Chinese-style dishes. The men drank beer and ate fruit; we talked, laughed, and sang. Though I was worried about the time and having to get home, I could not bring myself to call it an evening and leave. Soon it was past ten o'clock, then past eleven. No one made a move to leave, however; in fact, the men now started playing cards. Cards are my favorite pastime, so once again I let myself be drawn in. The next thing I knew, the sound of passing streetcars could no longer be heard. I ended up spending the night. The man who lived there rented a room off his for Hyeon and me.

When I awoke the next morning, my first thought was of the people at Great-Uncle's. Hanae's words the night before were ringing in my ears. Although I had not meant to deceive her, I had not in fact gone to see Kunō. I had gone to see Hyeon and not come home. I could not bear to think of the disgust and anger with which they would now view me.

We all gathered again in the room of Hyeon's friend. Once again he sent out for Western-style food. When the men had eaten they resumed the game of the night before. But I could neither eat nor take part in the game. I sat on the window sill facing the garden, lost in thought. "Matsumoto," I said at last, "couldn't you leave the game for a minute? There's something I want to talk to you about before I go home."

Hyeon got up reluctantly, and we went to the room we had stayed in the night before. "Look here, Hyeon," I said when we were seated, "going out and sleeping away from home like this . . . it's getting hard for me to stay on there. Well . . . what we talked about, what's happening? Why can't you hurry up and decide?"

Hyeon had promised at the very start of our relationship that we would rent a house and live together in a quiet place away from the city center. But since then he had not shown the least sign of intending to go through with it, and I was beginning to doubt his sincerity. The stronger my doubts grew, however, the more I seemed to cling to him. And now I was sleeping out so much that it was hard for me to go home.

"Oh that, you mean," he responded, clearly ill at ease. "Well, I'm looking for a house, but . . . in fact, there *is* a house. A friend of mine in Ueno is renting it, but . . . well, he's gone back to his home town right now. I'm afraid there's no way we can settle it. But I'll do something about it soon."

As always, nothing but evasion. He was just trying to find a way to get out of it without looking bad. What was there to say? I would just have to wait and trust in his vague promise. But there was still the problem of Hanae; I would have to make good on what I told her last night.

"All right. We'll leave it at that for the time being. But, you know, I told them I was going out to see Kunō last night. I can't just go home like this; I need something to show as proof that I've been to her place. I gave her a kimono of mine to pawn this spring. I want to take it home with me so they'll think that I really went to see her."

I was asking Hyeon for money, which, for two people in love, would not have been unusual. But if he were only using me, he could claim that I was asking for payment for sex, a thought I found repulsive. But my need to get that kimono overrode these considerations and I blurted out the request.

"Oh, yes. I see. I think that's fine. Why don't you do that." Hyeon searched his pockets, but finding nothing, asked me to wait while he went to his room for some money. He left the sliding door part-way open when he went out. Two maids, brooms in their hands, passed by in the hall. I overheard the one whisper, "Hey, Sumi, who do you think she is?" and the other reply, "Probably a whore who works the rooming houses."

Hyeon returned and pressed a five-yen bill in my hand. I swallowed my tears and took it.

The men were still carrying on in high spirits when I left the rooming house. It was past ten o'clock and raining, though not hard. I had neither an umbrella nor proper clogs for the rain, but as I had to use the money I had to get my kimono out of hock, I walked to Kunō's house in Sugamo in my low clogs. When I arrived I was soaking wet and splattered with mud. I hurriedly stepped into the entrance. "Anybody home?"

"Yes?" someone replied. But it was not Kunō who appeared.

"Excuse me, but is Kunō here?"

"Kunō? I don't know anyone by that name."

I left thoroughly bewildered and headed for the Rōdōsha (Workers' Society) nearby to try to find out what was up, but there was no one there whom I knew. They were at least able to tell me Kunō's whereabouts, however. "Kunō? She went with Mikimoto to Osaka," one of them said.

"Oh dear, that's too bad."

"Was there something you wanted to see her about? Excuse me, but what's your name?" The man invited me to stay, but I left without even telling them who I was. I knew where Kunō had pawned my kimono and went there.

"Yes, I did have that," the clerk said when I described the article, "but unfortunately the time limit was up and I disposed of it. I got after her a number of times about it, but she didn't even make a single payment."

I felt at that moment as if my one remaining lifeline had been severed. I was plunged into an abyss of despair where even tears were irrelevant. It was not that I wanted the kimono for itself; I just had to have it. But aside from my present need, I felt that what Kunō had done was so unkind! If nothing else, this incident has disabused me of the naive notion that "movement people" were a species of human beings set apart. This rude awakening was like being toppled from the pinnacle of a beautiful dream into the reality of a filthy mire.

My uncle from the temple had fallen sick and had come to my great-uncle's in Minowa. His health was now completely broken, and he was a pitiful sight of a man. Seeing him in this condition, I could no longer harbor any resentment for what he had done to me. In fact, I took him from one hospital to another in search of a cure, but nowhere could they offer him any hope. When, none the better for these efforts, Uncle finally left for home, I saw him off at Iidamachi Station. "Good-bye, and take care," I said.

"Thank you. And you study hard."

Although Uncle did not realize it, I knew that he was near death. The thought that this would be our "last parting" filled me with sadness. When his train had left I retraced my steps. I wanted to go somewhere and shake off this depression, but I stood there letting one streetcar after another pass by.

Gazing distractedly up at the street light, I felt that I had to be with a man. And the man I wanted to see was he whom I could not even call a lover any more. I hurried to a telephone and tried calling a number of places where I thought Hyeon might be until I at last got hold of him. "This is perfect," he said, "I've been wanting to see you to tell you something." We arranged to meet at Cho's place in Hongō.

I arrived at Cho's place two or three minutes after Hyeon. "What was it you wanted to tell me?" I asked.

"Well . . . umm, what I wanted to tell you was . . ." Then Hyeon went on in his roundabout way to inform me that he and Cho were going to Germany to study and that this would be good-bye. But it no longer seemed to matter.

"Oh, really? Well, that's nice."

"Let's have a good time for our farewell," Cho said. He sent out for some liquor and Western-style food.

I did not feel either sadness or humiliation, but a sense of despair was decidedly getting the better of me. I drank one glass of whiskey after another, how many I do not know, until I could not even stand up.

After this it was impossible to stay on at my great-uncle's. I left his place, brokenhearted over my lost love.

A Work of My Own!

AFTER LEAVING my great-uncle's, I found myself working at a small eating place in Hibiya. It was known as the "socialist oden's" because the owner was sympathetic to socialism; he seemed, in fact, to be a socialist himself. The place attracted people of an intellectual bent like journalists, socialists, office workers, writers, and the like. I waited on customers here during the day and went to school at night, the agreement being that the shop would pay my school fees and train fare.

Up to this time I had been attending day school, but I now switched to night classes where I made friends with a woman by the name of Niiyama Hatsuyo. Hatsuyo is probably the only woman of her sort that I will come across in my lifetime. How many things I learned from her! But it is not only what she taught me; thanks to Hatsuyo, I gained the warmth and strength of true friendship. After Park and I were arrested, one of the people at police headquarters evidently asked Hatsuyo who her closest woman friend was. Without a moment's hesitation it seems, she gave my name. She was certainly my closest friend, too. Hatsuyo, however, is no longer of this world. Oh, how I would like to reach out my hand to her right now! But I know there is no one there any longer to take it.

Hatsuyo was two years older than I, just twenty-one at

the time. She was extremely intelligent and had what you might call, in the good sense of the word, a "masculine" personality. She was strong-willed and did not let herself be ruled by those around her; she was a woman who had the strength to stick to her guns.

Hatsuyo's family was not well-off, but neither was it lumpen proletariat like my own. Which is not to say that she had an easy time of it. Her father had been a heavy drinker and had neglected his children; he died when Hatsuyo was in her second year at women's high school. Not long after that she came down with a lung ailment and had to go to her home town in Niigata to recuperate. At this time, it seems, troubled by the problem of death, she began studying Buddhism. Her illness was not too serious, however, and she came back to Tokyo to graduate with honors from either the No. 2 or No. 3 High School.

People realized her potential and urged her to go on for higher education. But with her father dead, her mother had her hands full just trying to raise Hatsuyo's younger sister. Hatsuyo would not think of adding to her mother's burden, and instead of continuing her education, she set about looking for a means to support herself. She attended typing school, became a typist, and went to work as a clerk in a company run at the time by an Englishman. At night she attended Seisoku to improve her English.

I do not remember exactly how I became friends with Hatsuyo, but the four or five women students at the night school were all seated together in the front of the classroom, so at first we merely exchanged polite greetings. But her seat was next to mine, and one day I overheard her debating with a male student on the problem of death: I took the opportunity to get in on the conversation. Of course, I had been attracted to Hatsuyo and everything she did right from the start and had wanted to get to know her. This is what she had to say on the problem of death.

"I have a lung ailment, which is why I have thought so

much about death. I believe that it is not so much death itself that people fear as the pain of that instant of passing over to death. The reason I feel this way is that people are not afraid of sleep even though the loss of consciousness in sleep is, you could say, a kind of temporary death."

Hearing this, I vividly recalled the feelings I had experienced the time in Korea that I had determined to die. I joined the conversation to say that, based on my own experience, I thought Hatsuyo's view was mistaken.

"I don't agree with you. I can state from my own experience that what people fear in death is the loneliness of having to leave this world forever. Though people may not be consciously aware of all the phenomena around them under normal circumstances, the thought that that which makes them themselves will be lost forever is a terribly lonely thing. In sleep, that which is ourselves is not lost, merely forgotten."

I do not, of course, think that either of our positions was entirely correct; but this discussion provided the occasion for the two of us to start talking to each other.

"Have you actually faced death?" Hatsuyo asked me.

"Yes, I have," I answered. The two of us continued the conversation on the way home after school let out; we were soon good friends. In retrospect, I believe I was influenced not so much by Hatsuyo herself as by what I read in the books that I got from her. I had always wanted to read books but had been unable to afford them. But when I became friends with Hatsuyo, I borrowed and read almost all of her books. It was she who lent me *Worker Sergiev*, a book that impressed me very much. She had also lent me *Night before Death* and had told me of the thought of, or at least the names of, Bergson, Spencer, and Hegel. The books she introduced me to that had the greatest influence on my thought were those of the nihilists. It was at this time that I learned of people like Stirner, Artsybashev, and Nietzsche.

It was getting on evening and the leaden sky portended imminent rain, if not snow. I left the oden shop at four o'clock, but as there were still two hours before classes began, I went over to see a friend of Hyeon's who lived in a lodging house near school.

"Come in," Jeong said as soon as he saw me. "I've been waiting for you to come. I've got something nice for you." He took a letter out of his desk drawer and handed it to me.

The letter was from Hyeon, and part of it was addressed to me. It said that he had received a telegram that his mother was in critical condition and he had had to leave for home in a great hurry. He apologized for not being able to say good-bye. This was a complete lie, however; he had decided some time ago to go home.

I flung the letter aside with a shrug, not even particularly angry. Jeong had nothing to say on the matter either. He seemed, in fact, to have been just waiting for me to finish so that he could show me three or four pages of galley proof, which he now took out. They were from an eight-page octavo monthly that he was going to publish, a project that he had spoken to me about before.

"Oh, it's out already," I exclaimed, eager to share in Jeong's excitement. The contents, however, turned out to be things that had been written some time back, all of which I had read in manuscript. But there was one item that caught my eye. It was a short poem in a corner of the last page.

Oh, what a powerful poem it was! Every single phrase gripped me. By the time I finished I was practically in raptures. My heart leapt in my breast, and I felt as though my very existence had been elevated to new heights. I was not familiar with the author's name, Pak Yeol, and thought at first that it might be a pen name. But no, the person who had written this poem could not be one of the Koreans whom I knew.

"Who is this . . . this Pak Yeol?" I asked.

"Him? Oh, he's a friend of mine," Jeong replied offhand-edly. "He's not very well known yet though. Quite a poor guy."

"Oh? But this man has great strength. I've never seen a poem quite like this."

If Jeong did not have the wits to recognize the author's worth, I certainly did. My reaction did not please him very much though. "What's so good about it?"

"It's not any one thing in particular; it's the poem as a whole. It's more than good, it's powerful! I feel like I've just discovered here in this poem something I've been searching for."

"Got really carried away, didn't you? Would you like to meet the author?"

"I sure would. Seriously, introduce me, will you?"

At that point I became aware of the gentle sound of a light, powdery snow falling outside. The clock in the hall downstairs struck six o'clock, and the boisterous voices of students trooping down the stairs could be heard. "Hey, don't you have to go to school?" Jeong reminded me.

"School?" I answered indifferently, "Who cares about school?"

"What do you mean?" Jeong looked puzzled. "I thought you were the struggling student, slaving away to put your-self through school."

"I was. In the beginning I was so full of enthusiasm that I wouldn't have missed a day even if it meant going without meals. But not any more."

"What happened?"

"Oh, nothing special. I'm just no longer interested in try-ing to get ahead in this world."

"What! But if you quit school, what are you going to do?"

"That's the question; it's been on my mind a lot. I want to do something, but I don't know what. I'm sure, though, that it's not slaving to put myself through school. I believe that there is something that I must do, that I have to do, no matter what, and I'm trying to discover what that something is."

Although I had once pinned all my hopes on putting myself through school, believing that I could thereby make something of myself, I now realized the futility of this all too clearly. No amount of struggling for an education is going to help one get ahead in this world. And what does it mean to get ahead anyway? Is there any more worthless lot than the so-called great people of this world? What is so admirable about being looked up to by others? I do not live for others. What I had to achieve was my own freedom, my own satisfaction. I had to be myself. I had been the slave of too many people, the plaything of too many men. I had never lived for myself. I had to do my own work; but what was it? I wanted so badly to find it and to set about accomplishing it.

It was no doubt Hatsuyo who influenced me to think this way. Besides the stimulus of the books that she let me read, there was the example of Hatsuyo herself and her lifestyle. But whatever their source, such thoughts had preoccupied me for some time.

"You're right," Jeong said in complete agreement. "I'm sure, too, that we all have something before us that we must do."

We went on to talk about a variety of things with a seriousness we had never had before. Then, remembering that there was a lecture that night on "socialist thought" at Seinen Kaikan in Mitsushiro-chō, I bade farewell to Jeong and went to school to invite Hatsuyo to the lecture. The two of us left school and walked through streets covered with snow.

I was gradually beginning to understand how society works. Up until then the true shape of reality had been thinly veiled, but now it all began to become clear. I understood why someone poor like myself could never study and get ahead in this world, why, too, the rich got richer and the powerful were able to do anything they liked. I knew that what socialism preached was true.

But I could not accept socialist thought in its entirety. Socialism seeks to change society for the sake of the oppressed masses, but is what it would accomplish truly for their welfare? Socialism would create a social upheaval "for the masses," and the masses would stake their lives in the struggle together with those who had risen up on their behalf. But what would the ensuing change mean for them? Power would be in the hands of the leaders, and the order of the new society would be based on that power. The masses would become slaves all over again to that power. What is revolution, then, but the replacing of one power with another?

Hatsuyo ridiculed the movements of people like the socialists, or at best viewed them coolly. "I can't," she said, "hold a fixed philosophy about human society. What I do is gather people around me who feel like I do and live the kind of life that feels right. That is the kind of life that is most realistic and has the greatest meaning."

One member of our group called that view "escapism," but I did not agree. I, too, believed it was impossible to change the existing society into one that would be for the benefit of all; neither could I espouse any given ideal for society. But in one thing I differed from Hatsuyo. I felt that even if one did not have an ideal vision of society, one could have one's work to do. Whether it was successful or not was not our concern; it was enough that we believed it to be a valid work. The accomplishment of that work, I believed, was what our real life was about. Yes. I want to carry out a work of my own; for I feel that by so doing our lives are rooted in the here and now, not in some far-off ideal goal.

One bitterly cold night I skipped my English conversation class to go to Jeong's, something I often did. I opened the sliding door to his room unannounced, as was also my wont, and called out a greeting. Jeong was sitting by the hibachi with a man I did not know; the two of them were discussing something in low tones. The stranger, who looked around twenty-three or twenty-four, was of medium height, slender, and had thick, jet-black hair that fell loosely down to his shoulders. He was wearing blue duck cloth workman's clothes and a brown overcoat, the buttons of which were hanging down by the threads in imminent danger of falling off. The sleeves of the coat were worn at the elbows, and the knees of the man's trousers were so threadbare that they had gaping holes.

"Come in!" Jeong called out in welcome.

The stranger gave me the briefest glance, then clammed up and directed his gaze at the smoldering coals.

"It's really cold, isn't it?" I said as I swept into the room and seated myself by the hibachi.

"I haven't seen you for a few days. Did something come up?" Jeong asked.

"No, nothing special," I answered, then addressed a few words to the stranger. "I'm sure I saw you standing by the stage the other day at the Russian famine relief concert at Chūka Seinen Kaikan. You were there, weren't you?"

"Oh was I?" he said, then quickly rose to his feet.

"Oh, you don't have to go," I said hurriedly to stop him. "Go on with your conversation. I didn't come for anything in particular."

The guest made no response; he merely stood there looking down coldly at me under thick eyebrows through his black, horn-rimmed glasses. His presence was overpowering. He then bid us an abrupt good-bye and left.

"Hey," Jeong yelled, jumping to his feet and running out to the hall after the stranger. "Where are you going to stay tonight? You can stay with me, you know."

"Thank you, but I'm going to stay at a friend's in Komagome tonight," he said with a hint of sad resignation.

I felt very small, like I had done something wrong.

"Jeong, what's that man's name?"

"Him? That's Pak Yeol, the author of that poem you got so excited about."

"What! That man is Pak Yeol?" I exclaimed, blushing.

"Yes, that's the man," Jeong calmly replied.

I asked all sorts of questions about Pak Yeol and learned that he had been a rickshaw man, ticket scalper, mailman, longshoreman, and many other things as well. He had no job at present, however, and slept at a different friend's home every night.

"Why, he lives just like a stray dog. Where does he get that powerful presence, then? He carries himself as if he were a king."

"All the while going around like that living off his friends, eh?" Jeong said with a touch of contempt. When he saw my displeasure, however, he added, "But he really is something, that man. How many of us think as seriously and act with as much conviction as he does?"

Oh, how right you are! my heart cried out. Something was stirring within me, about to be born. What was at work within this man? What was it that made him so strong? I wanted to find out and make it my own.

I left Jeong to go back to the shop, and on the way it dawned on me. "That's it! That's what I'm looking for, the work that I want to do! He has it within him. He is what I'm looking for. He has my work." A strange joy set my heart leaping. I was so excited that I could not sleep that night.

Early the next morning I went to see Jeong to tell him that I wanted to get to know Pak and to ask him to introduce us.

"But he's always drifting. It's hard to get hold of him when you want him," Jeong said.

"That's all right. Just tell him to come to my shop. All you have to do is pass that message on to him." Jeong agreed to help. But Pak did not come. After four or five days I went to see Jeong again. "Did you tell him?"

"Yes. I saw him at a meeting two or three days ago and told him."

"What did he say?"

"Nothing much, really. He just said, 'I see.' He didn't seem very interested."

I was somewhat discouraged. Perhaps he could not be bothered with somebody like me. But I did not give up, and I waited for the day when he would show up. Ten days passed, however, then twenty, and Pak still did not come to see me. By now I was desolate. His failure to come seemed to set the seal on my worthlessness. I even made a decision to get myself a profession, become a typist like Hatsuyo, perhaps, so that I could live on my own. Then, about a month after I had asked Jeong to convey my message—I think it was the fifth or sixth of March—Pak turned up at the shop. The sight of him set my heart pounding.

"Oh, you finally came," I said quietly, leaving the two groups of customers I had been waiting on to show Park to a table in the corner. "This is perfect. Wait for me a little while and I'll leave with you."

I brought Pak some rice, stewed daikon, and tōfu. When it was at last time for me to go to school, I went upstairs to get my things together. I had asked Pak to leave the shop a little ahead of me, and now I went out with my school bag on my arm as I always did. Pak was waiting for me outside, and we set out together for the street where the train passed. When we got there, however, Pak stopped short. "You're going to Kanda, aren't you? I have something to do in Kyōbashi, so I'll say good-bye here." He started walking off at a brisk pace.

"Wait a minute!" I said, running after him. "Come again

tomorrow. I'll have something nice for you."

"Thank you. I will." Then he was gone, leaving me feeling frustrated.

He came to the shop around noon the next day. I sat down beside his table and said in a low voice so that the other customers would not hear, "Would you meet me in front of school tonight? There's something I want to talk to you about."

"What school do you go to?"

"Kanda Seisoku."

"All right, I'll be there."

I felt assured at last and waited for evening to come. Sure enough, he was there just as he had promised, standing beneath the bare trees in front of school. "Thank you. Have you been waiting long?"

"No, I just got here."

"Oh, did you? Thank you. Shall we walk a bit?"

We chose a place were there were few people. We did not speak, however; what I wanted to talk about was not the sort of small talk you make on the street. I was looking for a place that would be quieter and more relaxed. When we came to Jimbō-chō Avenue, I saw a large Chinese restaurant. "Let's go in here," I said and strode up the steps. Pak followed me without a word. We sat down in a small room on the third floor and the boy brought tea. I asked him to bring two or three dishes, leaving the choice up to him. When the boy had left I lifted the lid from the tea cup.

"Do you know how you're supposed to drink this tea? If you drink it with the lid off, it seems like the tea leaves will get in your mouth. But it seems funny to drink it with the lid on."

"How *are* you supposed to drink it? I've never been in a fancy place like this, so I don't know," he said, taking the lid off, then replacing it as I had done. "But it's a drink, so I suppose any way that you can get it down will be all right. Surely there isn't a rule about it, is there?" He tilted the lid slightly and drank at the opening.

"Oh, I see. That must be the way to do it," I said as I followed suit. The tea was not very good.

We ate the food as the boy brought it. I was not making much headway with the meal, but Pak ate as if he were ravenous. I wanted to get onto the topic I had come to talk about, but the atmosphere was stiff and it was hard to speak. Finally, however, I made an awkward beginning. "Well, I think you probably heard from Jeong that I wanted to be friends with you."

"Yes. He did say something about that." Pak lifted his gaze from his plate and looked at me. Our eyes met. I felt acutely embarrassed, but having reached this point, there was nothing to do but come out with what was on my mind. I went on.

"Well, uhh . . . I'll get right to the point. Do you have a wife? Or . . . well, if not exactly a wife, someone like, say, a lover? Because if you do, I want our relationship to be just one between comrades. Well . . . do you?"

What a clumsy proposal! What a comical scene! When I think back on it now it makes me blush and want to burst out laughing. But I was dead serious at the time.

"I'm single."

"I see. Then, what I want to ask you . . . I hope we can talk absolutely frankly with each other."

"Of course."

"Well, then . . . you see, I'm Japanese. But I think I can say that I'm not prejudiced against Koreans. I wonder though if you have any feelings against me."

Knowing how Koreans felt about Japanese, I thought that it was necessary to ask this straight off. I was afraid of the emotions that Pak might harbor as a Korean.

"No. It's not ordinary people that I hate; it's the Japanese ruling class. And I even feel a bond with people like you who aren't prejudiced."

"Really? Thank you." I smiled with relief. "But there's something else I want to ask. Are you working in the nationalist movement? You see, I lived for quite a while in Korea, and I think I understand how the nationalists feel. But I myself am not Korean. I haven't suffered the kind of oppression by Japan that Koreans have, and I don't feel I can work in the independence movement with those people. So if you are in the independence movement, I'm sorry, but I can't work with you."

"There are points where I sympathize with the independence movement people," Pak said. "I myself tried to participate in the nationalist movement at one time. But not now."

"Are you completely opposed to the nationalist movement, then?"

"Not at all. But I have my own way of thinking and my own work to do. I can't participate in the nationalist front."

I felt tremendously relieved; there was nothing in the way now. Yet I still did not feel that the moment had come to bring up the main point. We made small talk once again. I sensed more than ever a strength in him, and I felt myself being more and more deeply attracted. At last I broached the subject. "I've found what I have been looking for in you. I want to work with you."

"It's no good," Pak said in a chilling tone. "I go on living only because I don't seem to be able to die."

It must have been close to eight o'clock by then. We agreed to meet again and asked the boy for the check. It came to three yen.

"I'll pay. I have some money today," Pak said as he emptied the outer pockets of his overcoat. They contained three or four Golden Bat cigarettes, a couple of rumpled bills, and seven or eight copper and silver coins. I stopped him.

"No. I'll pay. I think I'm richer than you are."

We left the restaurant together.

We saw each other often after that and could speak without any awkwardness. We were at ease because our hearts were one. At last we reached a final understanding. The matter was settled in the upstairs of a small restaurant in Misaki-chō; we finished at around seven o'clock. It was too late for me to go to school and too early to go home, so we strolled beside the dark moat in the direction of Hibiya. The nights were still cold, and we clasped hands in the pocket of Pak's overcoat, letting our feet take us where they would. There was not a soul in the park. The stillness of the night was broken only by the feeble echo of a distant train; the only light was the silent glistening of the stars in the sky above and the arc lamps on the earth below.

Pak spoke with an uncommon animation. He said that he had been born in a rural area in Gyeong Sang Bug Do. He came from a commoner family that had been peasants for generations, although there had been a number of scholars and persons in high social positions among his forebears. Pak's father died when he was four years old. His mother was an extremely gentle woman, and the young Pak clung to her to the extent that he could not sleep at night if their legs were not first tied together. Pak went to the village temple school when he was seven and then to the regular school that was built in the village when he was nine. An unusually bright student, he wanted to go on with his studies, but the family's fortunes declined at that time, and Pak's older brother decided that Pak would work on the farm. This he did until he was fifteen when, unable to suppress his desire to study, he ran away to Taegu and took the exam for regular high school. He passed with such a high score that his brother gave in and, although it was hard for the family, sent him his school expenses. Pak took correspondence courses from Waseda University from about that time and read works by Japanese writers. His thinking began to move steadily to the left.

It was about that time that he decided to join the independence movement. He quickly realized its falseness, however. As Pak saw it, even if the rulers changed, this would mean little as far as the people were concerned. Then, in the spring of his seventeenth year, he came to Tokyo.

Pak's life after coming to Tokyo was one long, bitter struggle, and he became increasingly closed in on himself. He had by now lost interest in movements dependent on the pen or the tongue and was determined to forge a path by himself.

Pak did not tell me all of this at one time. In fact, he is not a man to talk a lot about himself. He told me only fragments, and I put the fragments together from what other people later told me. It was of the future, not the past, that we mostly talked. We cherished vague hopes and spoke of the tasks that lay before us. Then Pak brought up something that had been on his mind.

"Fumiko, I want to move into a flophouse to do serious movement work. What do you think?"

"A flophouse? I think it's a good idea."

"But it would be filthy, you know. There would be bed-bugs and things. Do you think you could put up with it?"

"I think I can. If you can't put up with little things like that, you might as well not try anything in the first place."

"Of course you're right." After a brief pause Pak began again. "Fumiko, they say that the bourgeoisie go on honey-moons when they get married. But how about us com-memorating our living together by putting out a secret publication?"

"That sounds interesting; let's," I said without giving it much thought. "What shall we publish? I have *The Con-quest of Bread*. We could translate that."

"That's already been translated. And besides, I don't want to put out anything by others. It's better if the two of us write something ourselves, even if it isn't so great."

We became completely wrapped up in planning this venture, and before we knew it we were out of the park and on a busy street. It seemed to have gotten rather late. "I wonder what time it is. I have to go home at nine o'clock," I said reluctantly.

"I don't know. But wait here; I'll go and see." Pak went over to look at the clock at the police box in front of the trolley intersection. Neither of us had ever owned a watch. "It's seventeen minutes to nine," he said when he returned.

"Oh, then I'll have to be going home."

"You can stay another thirty minutes, can't you? After all, school lets out at nine, and then it takes you ten minutes on the train, right? So you've still got twenty-five or thirty minutes."

"Thank you, sir. What would I do without you?"

We held hands again and went back into the park, found a bench under some trees and sat there, perfectly still, our frozen cheeks pressed together, until it was time to leave. We got up reluctantly and made for the park exit. At last I broke the silence. "Where will you be spending the night?"

Pak thought for a while then said in a melancholy voice, "I guess I'll go to a friend's house in Kojimachi."

"Well, that's fine. But aren't you lonely like this with no home?"

"Sure I'm lonely," Pak murmured, not taking his eyes off the ground. "It's all right when you're well, but when you're sick. . . . Even people who are normally kind don't want to be bothered at times like that."

"That's true. People can be cold, can't they. You're a little thin, but have you been seriously ill, I mean, since coming to Tokyo?"

"Yes, last spring. I had a bad case of flu and no one to look after me. I spent three days in a flophouse in Honjo, not eating or drinking, just lying there moaning. I was afraid I would die like that."

I was overcome by emotion, and my eyes filled with tears. I squeezed Pak's hand. "If only I had known. . . ."

Soon, however, Pak said in a perfectly composed voice,

"Well, good-bye. Be seeing you." He dropped my hand and jumped on a car for Kanda. I prayed in my heart as I watched him go: Please wait. It won't be long. We'll be together just as soon as I finish school, and then I'll always be with you. I'll never let you suffer from sickness or things like that. If you die, I'll die with you. We'll live together and we'll die together.

Afterword

I END the account of my life here. I am not free to record anything of what happened after this except for my life together with Pak. But in writing this much I have accomplished my purpose.

What made me the way I am? I have nothing more to say on this. It is enough that I have laid out my whole life here. The reader with feeling will, I believe, understand well enough from this record. My presence will shortly be effaced from this earth. I believe, however, that every phenomenon continues as such to exist in eternal actuality even though it be physically obliterated. I now lay down the pen with which I have written this clumsy account, perfectly calm and at peace. A blessing on all those whom I love!

Glossary

akebi	reddish-purple fruit that grows on a vine in forests; *Akebia quinata* Decne
Bon festival	Buddhist festival in August featuring visits to ancestral graves, traditional communal dancing, etc.
chō	approximately 109 meters; in this work, rendered as "block" when referred to in urban settings
daikon	long white radish
donburi	large rice bowl; rice dish served in large bowl
go	board game played with black and white pebbles
haori	long, loose, coat-like garment
happi	workman's livery coat
hibachi	charcoal stove used indoors
Jintan	brand name of common breath tablets
jōruri	a ballad drama
kana	Japanese syllabic script
kasuri	splash pattern or cloth woven into such a pattern
katakana	one of two forms of kana
kin	1.323 pounds
Kōdan kurabu	"Story Club"
kotatsu	foot-warmer covered with a quilt
koto	musical instrument with strings stretched over long, convex sounding board
kotobuki	"felicitations"
kyōgen	comic interlude performed as supplementary entertainment during a Noh program

meisen	common fabric such as might be used for cushion covers
miso	bean paste
mochi	rice cake eaten as a staple at New Year's meals
obi	long, broad sash worn with a kimono
oden	stewed dish
okamisan	used to refer to married woman of common status
okusan	used to refer to married woman of solid middle class or above
ominaeshi	perennial plant with yellow flowers of the family *Valerianaceae*; *Patrinia scabiosaefolia*
ri	2.44 miles
rin	1/1000 yen
sen	1/100 yen
shamisen	three-stringed instrument with long neck played with plectrum
shō	0.477 U.S. gallon
soba	buckwheat noodles
tabi	digitated socks
takashimada	court attendant's hairstyle popularized as a bridal coiffure since the Meiji era
tatami	thick, woven straw mats tightly fitted together as a floor covering; room size expressed in terms of number of tatami mats
to	4.765 U.S. gallons
tōfu	bean curd cake
tsubo	3.954 square yards
tsumugi	pongee; Ōshima tsumugi is woven in the Amami Islands in dark-colored patterns favored by middle-class matrons
udo	edible wild perennial found in mountainous areas in spring; *Aralia cordata*
ukiyoe	color print depicting everyday life in old Japan
warabi	edible bracken found in mountainous areas; *Pteridium aquilinum* Kuhn
wasabi	thick-rooted perennial used in Japanese cuisine; Japanese horseradish; *Wasabia Japonica* Matsum
yukata	light cotton kimono worn in summer and as sleepwear
zori	sandal-type footwear

Index

JEAN INGLIS studied Indonesian history at Gadjah Mada University in Jogjakarta and anthropology at Catholic University in Washington. Residing in Japan since 1970, she has worked as a freelance editor with Tokyo University Press, *Ampo: Japan-Asia Quarterly Review*, and *New Asia News*, and since 1975 has been doing freelance translating for *Japan Quarterly*, Fukuinkan Shoten, *Ampo*, and Lingua Guild. Her books include *Ohkuno Island: Story of the Student Brigade, Japanese Transnational Enterprises in Indonesia*, and *Drug Crime: The Hidden Story of Chloroquine* (forthcoming). Ms. Inglis is also active writing and speaking on the East Timor issue, is co-editor of *Higashi Chimoru tsushin* (East Timor news), and is a founding member of the Free East Timor Japan Coalition.